DISCARDED

Teaching Constructivist SCIENCE K-8

This book is dedicated to the memory of Neil Postman, 1931–2003, who taught at New York University for 40 years. Although he was not a science educator himself, his book Teaching as a Subversive Activity *(1969), with Charles Weingartner, introduced many teachers in our generation to the inquiry method, a student-centered method of education focused on asking questions. Postman claimed that the activities and behaviors of intelligent people at all stages in life relate to the process of inquiry, not to a result of static knowledge, and his claim is as relevant today as it was four decades ago. The inquiry method is different from the way most of us were taught. Following Postman, the kind of K–8 classrooms we envision are places where students are encouraged to ask questions that are meaningful to them, including those without easy answers. We envision classrooms in which teaching-by-telling is minimized and active "hands-on, minds-on" learning is the norm. Our hope is that you will become an inquiring teacher and pass it on.*

Teaching Constructivist Science

SCIENCE K-8

Nurturing Natural Investigators
in the Standards-Based Classroom

Michael L. Bentley | Edward S. Ebert II | Christine Ebert

CORWIN PRESS
A SAGE Publications Company
Thousand Oaks, CA 91320

Copyright © 2007 by Corwin Press

All rights reserved. When forms and sample documents are included, their use is authorized only by educators, local school sites, and/or noncommercial entities who have purchased the book. Except for that usage, no part of this book may be reproduced or utilized in any form or by any means, electronic or mechanical, including photocopying, recording, or by any information storage and retrieval system, without permission in writing from the publisher.

For information:

Corwin Press
A Sage Publications Company
2455 Teller Road
Thousand Oaks, California 91320
www.corwinpress.com

Sage Publications Ltd.
1 Oliver's Yard
55 City Road
London EC1Y 1SP
United Kingdom

Sage Publications India Pvt. Ltd.
B-42, Panchsheel Enclave
Post Box 4109
New Delhi 110 017 India

Printed in the United States of America.

Library of Congress Cataloging-in-Publication Data

Bentley, Michael Lee.
Teaching constructivist science, K–8: Nurturing natural investigators in the standards-based classroom / Michael L. Bentley, Edward S. Ebert II, Christine Ebert.
    p. cm.
Includes bibliographical references and index.
ISBN-13: 978-1-4129-2575-4 (cloth)
ISBN-13: 978-1-4129-2576-1 (pbk.)
   1. Science—Study and teaching (Elementary) 2. Science—Study and teaching (Middle school) I. Ebert, Edward S., 1953– II. Ebert, Christine, 1946– III. Title.

LB1585.B365 2007
372.3'5—dc22   2006034104

This book is printed on acid-free paper.

07   08   09   10   11   10 9 8 7 6 5 4 3 2 1

Acquisitions Editor:	Jean Ward
Editorial Assistant:	Jordan Barbakow
Production Editor:	Diane S. Foster
Copy Editor:	Carol Anne Peschke
Typesetter:	C&M Digitals (P) Ltd.
Proofreader:	Caryne Brown
Indexer:	John Roy
Cover Designer:	Michael Dubowe
Graphic Designer:	Scott Van Atta

Contents

List of Figures

List of Tables

List of Activities

About the Authors

 **Michael L. Bentley** is an associate professor of science education at the University of Tennessee, Knoxville, where he teaches courses in environmental education and methods of teaching K–8 science. Dr. Bentley has written science books for young readers and curriculum materials and numerous professional articles and chapters in books. He has also been involved with the creation of several innovative schools and has been an officer on two school boards. Dr. Bentley's interests include teacher education, the public understanding of science, curriculum studies and international education, and the history, philosophy, and sociology of science as applied to science education. He lives in Salem, Virginia, with his wife, the Rev. Susan E. Bentley, a daughter, Sarah, and sons Alex and Matthew.

 **Edward S. Ebert II** is a professor of education at Coker College in Hartsville, South Carolina. With a degree in psychological foundations of education, Dr. Ebert teaches courses in educational psychology, elementary science methods, child development, classroom management, assessment, and creative problem solving. He has written several books on elementary science methods, creative thinking and science teaching, introduction to education, and classroom pragmatics management and assessment. Dr. Ebert has done numerous presentations nationally and internationally and has taught science education and educational psychology for a semester at Shanghai International Studies University. He resides in Columbia, South Carolina, with his wife, Christine Ebert.

 **Christine Ebert** is associate provost, dean of the graduate school, and professor of science education at the University of South Carolina. Her work in science education focuses on conceptual change and development in students' understanding of science principles. In addition, she has taught courses in thinking and reasoning and is extensively involved with collaboration between elementary schools and the university. Dr. Ebert serves regularly as a program evaluator for national federally funded science initiatives. She has coauthored three other books related to science education and conceptual development. Dr. Ebert has presented her work on science education and creative thinking at conferences across the country and around the world. She and her husband live in Columbia, South Carolina.

Preface

Those who have meditated on the art of governing humankind have been convinced that the fate of empires depends on the thorough education of youth.

—Aristotle

This book is about the teaching of science in elementary and middle school. It is written for teachers who want to become more skilled and those of you who are preparing to teach. It is written for teachers who share our perspective that teaching involves much more than the transmission of information and that education is a profession of inquirers who can communicate the beauty and value of well-developed human thought.

From the beginning, it is only fair to acknowledge that a study of science teaching is complex and challenging enough to keep one learning throughout years of classroom experience. For this reason, we have written this book to be useful as a guide and as a resource to return to over many years of teaching.

Three of us worked together to write this book. Combined, we share nearly a century of experience in teaching science and in helping individuals prepare and grow as science teachers. We hope that what we have to share in these pages will help you meet the challenges of the classroom and help you to better understand the nature of science and science education.

The book contains 10 chapters clustered in three sections. The three chapters of the first section are provided to help you further develop your own perspective of science and its place in the elementary and middle school curriculum. One piece of this is an introduction to the national standards that now frame the science instruction and curriculum in U.S. schools. A strong foundation in the nature of science, an understanding of the science learner, and a solid repertoire of effective and complementary pedagogical strategies will support you as you plan and enact an engaging and exemplary program of science education in your classroom.

Part II focuses on the teaching of science, with the philosophy of constructivism as its referent. Everything we present will be offered as a component of a dynamic, interactive, hands-on and minds-on approach to education that capitalizes on the inherent curiosity of children and tweens. Supporting your effort to develop meaningful science lessons for a given topic in the curriculum is the goal of this book. Taken together, these chapters are intended to help you make science the most exciting time of each class day.

In Part III we shift to a discussion of classroom pragmatics: the nuts and bolts of organizing and managing an inquiry-based science program. Also included in this section is a discussion of assessment. In a time of clarion calls for school accountability, it is more important than ever that the classroom teacher be able to accurately determine the gains made by children as a result of instruction. Part III concludes with a compendium of resources and practical guidelines and a bibliography of current professional literature relevant to K–8 educators. This portion of the book will help you extend your teaching by using the many resources available to you as a classroom teacher and offers direction for pursuing any aspect of this book for further exploration. We hope and expect that you will make frequent use of the information provided in Chapter 10.

You will probably notice very early that each chapter begins with a quotation. All are from people we consider wise and erudite. In some cases their wisdom was born of many years of considering this world. In other cases, it is the wisdom that can come only from those yet to arrive at their tenth birthday. We can learn from each.

A last, more personal word. While we have been occupied in the writing of this book, three children and two grandchildren have been born into our families. Even experienced educators are reminded of the degree to which children depend on the nurturing care of loving family members. What develops is a physical, emotional, and intellectual exchange that will continue throughout their lives. And when those children go off to school, it will be the nurturing guidance of teachers, professionals such as you, to whom they will turn. Your influence will last an eternity.

It is an awesome responsibility for all teachers, but it is one that each of us can hope to address by being a teacher who not only knows the content but also knows how children learn and how to value their thinking. That bigger picture is what this book tries to convey. As you hone your professional skills, you may find yourself challenged to change some of your own attitudes about science. However, as good teachers know, it is never too late for curiosity and growth in our profession.

Indeed, the responsibility of being a teacher is awesome, but it is a career in which you truly can make a difference in the world.

Michael L. Bentley
Edward S. Ebert II
Christine Ebert

Acknowledgments

Corwin Press gratefully acknowledges the contributions of the following individuals:

Bena Kallick
Educational Consultant
Westport, Connecticut

Christine Anne Royce
Assistant Professor of Education
Shippensburg University
Shippensburg, Pennsylvania

Diann Musial
Distinguished Teaching Professor, Foundations of Education
Northern Illinois University
DeKalb, Illinois

Susan Illgen
Oklahoma State Teacher of the Year, 2005
Oklahoma City, Oklahoma

K. T. Willhite
Center Coordinator
Southern Illinois University–Carbondale
Carbondale, Illinois

Rachel A. McBroom
Science Education Program Coordinator
University of North Carolina at Pembroke
Pembroke, North Carolina

PART I

Foundations for Teaching Science

P art I contains three chapters that share the common theme of describing science, each in a different context. The chapters progress from a consideration of the nature of science, to a discussion of science as it is represented by educational curricula, and finally to a discussion of children's cognitive development and how to elicit their science understanding before instruction.

Chapter 1, "The World of the Scientist and the Nature of Science," looks at science in terms of its characteristics, relationship to our culture, and philosophy. Science is much more than just a collection of facts in a textbook. Good teachers recognize the importance of understanding the nature of science before teaching it.

Chapter 2, "The Content of K–8 Science," looks at curriculum and particularly at efforts on the state and national levels to build frameworks that identify the most appropriate and important domains of science for children to experience in school. In contrast to Chapter 1, with its focus on scientific investigation as human endeavor, this chapter is concerned with the social and sometimes political aspects of science curriculum.

"Characteristics of the Science Learner: Development in Childhood and Adolescence," Chapter 3, offers a discussion of how children's science is similar to and different from scientists' science. The construction of knowledge uses all the experiences a child has had, most of which occur outside a classroom. This chapter presents a stepwise model to help clarify the task of systematically moving children from one level of understanding to the next.

It also provides a method for finding out just what makes scientific sense to your students. Often what teachers think students believe does not match what they actually believe. Interviews with students can elicit this information. The interview is a distinctly noninstructional tool used solely to determine what students really know or believe about a topic before planning instruction. For this reason, we have placed it in this foundation section rather than with teaching methods or assessment.

1

The World of the Scientist and the Nature of Science

What Is Science?

Science and Culture

Science and Technology

Science and Philosophy

Your Academic Roadmap

This chapter should help you to understand the following ideas:

- The study of science is open to all.
- Science is a multidimensional human endeavor with complex interrelations with society.
- Science is creative and inquiry oriented.
- Science is dynamic and tentative as scientists continue to understand the natural world.
- A constructivist philosophy values children's inherent curiosity as teachers provide opportunities for experiences that foster their construction of knowledge.

Our century is a century of explorations: new forms of art, of music, of literature, and new forms of science.

—Illya Prigogine
(1980, p. 215)

WHAT IS SCIENCE?

Science, like *art* or *creativity,* is a term that most people assume they understand. "What is science?" is a question few people wrestle with unless specifically put on the spot. Yet isn't it an important term for us to understand? Certainly the scientist herself should understand it to conceptualize the work she is to do and to internalize the purpose of that work. Teachers of science certainly need to understand the term to teach their students appropriately. Students benefit from understanding the nature of science because it helps them organize their experiences of science in the curriculum. A literate person in a democratic society should be able to verbalize a contemporary conceptualization of the nature of science, if for no other reason than that science contributes much to our culture and our lives.

What Distinguishes the Scientist?

When you think of a scientist, what image first comes to your mind? Over the years this question has been presented to a lot of children as the "Draw-a-Scientist" Test (DAST; Figure 1.1). Try asking some children to draw the first picture that comes to mind when they think of a scientist. Do you think they would respond as you did? Many children draw the familiar, stereotypical image of the scientist, the one that probably flashed in your own mind: a Caucasian man dressed in a white lab coat and surrounded by the stuff of his trade: test tubes, flasks, Bunsen burners, microscopes, maybe computers or other fancy equipment, and, of course, a pocket liner with pens sticking out. Typically, fewer children spontaneously represent their scientists as women or ethnic minorities. Researchers have found that children do indeed perceive scientists stereotypically, more and more so as they progress through successive grade levels (McComas, Almazroa, & Clough, 1998).

Stereotyping by gender and ethnicity is just one way children (and many adults) misconceive scientists. So what do you think *really* characterizes a person in the profession of a scientist? The distinction between science and other pursuits can be fuzzy; not everyone agrees on which disciplines belong under the *science* umbrella. To complicate matters further, there is the demarcation between science and technology. Little wonder then that defining *science* is not as easy as it first appears! Having determined that gender and ethnicity are not relevant characteristics of a scientist, let's try to look more closely at what science *is* and what scientists *do* in order to address our initial question. To begin, complete Activity 1.1 on your own, and then discuss your ideas with one or more of your colleagues. There is no single correct response to any of the statements, but you may find some of your opinions changing by the time you have read the rest of this chapter.

Figure 1.1 Children's Drawings of Scientists

Rowshan

I found the sugar cubes. It is cool to find it

mossy seed

gills

roots

rockes

wolf

My scientist is experimenting if cloroem and acsid will explod.

Very interesting

Activity 1.1   **Your Opinions About Science**

Think about the following and then discuss your ideas with a colleague:

What *is* science? What features or characteristics distinguish science from nonscience?

1. What do you think about the statement that science is the search for truth?

Strongly disagree   1   2   3   4   5   Strongly agree

2. Compared with knowledge in other disciplines, scientific knowledge is more objective and unbiased.

Strongly disagree   1   2   3   4   5   Strongly agree

3. In research, scientists use the scientific method to solve problems and verify findings.

Strongly disagree   1   2   3   4   5   Strongly agree

4. In science, if a theory is supported as true, it becomes a law.

Strongly disagree   1   2   3   4   5   Strongly agree

5. Biological knowledge would be different today if the historic proportion of male and female biologists had been reversed.

Strongly disagree   1   2   3   4   5   Strongly agree

6. Most of the new ideas in science are produced by brilliant individuals.

Strongly disagree   1   2   3   4   5   Strongly agree

7. If experimental results fail to support a theory, scientists reject the theory and seek alternatives.

Strongly disagree   1   2   3   4   5   Strongly agree

8. Disagreements between scientists about a theory normally are solved when new data are generated related to the problem.

Strongly disagree   1   2   3   4   5   Strongly agree

An Operational Definition of Science

Science is a term that encompasses many scholarly fields, or disciplines, and so when we ask "What is science?" the question goes to the *nature of the endeavor* rather than simply the content of a particular discipline, such as astronomy, chemistry, or geology. A science teacher's goal should be to help students develop not only their *scientific knowledge* but also their *knowledge of science.* Every science lesson that you teach is both a lesson about a scientific topic, such as the water cycle, and a lesson about science itself, how scientists find out about such a thing, and why (Lederman, 2002). In fact, communicating the nature of science is now widely recognized as one of the general goals of science education. In its Project 2061, the American Association for the Advancement of Science identifies the nature of science as one of four categories of knowledge, skills, and attitudes essential for all citizens. Three principal aspects of the nature of science are emphasized:

- *The scientific world view:* The world is understandable, scientific ideas can change, scientific knowledge is long lasting, and science cannot provide complete answers to all questions.
- *Scientific methods of inquiry:* Science demands evidence, science blends logic and imagination, science explains and predicts, scientists try to identify and avoid bias, and science is not authoritarian.
- *The nature of the scientific enterprise:* Science is a complex social activity, science is organized into content disciplines and is conducted in various institutions, ethical principles govern the conduct of science, and scientists participate in public affairs both as specialists and as citizens (American Association for the Advancement of Science, 1990).

Your own concept of the nature of science is an important part of your content background and comes into play when you make decisions about what to teach and how to teach it. What you believe about the nature of science—how scientists come to know what they know, how they organize and warrant knowledge—influences what you present as science in your classroom and your own motivation to learn more science.

The word *science* is based upon the Latin *scire* ("skee-ray"), meaning *to know.* In this case, the term means to know about *nature,* the physical environment and phenomena. Just over a century ago people we call scientists today thought of themselves as "natural philosophers," and what they did was simply *systematic inquiry.* The German word for science, *Naturwissenschaft,* translates as systematic scholarship about nature, or "inquiry into the external world" (McCloskey, 1995, p. 19). The English meaning for science today is much the same as its counterparts in Japanese, French, Tamil, Turkish, and many other languages; the enterprise has become nearly universal, or at least *global.*

Danish physicist Niels Bohr said that the aim of science is to extend our experience and reduce it to order. But other aims of science are also found in the literature, including aims such as simplicity of explanation, instrumental control, problem solving, convergence on truth (while never being able to be absolutely certain of attaining it), and even the free flow of ideas and technological gain.

Science is *naturalistic,* which mean its scope is limited to what can be tested empirically (*empirical,* i.e., derived from experience and observation). Anything regarded as *supernatural* cannot be tested and therefore is outside the scope of science. Science is intimately tied to nature, and its explanations of nature are always open to question. Scientists specifically strive to ask questions that force us to reconsider, or consider further, what we know.

Questions of a religious nature, such as those about the human purpose on the planet, are less empirically decided, more dependent on faith. Of course faith holds *any* system of beliefs together, including those of science, even when evidence might call those beliefs into question. In both science and religion we seek explanations for nature and our place in it. Both are human endeavors. Science seeks to understand the world in a bottom-up, systematic way, with full awareness that our understanding is a work in process and that further questions and revision are to be expected.

Science as Problem Solving

If science is considered to be the process of understanding nature by finding answers to myriad questions from multiple perspectives, then *problem solving* is certainly an aspect of it. Obviously, questions provide the impetus for scientific investigation. Yet we all face questions every day. "How will I get to class if it rains today?" "What do I need at the grocery store?" "Where did I leave my keys?" These are everyday problems to be solved. But are they *scientific* problems? In answering them you would be accessing information already known. You would be problem solving, but you would not be doing the particular kind of problem solving that characterizes science.

The questions—the problems—in scientific investigation differ from the types of questions people typically face. For one thing, the answer in a scientific investigation is not already known. For another, the answer often produces *new* information. If the investigation replicates a previous research study, the additional result changes (strengthens or weakens) earlier findings. For this reason, problem solving in science is called *creative* problem solving (Ebert & Ebert, 1998). It is creative because investigations in science must necessarily question the implied or received parameters of the problem in order to gain a new perspective or response. If we do not question the "rules" of the problem, nothing new is likely to emerge.

Curiosity is what motivates us to ask questions, and kids are always asking questions. They want to make sense of the world around them, yet they have limited information. They ask questions, of themselves and others, that require knowledge beyond what they understand. Furthermore, young people rarely confine themselves to particular rules for finding answers to their questions. Scientists work by rules or conventions determined by their professional communities, often continually negotiated, and they have to be learned. Science is a systematic exploration with a willingness to change what one already knows.

The Processes of Science

Despite what you may have been taught, the processes of knowledge building in science cannot be reduced to a single method, the "scientific method." Scientists don't actually do their work through any particular series of steps (Latour & Woolgar, 1986). Sociologists who have studied scientists' work report that those familiar steps are more like the format used by scientists in writing up their work for peer review than a description of an investigation. The journal article is more a reconstruction of what actually went on in an investigation (Weininger, 1990).

One sure thing about science is that it is *empirically based,* that is, derived from experience, but in practice scientists use many different methods, and some are particular to the disciplines. For example, whereas chemists rely heavily on experimenting, archeologists and astronomers primarily observe and document. Because of the nature of their subject matter, the latter rarely use experimental methods. Whereas the stereotypical scientist wears a white coat and is surrounded by lab equipment, some scientists spend most of their time in the field. Others, such as theoretical physicists, work mostly with mathematical models and, like Einstein, do *gedanken* (thought) experiments.

Science has been conceptualized as a dialectic activity involving both thought and action (Bohm & Peat, 1987). The cycle of thought and action in science leads to the accumulation of ideas. The thought aspect is part of the natural curiosity that students bring to your class along with rudimentary skills in inquiry. The action is represented by the methods, or investigative techniques, that scientists—and students—use in answering their questions. Taken together, these processes of thought and action will enable your students to *do* science rather than simply *read about* science. The good news is that your students are natural investigators; that is, they bring these capabilities to your classroom. Your task is to help them refine their skills and systematize their investigations and their thinking.

SCIENCE AND CULTURE

Science and technology influence culture, and, reciprocally, culture influences science and technology. For instance, electric lights used for sporting events took what was an afternoon and weekend pastime and made it available at night. What effects do you suppose this had on patterns of family interaction? On the other hand, prevailing cultural priorities determine to a great extent which scientists' research is funded. Furthermore, as in ages past, science today provides rich material for writers and artists. Contemporary writers such as Michael Crichton and Stephen King often use science in their writing, but even Chaucer wrote about the astronomy and medicine of his day (Weininger, 1990).

Science is *culture laden.* Western scientific ideas are now widely disseminated, but they emanate from our particular cultural context and permeate the science of other countries to the extent that they are culturally compatible. But science is also influenced by non-Western knowledge and culture. In his book *Science Education for a Pluralist Society,* Michael Reiss (1993) says that many students "have no idea of the extent and significance of the contributions made to science by non-Western cultures" (p. 13). He argues that every science is an *ethnoscience,* such that "a scientist's *perceptions* of the natural world, as well as her interpretations, come through her senses, herself as a person, and her culture. There is no single, universal, acultural science" (Reiss, 1993, p. 24).

Science and Language

Language is another aspect of science as a human enterprise. Every language is a system of communication with sociocultural roots. Scientific knowledge is built on a framework of metaphor. Theories and models draw on cultural metaphors, and metaphors play an important role in communicating scientific ideas. Gloria Snively (1995) reminds us, "Language is a necessary medium for thinking and learning" (p. 59). Precision in language often is associated with science. Yet technical terms often cover a whole range of meanings, even among scientists. Sometimes this is a problem, but flexibility of concepts also can be helpful. Somewhat open-ended scientific metaphors enable scientists to find further applications for concepts and theories and also their limits (Weininger, 1990). Scientists also use common expressions to communicate special scientific meanings. The words *living* and *acceleration* can mean different things to scientists working in their fields than what they mean when used in everyday conversation. *Equilibrium* was first used in science but now has moved to the wider culture and acquired everyday meanings.

Hypotheses, Models, Theories, and Laws

Scientific investigations ultimately lead to the various *products* of science, taking such forms as facts, models, stories, and theories. Scientists tell stories and build models as ways of explaining their findings. Scientific work involves creating the stories and models and then testing them. Newtonian physics turns out to be mostly mathematical modeling, whereas Charles Darwin's biology is almost entirely story with no mathematical models (McCloskey, 1995). Such products of science as models, principles, theories, laws, and hypotheses are idealizations that represent the physical reality that itself is beyond our reach. By the middle grades, students should be able to describe and distinguish these products of science.

Models and theories differ in that theories need the support of more evidence than models and often encompass models. More specifically, models seek to explain *how* parts interact, whereas theories go further by attempting to explain *why* parts interact as they do. For example, a model of our solar system would show how the planets are arranged relative to the Sun but not necessarily explain *why* they are as they are in their orbits, which is explained by the solar nebular theory, the most widely accepted explanation of the formation of the solar system. In like manner, the big bang theory attempts to explain why the universe got started and why it is as it is today.

Theories and laws are the "Holy Grails" of science. However, contrary to the widely held misconception, theories *do not* become laws when they are proven. In fact, the inductive reasoning process used in science cannot lead to a proof for either theories or laws (one can prove things in geometry if the given axioms are accepted, but science doesn't start with axioms). But besides that, theories and laws are different categories of representations, just as apples and oranges are different categories of fruit. In science a theory is an *explanation* in which scientists place a great deal of confidence because it is supported both by substantial evidence and by logical inferences. Laws, on the other hand, are *descriptions,* often mathematical, of natural systems whose behavior has been observed repeatedly (Chalmers, 1999).

Many scientific laws were known before the theories that were later developed to explain them. For example, you may recall Boyle's law from your chemistry class. Robert Boyle performed a number of significant experiments on gases in the seventeenth century. From those experiments came Boyle's law: The volume of a confined gas whose temperature is held constant will vary in inverse proportion to the pressure on the gas. You'll notice that Boyle's law does not explain *why* gases behave in this way; rather, it describes the behavior of gases as repeatedly observed. And that is what laws are: *descriptions.* Boyle's law and the other ideal gas laws are explained by kinetic molecular theory, which describes gases as made up of tiny particles in motion.

Here's an example of theory and law in everyday terms. The law may be that the maximum speed for driving on the freeway is 65 mph. That is, 65 mph is the maximum rate at which an automobile may be operated (description of behavior) without being cited for a violation. This law can exist in the absence of any theory (explanation) of why there is such a law.

The *hypothesis* is yet another category of the products of science. Cultural dilution has affected the meaning of this term, and many inappropriately define a hypothesis as an educated guess. However, there is much more behind a well-formed hypothesis than just an educated guess. Hypotheses are *tentative explanations* or descriptions that guide investigations. As a description a hypothesis may state an *anticipated relationship* based on the available information. Testing the hypothesis may yield information that strengthens or weakens the scientist's confidence in the model, theory, or law under consideration. Many teachers mistakenly use the term *hypothesis* when they really want students to make a prediction. Predicting and hypothesizing are subtly different.

Models and theories, then, are *explanations* of observations. Laws are *descriptions* of natural systems that have been repeatedly observed. And hypotheses are tentative statements of an anticipated relationship or explanation.

SCIENCE AND TECHNOLOGY

Distinguishing between science and technology is difficult for many students. In fact, many adults often don't distinguish between the two. The relationship actually is mutually beneficial in that each facilitates the work of the other (Ebert & Ebert, 1998). Nevertheless, science and technology are distinctly different: "Simply stated, science seeks to understand the world around us, and technology takes scientifically generated knowledge and gives it *practical value* by developing processes and machines that extend capabilities" (p. 56).

Henry Nielson (1992), author of *The Endless Spiral,* suggests another perspective on technology: "Technology is changing materials, information, and energy from one form into another." Science and technology can be contrasted in other ways as well. In science, theories are warranted through observations of natural phenomena, whereas in technology tools, materials, and processes are applied to develop human adaptive systems (Sanders, 1993).

From a sociocultural view, Ryan and Aikenhead (1992) assert that the social purpose of science is to generate new knowledge, and the social purpose of technology is to respond to human and social needs. In other words, science seeks understanding, whereas technology seeks to solve problems.

SCIENCE AND PHILOSOPHY

What people think about the nature of science has changed over time. Science to contemporary scholars is a different kind of enterprise from what it was thought to be only a few generations ago. The degree of change amounts to what philosopher of science Thomas Kuhn (1962) has called a *paradigm shift*, meaning that the whole picture has changed. Although scholars still differ on many issues, the consensus is that *positivism*, the earlier view, has been discredited. Even when positivism was the dominant view, a minority argued for an alternative. Thinkers who planted the seeds for what is now called *constructivism* were Immanuel Kant, Henry James, Charles Sanders Peirce, and John Dewey. Crafters of postpositivist philosophies of science include Thomas Kuhn and other historians, philosophers, and sociologists of science. Despite decades of conversation about the nature of science, there is no uniformity of opinion. There are many unsettled issues about the nature of science and knowledge.

Our own view is that scientists' work is *creative* and takes many diverse forms. As we see it, the main goal of scientific work is to create explanations of nature that are warranted by evidence, help us make sense of our experience, and are useful. "The great game of science," as Hestenes (1992) states, "is modeling the real world, and each scientific theory lays down a system of rules for playing the game. The object of the game is to construct valid models of real objects and processes. Such models comprise the core of scientific knowledge. To understand science is to know how scientific models are constructed and validated" (p. 732).

The evolution of what might be called the contemporary view of science began in the eighteenth century. As the 1700s began, natural philosophers pondered the mysteries of the natural world. Those early explanations couldn't help but be influenced by the political and religious thought and social contexts that shaped those times. The radical ideas of the Enlightenment were especially influential.

Positivism

Nineteenth-century philosopher Auguste Compte coined the term *positivism*, but its roots can be traced back to Francis Bacon, the "Father of Modern Science" (Isaac Newton and René Descartes are also regarded as founders of modern science). The positivist conception of science gradually developed and took its most extreme form in nineteenth-century Europe. The basic assumptions that underlie and characterize positivism as a philosophy of science include the following:

- That a single, tangible reality exists "out there" that can be broken apart into pieces and studied independently (thus the whole is just the sum of the parts)
- That the observer can be separated from the observed, the knower from the known
- That observations are separated in time and context, such that what is true at one time and place is true at another time and place
- That causality is linear, that there are no effects without causes and no causes without effects
- That objectivity is possible, and methodology guarantees that the results of an inquiry can be free from the influence of values and beliefs (Lincoln & Guba, 1985)

Scholars today do not consider the assumptions of the positivists to be logically defensible. The problem for teachers is that many science textbooks and classroom programs may still reflect outdated positivist views. For example, students still might find it written in a textbook or trade book that scientists have "proven" this or that. Science depicted as nothing more than an accumulation of facts is also positivistic. Why do the old ideas still linger? For one thing, it often takes a long time for a new idea to be discussed and negotiated. Cultural historians consider a century to be the time needed for the dissemination of a major concept through culture.

Constructivism

Constructivists perceive science as a complex of meanings *negotiated* in a community of practitioners. From a constructivist view of science, instead of seeking proof, scientists work to convince their peers that what they propose reasonably fits the available data, aids understanding, and is useful in making predictions and decisions. In other words, scientists seek to show that their idea meets criteria of *warranted assertability* and *viability* (von Glasersfeld, 1989). Constructivists also make assumptions. Established in the twelfth and thirteenth centuries by the Scholastics, science assumes the susceptibility of the physical universe to human ordering and understanding. Then there is the assumption that, ultimately, science is driven by curiosity and that science aims at both comprehensiveness and simplification in its explanations of nature. Other assumptions include that the process of explaining nature in science involves the use of multiple methods in open social interaction between researchers that is dynamic and ongoing. These methods of science are characterized by more than procedural attributes and extend more toward the realm of values than techniques. There is another assumption: that science cannot guarantee truth, cannot prove its explanations. Thus tentativeness and uncertainty characterize all science.

Constructivism and the Teaching of Science

You can weave more explicit instruction about the nature of science into your program, gearing the content to your students' readiness. With your help, your students can develop a richer and more contemporary conception of the nature of science as they work with each other in conducting investigations and constructing knowledge. First, you need to be aware of your students' initial conceptions and challenge them to think more about their ideas (just as we have been challenging you to think about your ideas throughout this chapter).

A number of aspects of the nature of science have been extracted from eight current international curriculum standard documents. Notice that these ideas are complementary:

- Scientific knowledge, though durable, has a tentative character.
- Scientific knowledge relies heavily, but not entirely, on observation, experimental evidence, rational arguments, and skepticism.
- There is no one way to do science (therefore, there is no universal step-by-step scientific method).
- Science is an attempt to explain natural phenomena.
- Laws and theories serve different roles in science; therefore, students should know that theories do not become laws even with additional evidence.
- People from all cultures contribute to science.
- New knowledge must be reported clearly and openly.
- Scientists need accurate record keeping, peer review, and replicability.
- Observations are theory laden.
- Scientists are creative.
- The history of science reveals both an evolutionary and a revolutionary character.
- Science is part of social and cultural traditions.
- Science and technology influence each other.
- Scientific ideas are affected by their social and historical milieu (McComas et al., 1998, p. 513).

In addition, a number of implications for teaching practice have been discussed in the science education literature (Duschl, 1989; Duschl & Hamilton, 1992; Flick & Lederman, 2004; Keeley, Eberle, & Farrin, 2005). We need to create a classroom climate in which students feel comfortable in sharing their beliefs about science, their naive theories. Students need to recognize how one's expectations and beliefs affect observation and data selection in scientific work. You can help students make their ideas more explicit by asking them why they have said such-and-such and encouraging them to elaborate in their explanations. We recognize that the theory side of scientific investigations has been neglected in the curriculum and that we need to pay more attention to theory to balance our attention to the empirical side.

Another suggestion is that classroom activities and investigations should be less like cookbook recipes and more like the open-ended investigations of real scientific work. The danger in teaching the old list of steps for the scientific method without students actually internalizing how to study something scientifically is that students come away with the misconception that one just goes through the steps, and the answers will appear at the end. They do not grasp the real nature of the work: the reviewing of previous work and input of colleagues, the false starts, dead ends, and trial and error, or the value of failure as part of science. When they do an investigation with results different from their hypothesis (assuming they have one), they conclude, "It didn't work!" and think that they have failed.

To model real science in the making, instructional activities and situations should engage students in more student-to-student discussion of scientific ideas and more cooperative group work (Dickens, 2005). Students can also experience an aspect of the nature of science by using special tools, as scientists do in their investigations. Such tools include simple rulers, tape measures, and trundle wheels (all for measuring length or distance), measuring cups or graduated beakers (for capacity), thermometers, spring scales (for weight), equal-arm platform balances (for mass), and stopwatches, sundials, hourglasses, and clocks (for time). More complex instruments include microscopes and telescopes.

After students have used the tools, taken their measurements, and organized and analyzed their data, you can help them critique their work and call their attention to the process of their investigation and the value of using the tools. This kind of metacognitive activity is instrumental in students' epistemological development.

Of course, computers are a major tool in science and other endeavors. Scientists use them in a variety of ways. Like scientists, children can use computers with probe attachments containing sensors that directly measure phenomena such as temperature. Also like scientists, students can use computers for modeling and simulating physical systems. A simulation creates a "microworld" in which students can observe contrived systems and make and test their hypotheses and predictions.

Finally, we recommend that you give more attention in your classroom curriculum to the history of science and technology. This content can be shared with your social studies program. Studying historical exemplars that illustrate the creation and negotiation of scientific knowledge can help students learn about the human face of science.

CONCLUSION

It is not necessary to adopt a constructivist philosophy in order to teach science. A philosophy is a personal choice, and that sentiment is very much in keeping with a constructivist view. Whatever your perspective, it will have a profound influence on your approach to the teaching of science. For example, constructivists recognize the value of the inherent curiosity that students bring to school and see science as dynamic rather than static, a continual process of understanding the natural world. Constructivists view the construction of knowledge as occurring through one's interaction with people and phenomena. From this perspective, your task as a teacher is to provide opportunities for the engagements that will allow your students to construct knowledge, and to continually monitor that process in order to ensure that your instructional goals are being met.

This chapter has focused on developing *your* understanding of the nature of science and of how science is a human endeavor. This is particularly important for you as a teacher to understand. Why? Because your students will bring to your classroom a lot of naive ideas about science that they have developed over the years. Indeed, it might be easier for you if each of your students came to you *tabula rasa* (a blank slate), as Locke supposed. However, that will not be the case.

Many teachers are still unfamiliar with contemporary ideas about the nature of science. The view of science still being communicated in many classrooms is that science is a body of knowledge compiled through the steps of the scientific method. This is not surprising because some textbooks still inappropriately and inaccurately depict science as objective, value-free knowledge that accumulates as experiments prove or disprove hypotheses and theories.

As you consider what we've discussed in this chapter you will realize that there are many warranted answers to the question "What is science?" Throughout this book we will discuss ways in which teachers can orient classroom practice in order to help their students develop more sophisticated notions of science. The key recommendation in the National Standards is that children become engaged in active *inquiry* and through their own investigations be provided opportunities to reflect on what they believe about science and scientists. And it all begins here and now as you consider your own ideas about the nature of science.

2

The Content
of K–8 Science

The Scope of K–8 Science

K–8 Content in the National Science Education Standards

Obstacles to Implementing a Depth-Oriented Science Program

Your Academic Roadmap

This chapter should help you to understand the following ideas:

- An effective science education program is one that emphasizes depth as opposed to breadth.
- A framework approach to the development of a science curriculum makes connections between one topic and another more apparent.
- The National Science Education Standards (National Research Council, 1996) address curriculum content and programmatic standards from classrooms to school systems and also speak to teacher education.
- Professional wisdom suggests a move away from the textbook-dominated "read-about" approach to science education.
- Many resources are available to enrich the classroom science program.

The present curricula in science and mathematics are overstuffed and undernourished.

—Rutherford and Ahlgren
(1990, p. xvi)

THE SCOPE OF K–8 SCIENCE

The scope of science itself is enormous, and so is the scope of the K–8 science curriculum. It is unlikely that any teacher would be familiar with *all* the science content for such a span of grades, but then again, teachers periodically are called on to teach unfamiliar subject matter. The curriculum prescribed by typical state curriculum guides that are based on the National Science Education Standards includes the physical, life, and earth and space sciences, as well as additional content related to inquiry, the nature of science, and science in personal and social interactions. In the elementary grades, some aspect of each of these content areas is to be taught each year. Thus teaching science may seem challenging for anyone who was never seriously interested in studying science and may never have developed a conceptual framework with which to meaningfully structure the subject matter.

In terms of structure, having a science textbook may help, but it's unlikely that a textbook will provide all the background information you need to plan your science lessons. Sometimes the task of planning and enacting the classroom science program may seem overwhelming. However, if you can grasp the big picture and develop a basic framework, you can move forward. Having on hand some appropriate resources will help you get the details together. The good news is that the longer you teach science, the more you will assimilate the content yourself, so that you can count on your own knowledge, and your confidence will grow with each successive year in the classroom.

The science content discussed in this chapter is based on the framework developed by the National Science Education Standards, published in 1996 by the National Research Council (NRC) of the National Academy of Sciences. These standards represent a broad framework for planning a classroom science program. They also influenced the development of many state standards. Regardless of where you teach, you will find it useful to understand the content framework of the National Science Education Standards. However, we would be remiss if we did not point out that standards are just part—the framework, if you will—of an overall approach to science education. Also involved are issues such as the appropriate content preparation of teachers, curriculum development, support for the new curriculum, and provisions for assessment and accountability (Sunal & Wright, 2006).

Less Is More

The notion of "less is more" can be traced back to the Greek poet Hesiod (~700 B.C.E.), but the phrase is most associated with Mies van der Rohe, the architect of unadorned, functional buildings who adopted the phrase as a guiding principle for his work. The idea was applied to education in *Horace's Compromise,* a book by Theodore Sizer (1984) that focuses on improving U.S. secondary schools. It was then picked up by the American Association for the Advancement of Science in its Project 2061 (AAAS, 1990) and then by the National Science Education Standards. Thus, for science education at all levels, there is now an emphasis on science's "big ideas," and the charge for teachers is to address fewer concepts in greater depth, with more emphasis on understanding and less emphasis on the recall of vocabulary. As a guiding principle in planning units and lessons, "less is more" means *depth* is preferred over *coverage.*

Think about this: "To cover" refers to concealing something rather than exposing it for consideration. When teachers try to cover too much content, their students tend to get stuck at a low level of thinking, which is all that is needed for simply remembering information. Wouldn't you prefer that your students comprehend the richness and complexity within a few topics than being superficially exposed to many topics? Studying something in depth leads to better retention and increases the chances that what has been learned will be applied in new situations. Instead of being overwhelmed by too many facts and new terms, students engaged in in-depth studies are more likely to experience the satisfaction of mastering some particular content. Unfortunately, few students today have the intellectual experience of reaching the point in their studies where they can perceive the limits of knowledge and where they can generate new questions that lead them into creative inquiry. We hope you will agree and that your students will be able to "go beyond simple declarative statements to differentiation, elaboration, qualification, and integration" (Newmann, 1988, p. 346).

Frameworks for Science Content

Because schooling is an intentional process ultimately directed by the larger society, people at many levels have a stake in what gets taught, and politics is involved. As a teacher, you will have ample opportunity for your own creative curriculum making, but you will also be constrained by society's dictates. These dictates range from local school board policies (e.g., on the use of animals in the classroom or field trip policies) to your state's standards documents. In order to constrain the constant addition of new material to the science curriculum, state frameworks have been mandated by the No Child Left Behind Act to delineate the categories of content and the key concepts to be addressed at each level. These frameworks specify content but leave the pedagogy to you, the teacher. The science program that results from the combination of content and pedagogy encompasses of all the science-related opportunities available for students to experience under the aegis of the school.

In the past, the science content of the K–8 curriculum was divided into two broad categories: physical science and life science. Later, science was divided into physical science, life science, and earth and space science. In other schemes, such as the AAAS-sponsored program of the 1970s, "Science: A Process Approach" (SAPA), the science processes (e.g., observing, measuring) were emphasized, and conceptual content was secondary. Thus science can be organized in different frameworks, and each approach has had its advocates. In this chapter we will use the framework adopted by the National Science Education Standards (Table 2.1; National Research Council, 1996).

In the best of all possible worlds, all teachers would be thoroughly familiar with every topic before teaching it, but it is in the practice of instruction itself that teachers often learn the content in depth and come to feel comfortable with it. We recommend that you be less concerned about covering all the content specified in your state standards or in the textbook and instead focus on creating units that enable your students to explore one or more aspects of the content in depth. Start your unit planning by thinking about the major ideas related to the area. If you are developing a physical science unit for primary grades, for example, a major idea will be "properties of matter." Create an outline or sketch out a graphic organizer, such as the one in Figure 2.1. This "framework" approach will help you see connections between ideas and structure the development of relevant learning activities.

K–8 CONTENT IN THE NATIONAL SCIENCE EDUCATION STANDARDS

In the National Science Education Standards, science content is considered in clusters of grades rather than grade by grade, as is the case in many state standards. On the basis of children's cognitive development and teacher experience, grades are grouped as levels K–4 and 5–8. At each level the National Science Education Standards address major concepts in the physical, life, and earth and space sciences and the five additional content categories indicated in Table 2.1. We will first summarize the content of the traditional categories of physical, life, and earth and space science and then look at the five other content areas.

Table 2.1 A Framework for Science Program Content Devised by the National Science Education Standards

In the National Science Education Standards, Grades K–8 science is divided into eight content categories:

Science as inquiry

Physical science (physics and chemistry)

Life science (biology and ecology)

Earth and space science (astronomy, meteorology, oceanography, and geology)

Science and technology

Science in personal and social perspectives

History and nature of science

Unifying concepts and processes

Figure 2.1   Concept Map: Properties of Objects and Materials for a Primary Unit

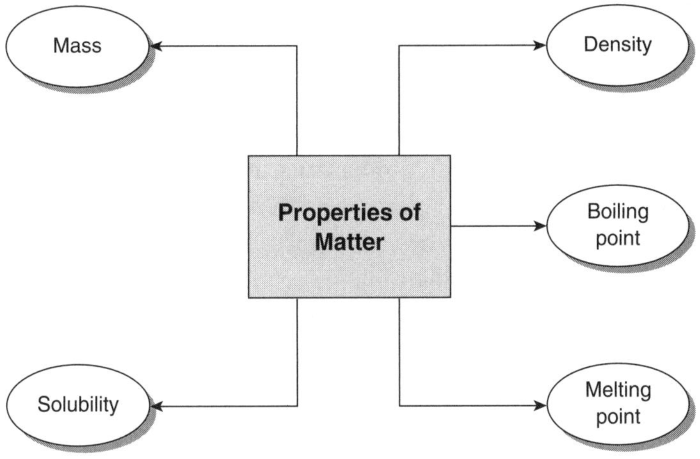

Physical Science

The physical science content in the K–8 curriculum is chiefly about forces, motions, matter, and energy. Forces include pushes and pulls, friction, and gravity. Motions vary in starting position, speed, and direction. Forces and motions are also related to machines. Matter is studied through investigation of the properties of things. Energy includes mechanical energy, sound, light, heat, electricity, and magnetism. The study of energy also includes potential and kinetic energy, the transformation of energy from one type to another, and sources of energy.

According to the National Science Education Standards, students in Grades K–4 are to understand

Properties of objects and materials

Position and motion of objects

Light, heat, electricity, and magnetism

Students in Grades 5–8 are to understand

Properties and changes of properties in matter

Motions and forces

Transformations of energy

Physical Science for Grades K–4

Young children explore the physical world in their everyday environment by observing and manipulating objects. They need many experiences with different things and in different contexts so that they can compare, sort, and describe these experience as their understanding develops and expands.

Younger children describe objects and materials and how they behave and change in *qualitative* terms. As their knowledge develops they will begin to use *quantitative* descriptions.

Investigations children carry out in their early years can provide a basis in experience for conceptual growth. Experiences with heat that focus on changes in temperature, for example, can later be drawn on when children grapple with the difference between degrees in temperature and calories of heat.

As they go through school, children find that they can extend their descriptions by measuring things. First they use nonstandard units (e.g., hand lengths, pencil lengths) and measuring devices they've made (e.g., markings on a stick), and later they use standard metric units and instruments such as rulers, meter sticks, measuring cups, thermometers, scales, and balances. By recording and graphing the measurements they make, children begin to recognize patterns and order in the physical world.

Physical Science for Grades 5–8

In the upper elementary grades students move from the properties of objects and materials to studying the properties of the substances from which the materials are made. These properties include solubility, density, and boiling and melting points. They also study simple chemical changes and learn about elements and compounds. Students learn that some substances share characteristics and can be grouped into categories, such as acids or metals.

Another area of physical science is force and motion. Students can experience the motions of simple objects, such as marbles, balls, and toys, and can move from qualitative descriptions in the early grades to more quantitative descriptions. They can learn to represent motion on a graph, and they can describe the forces acting on objects, such as friction, a force that slows down a ball rolling across the floor.

Students' understanding of energy is developed through early experiences with sound, light, heat, electricity and magnetism, gravity, and objects in motion. From such experiences students develop the idea that energy comes in different forms and from many sources. They learn to identify the Sun as the major source of energy for the Earth (but not the *only* source because there is also geothermal energy from within the Earth). In the upper elementary grades students begin to tackle more complex ideas (e.g., that light consists of different wavelengths and that energy can be transferred from one form to another). In studying energy, students should be provided with opportunities to experience a variety of energy transformations, such as the conversion of chemical energy to light or heat in fire, magnetism to electricity, and electricity to sound.

Life Science Content

Life science content specified in the National Science Education Standards includes the study of different kinds of organisms, their behaviors and functioning, habitats and life cycles, and interactions and relationships. Life science is also about the constituents of an organism, including the structure of the parts and how they function. The life science emphasis in grades K–4 is on plants and animals.

All grades K–4 students are to develop an understanding of

Characteristics of organisms

Life cycles of organisms

Organisms and environments

For Grades 5–8, the National Science Education Standards specify that students understand

Structure and function in living systems

Reproduction and heredity

Regulation and behavior

Populations and ecosystems

Diversity and adaptations of organisms

Life Science for Grades K–4

In the early grades children should be able to experience and study different kinds of living things and their habitats. From their observations children can begin to distinguish living from nonliving and can begin to categorize living things in a scientific manner. Young children also begin to understand the needs of living things and how organisms behave to meet their needs. They can understand that organisms possess different structures that function in particular ways to help them meet their needs. Early experience with living things is the basis for understanding biological diversity and the dependence of organisms on the living and nonliving environment for survival. Such experience also is the basis for the realization that all organisms cause changes where they live, *including humans,* and that such changes may be beneficial or harmful to them and to other organisms.

Young children also should have experiences with organisms in the different stages of their life cycles. In the early grades, children may not grasp the continuity of life through different stages, such as, for the frog, from egg to tadpole to adult. Although young children realize that organisms resemble their parents, they are not likely to understand the inheritance of traits. They may think traits come from only one parent or are just a blend of each parent's characteristics. In addition, they should learn that features of an organism may be changed or become developed through the organism's interactions with its environment.

Life Science for Grades 5–8

In the upper elementary and middle school years, students move from a focus on individual organisms to both the larger context of ecosystems and the smaller dimension of the units of organisms and cells. Older children begin to develop concepts of nutrient and energy flows in an ecosystem ("matter cycles, energy flows"). They can relate heritability of characteristics across generations to adaptation and evolution. In learning about ecosystems, older students can grasp concepts of food webs, food pyramids, and trophic levels (producers, consumers, decomposers). They also can understand the concepts of ecosystem carrying capacity and niche. Their investigations can be increasingly quantitative, and they can learn to use instruments such as the microscope.

In the upper elementary grades, students can recognize that structures and functions are complementary at different levels of organization: cells, organs, systems, whole organisms, and ecosystems. Students can understand more about the nature of disease, such that some diseases result from the failure of a bodily system, whereas infectious agents cause other diseases. They can understand the difference between asexual and sexual reproduction, the role of specialized cells, such as sperm and eggs, and how hereditary information is carried by genes on the chromosomes of every cell.

Students in the upper grades are particularly interested in their own bodies, which makes this a good time to help them relate life science concepts to the human organism and our environment. Preteens become involved in activities such as sports, music, and the arts. One way to help them realize the relevance of life science to their lives is to help them see how their performance in sports or on the stage is related to the coordinated functioning of their bodily organs and systems (concepts of metabolism and homeostasis).

Earth and Space Science Content

The earth and space science content in the National Science Education Standards includes a range of topics from several scientific disciplines. These include physical and historical geology, astronomy and cosmology, meteorology and climatology, and physical oceanography and marine science.

In Grades K–4 the National Science Education Standards specify that students develop an understanding of the following topics in the earth and space sciences:

Properties of Earth materials

Objects in the sky

For Grades 5–8, the National Science Education Standards call for students to understand

The structure of the earth system

Earth history

Earth in the solar system

Earth and Space Science for Grades K–4

In the early grades, science instruction in this area should be focused on the concrete everyday world that children experience. Young children should be encouraged to use their observational skills to become aware of interesting details of their environment and changes that occur in their surroundings. They should develop their abilities to describe and explain what they observe. It is through talking about what they think and drawing what they see that children create the background for understanding more abstract concepts later.

Primary children can study the properties of earth materials (rocks, soils, water, and air). They can learn that the properties of these materials make them *useful,* such as for making things and for supporting life. They also can learn that such materials may be made up of parts or may be composed of different kinds of materials. For example, children can observe different constituents in typical rocks such as granite, gneiss, and conglomerate. At this level, it isn't important that they identify the constituents as minerals, that they learn what geologists call the rock, or even that they can classify the rock by its source (sedimentary, igneous, or metamorphic). Such ideas certainly will become relevant as these students move into the intermediate and middle grades. However, younger children can describe how different rocks and their different constituents look and feel. They also can begin to collect rocks, fossils, shells, and leaves, and such collections can be used in various investigations.

In their study of life and earth science children should regularly visit outdoor study sites. By observing changes in a specific place on a regular basis, children come to realize that change is the normal state of nature and that some of the changes occur in predictable ways and in patterns. The idea of change can be extended so that children may come to realize there are many time scales for change. For example, even young children can appreciate that fossils are evidence of creatures that lived in the distant past.

As early as first grade, children can keep science journals or nature logs as a way of recording and processing their experiences (Gallas, 1995). Later, they can use instruments such as thermometers and meter sticks to take and record measurements in their journals. They can be taught to organize their measurements in charts and simple graphs. For example, primary grade children can study the changes in the position of objects in the sky, such as the Sun and the Moon. They can draw the shape of the Moon as it changes through a lunar cycle. These drawings can be arranged in sequence and displayed in the classroom as a reminder of this predictable cyclical change. Young children can understand that moon phases relate to changes in the position of the Moon relative to the Sun and the Earth.

Earth and Space Science for Grades 5–8

By the middle grades students are more able to understand the positions, distances, and dynamics between the Earth, the Sun, and the Moon, ideas that are too abstract for the very young. These students also can work with models of the Earth-Sun-Moon system and the solar system. Furthermore, older children are able to consider the Earth as a *system* in which four components interact: geosphere, hydrosphere, atmosphere, and biosphere.

As for the hydrosphere, students at this level can understand the unique physical and chemical properties of water. For example, they can grasp that water is a solvent that dissolves minerals and gases and carries them to the oceans, and they can understand that water exhibits many unique properties, such as that it expands when it freezes and that its unusual surface tension is the result of the structure and polarity of its molecule.

Middle-level students can understand the theory of plate tectonics and grasp the sequence of events during Earth's history. They can speculate on how trends in the movements of the tectonic plates will make the Earth appear differently at various times in the future.

Middle-level students also can understand more about geophysical and geochemical cycles, such as the rock cycle, the water cycle, and the carbon cycle, and the processes of weathering, erosion, evaporation, and condensation. Students can understand how some geological events or processes are destructive, such as earthquakes and erosion, whereas others are constructive, such as mountain building through volcanic eruptions or sea floor spreading. Most students of this age will have little trouble conceptualizing evaporation, but condensation is likely to be more challenging.

The Additional Content Areas

In addition to the traditional subject matter areas of physical, life, and earth and space science, the National Science Education Standards add five other categories of content:

Science as inquiry

Science and technology

Science in personal and social perspectives

History and nature of science

Unifying concepts and processes

Science as Inquiry

The content standard for scientific inquiry and the standard on the history and nature of science overlap. As to the former, the National Science Education Standards state that as a result of activities, all students in kindergarten to Grade 8 should develop skills necessary to *do* scientific inquiry and develop an understanding *about* scientific inquiry. According to the National Science Education Standards, scientific inquiry consists of the many ways scientists study nature and propose explanations for natural phenomena based on the evidence derived from their work. In the classroom, inquiry consists of the activities in which children develop their understanding of scientific ideas and their understanding of how scientists conduct their work (NRC, 1996). Note that the standards also refer to inquiry as an approach to teaching in which students are enabled to conduct investigations themselves.

History and Nature of Science

The standard for the history and nature of science states that as a result of classroom activities, all K–8 students should develop an understanding of science as a human endeavor. For Grades 5–8, students should expand their understandings of the nature of science and the history of science. Science is a human endeavor in that people of different cultures have always sought to understand the world and to solve problems encountered in their environment. Since the earliest days of our species, people of many cultures have learned from their experiences and have contributed to the understandings of nature that we have in science today. Today many people from various ethnic and cultural backgrounds work in a science-related career. There are many types of employment in science fields from which people of different educational levels can both earn a good living and gain satisfaction in their work. A PhD is not a prerequisite for a science career.

Teachers typically have not emphasized the development of students' conceptions of the history and nature of science (NRC, 1996). Yet students can gain much insight from studying the history of science. Through the use of short stories teachers can integrate into instruction examples of people from the past and from different cultures and from various ethnicities who have contributed to science.

Science and Technology

Regarding science and technology, the National Science Education Standards state that as a result of classroom activities, all K–4 students should develop

Abilities to distinguish between natural objects and human-made objects

Abilities of technological design

Understanding about science and technology

The latter two aspects of the standard are also repeated for Grades 5–8. The science and technology standard extends the idea of *inquiry* in science to the parallel idea of *design* in technology. Young children often are able to carry out design activities with more understanding of the processes involved than is the case with inquiry activities. Older children can tackle more complex problems and can begin to distinguish between science and technology.

Science in Personal and Social Perspectives

The standard for science in personal and social perspectives states that as a result of activities all K–8 students should develop their understanding of personal health. Additionally, K–4 students should develop an understanding of

Characteristics and changes in populations

Types of resources

Changes in environments

Science and technology "in local challenges"

Students in Grades 5–8 also should develop understanding of

Populations, resources, and environments

Natural hazards

Risks and benefits

Science and technology in society

The content specified in this standard represents a foundation for students' developing understandings required of citizens in a democratic society and of the kind of actions they can and should take as citizens of their towns, states, and nations and as citizens of the world. This standard also connects science in the curriculum with social studies and health education, which makes it a great focus for curriculum integration. Younger and older children alike can learn about and act on problems and issues related to science and technology in their own communities.

Unifying Concepts and Processes

The standard for unifying concepts and processes lists the following major themes found across the sciences, which are to be integrated into content for the curriculum from kindergarten through Grade 12:

Order and organization

Evidence, models, and explanation

Constancy, change, and measurement

Evolution and equilibrium

Form and function

These are some of the interdisciplinary "big ideas" that can be found as threads in the fabric of science. Other major curriculum documents, such as *Benchmarks for Science Literacy* (American Association for the Advancement of Science, 1993), have different lists of the important conceptual themes but nevertheless emphasize the value of such "big ideas" in organizing the science curriculum.

The five new content categories discussed here can and should be integrated into the three basic subject matter categories of physical, life, and earth and space science. Taken together these five content categories provide the themes and the tone of science instruction. For instance, a life science unit about plants might include something about one or more of the scientists, such as Barbara McClintock, who made important contributions. The content of the same unit might include consideration of the methods and technologies used by scientists in the life sciences. A good example would be Stephen Hale's fascinating experiments to determine where plants obtain the materials for their growth. He was the first to show that "it is the evaporation of water from the leaves, not the pressure of water in the roots that is the prime mover in the circulation of the sap" (Harré, 1981, pp. 60–61). He also hypothesized that a great proportion of the weight of the plant must come from the air and not from the soil (you might find that many of your students mistakenly believe that plant growth comes from soil. While the soil may provide some mineral nutrients, green plants make their own food).

OBSTACLES TO IMPLEMENTING A DEPTH-ORIENTED SCIENCE PROGRAM

There are many obstacles to creating an in-depth and inquiry-oriented science program. One obstacle is that few elementary teachers, as students, have ever experienced this kind of science teaching. The cliché that one teaches as one has been taught points to the need for positive role models for teaching science. If you are typical of most K–8 teachers, your own experience was dominated by "chalk 'n' talk," coverage-oriented science (see Activity 2.1). Designing a depth-oriented inquiry classroom program will be challenging simply because it is new and unfamiliar.

Activity 2.1　**Standards Around the United States**

All 50 states have their own frameworks or standards for the science curriculum. These can be found on the Web by doing a search or accessed at http://www.academicbenchmarks.com/.

1. Locate your state's science standards or framework.

2. Compare your state's standards to the National Science Education Standards discussed in this chapter.

What are the content areas in your state's science program?

Select any grade level and look to see in what ways the content for your state is similar to and different from the nationwide standards.

Another obstacle you may face is finding appropriate teaching resources. Many materials are not designed to support an inquiry approach. If you are unfamiliar with the subject matter, you might find textbook readings, worksheets, and "cookbook" activities appealing because they provide structure and anchors in your lessons. Unfortunately, activities of this sort, which culminate in a single right answer or depict science as authoritarian, unintentionally misrepresent the nature of science (McGuiness, Roth, & Gilmer, 2002). Furthermore, typical textbooks cover too wide a range of topics and consequently tend to treat each topic superficially.

Still another obstacle to designing and implementing an in-depth inquiry approach is that many of your students have been culturally conditioned to expect to be taught in the traditional way. Because so many teachers in the past have relied exclusively on textbooks as their curriculum guide, many students have learned that they can succeed in science class just by completing discrete tasks and relying on rote memory.

Also playing into this is the culturally conditioned attitude many American students hold about their schoolwork that undermines sustained concentration on any one topic. Many students have spent far too many hours watching television or playing electronic action games. The media have dubbed children between the ages of 8 and 18 "Generation M," which stands for either "Generation Media" or the "Millennial Generation." These young people, who are growing up in the early twenty-first century, differ in their values and social structures, and, according to Royal van Horn (2006), "they not only use technology, they embrace it" (p. 727). Van Horn cites a recent Kaiser Family Foundation study (http://www.kff.org) that found that each day Generation M averages 3:04 hours watching TV, 1:11 hours watching recorded videos, 0:43 hours reading print, 1:44 hours listening to audio media, 1:02 hours on computers surfing the Net, and 0:49 hours playing video games. That makes for a total exposure to media of 8:33 hours per day, but the total time spent amounts to 6:21 hours because most kids are multitasking. These students tend to have less patience for in-depth studies and expect quick, simple, unambiguous answers, or soundbites.

It is also inevitable that a student in your class will ask you science questions that are far beyond your knowledge. Because your own experience as a student has convinced you that teachers should be subject matter experts, you may feel inadequate as a result. K. C. Cole (1982), a physicist and award-winning science writer, describes an experience she had years before, just after she had completed a book on light and optics. She was sailing on a sloop in the Virgin Islands and noticed the brilliance of the shimmering deep blue and green colors of the sea. So she asked her sailing companions about the cause of this effect. They quickly and unambiguously replied that the colors depended on the angle of the Sun, the shade of the sky, and the contour of the shore. Feeling ashamed and embarrassed at her own ignorance, Cole "crawled back into the cabin, vowing never to let my stupidity out in public again" (p. 18). But the story does not end there.

Later, back in the science museum where she worked, Cole asked three physicist friends why the waters of Tortola glimmered so in blues and greens: "To my surprise and delight, they argued about the issue for days—and no one pretended to have a single right answer" (p. 18). Cole's anecdote illustrates a very important point: In science, there are no stupid questions. Cole goes on to say,

Many people shy away from science because they are afraid to ask stupid questions. Somewhere along the line they have been led to believe that all scientific questions have clear, unambiguous answers. They have been taught that science is all work and no play, all logic and no guesswork, all knowledge and no wonder. The truth is that the more complete the answer in science, the juicier the next question. . . . Mark Twain used to say that the best thing about science was the enormous amount of conjecture one earned for such a trifling investment of fact. (p. 18)

The experience of many top scientists has been that the more they learn, the more they are aware of what they still don't know. "The greatest of all the accomplishments of twentieth-century science," notes scientist and physician Lewis Thomas (1978), "has been the discovery of human ignorance" (p. 15). As Cole (1982) concludes, "Asking stupid questions is usually worth the price in humility or embarrassment; because asking stupid questions is often a very good way to get smart" (p. 18).

Our point is that you should never feel as if you should have all the answers to students' questions, because nobody does. Nor should you ever communicate to a student that his or her question was a stupid one. If you don't know the answer, just say so. You might be tempted to add, "but we can find out together." But we recommend that you do not because there might not be an answer that can be derived through the methods of science. Remember, science is terrific, but it is a *limited* human endeavor.

Finally, there is one other very real obstacle to the implementation of an inquiry-oriented science program, particularly on a schoolwide basis. Believe it or not, it is the teachers themselves. In one study (Enyedy, Goldberg, & Welsh, 2006) it was found that because teachers bring their own experiences to an inquiry approach, it is not unreasonable that different teachers will have different interests and different emphases, and consequently their classes can be expected to go in different directions despite starting from the same topic. On one hand, this offers the opportunity for an even wider range of experiences if students from different classes can compare notes. On the other hand, it points out just how important it is for grade-level teachers to discuss with each other the objectives they collectively want to meet.

CONCLUSION

This chapter was intended to help you think about the overall picture of the science content of the elementary and middle school curriculum. We noted the current trend to teach fewer topics in exchange for greater depth. We looked at the content standards of the National Science Education Standards as a model framework for a K–8 science program. The first area of content in the National Science Education Standards is *science as inquiry,* but we also acknowledged that many teachers have found obstacles in switching to an inquiry-oriented, depth-oriented approach to curriculum. Not least among the difficulties is the process of transcending a textbook-dominated curriculum and the mistaken belief of many students that the teacher should know everything.

Your state standards, the National Science Education Standards framework, and a science textbook are not your only guides as you plan your classroom science program. Your school or school district is likely to have a curriculum guide as well. You should also have access to a *professional resource library* in your school or district, and of course there is the ever more useful World Wide Web. Chapter 10 features resources that we recommend.

Although some schools use multiple resources for science instead of a single science textbook, it is likely that you will have a textbook to help you with the content and organization of your classroom program. If a textbook is available, compare the content of the local or state curriculum framework with the content of your textbook. The two probably will not match perfectly. Note which chapters of the textbook match the content designated in the local or state curriculum framework for the grade you teach. Note whether there are topics for your grade that are *omitted* in the textbook. Find out whether topics in your textbook are designated to be taught in earlier or later grades. Finally, you may find it helpful to create an outline or concept map of the basic material you will be teaching.

3

Characteristics of the Science Learner

*Development in
Childhood and Adolescence*

Children's Science and Constructivism

Intended and Actual Outcomes of Instruction

Children's Science Versus Scientists' Science

Constructivism in Practice

Students' Conceptions

The Dynamics of Interviewing Students

Designing Interviews

Conducting Interviews

Analyzing Interview Responses

Finding Time for Interviewing

Your Academic Roadmap

This chapter should help you to understand the following ideas:

- The teacher's intended results, the learning outcomes, are not necessarily the same as the actual outcomes of instruction.
- Children and scientists both construct knowledge from what is available to them.
- Teachers provide opportunities for experiences that facilitate conceptual development.
- A student develops his or her understanding of science concept if the new explanation is as personally satisfying as the student's prior knowledge.
- The interview is a tool for designing lessons based on what the students actually know.
- Interviewing informs the teacher of individual beliefs and classwise conceptual tendencies.
- There are effective time management strategies to allow for interviews and the design of more appropriate lessons and classroom experiences.

What is science?

> *"You find out all the things about the Earth. You find out about animals. . . . It's asking questions and finding out why. That would probably cover it."*
>
> —Stephanie, 8 years old

Where does a shadow come from?

> *"It comes from your body, because your body makes it when it gets dark. A glow comes from your body, a dark glow."*
>
> —Jessica, 6 years old

CHILDREN'S SCIENCE AND CONSTRUCTIVISM

Whether or not children attend school, they do learn. Children are naturally curious and eager to make sense of the world around them. In that regard, they are very much like scientists in that both search for explanations as to how things work and why things behave as they do. However, one's knowledge of the world must be based on one's experience in the world. The result is that what makes sense to one person may not make sense to someone else. For instance, long ago the idea that the world was flat made sense to people based on their experiences of the world around them. From our wider experience today such a belief is unacceptable. Yet it remains true that we all construct knowledge with the inputs we have available.

By acknowledging the personal and social nature of sense making, a constructivist approach to education offers insight about what students bring with them as they enter the classroom, what occurs during instruction, and how to account for the eventual outcomes of instruction. By comparing the intended outcomes of instruction with the actual outcomes, we are better able to understand the difference between the more naive "children's science" and the more sophisticated and studied "scientists' science." Recognizing this distinction is one of the values of constructivism as a referent for instructional planning. It will be important also to draw another distinction, that of incomplete understanding versus misconception (in the sense of being an idea contrary to the accepted science). You will also see the term *alternative conception* used in the literature. This term doesn't communicate so much that the student is wrong as that his or her idea is not consistent with the science but still works for the student in some way.

As teachers, we have to begin with what our students already know. That is, we need to be aware that students come to us with a wealth of experiences and beliefs about how the world works (Colburn, 2000). We need to find out what our students know in order to design effective instruction. If you want to know what someone thinks or knows about a particular topic, how do you find out? Would you check the teacher's edition of the science textbook? Would you look it up in your old college human growth and development textbook? Each of these might provide you with some information about children in general but not specifically about the students in *your* classroom. Just as physicians must diagnose each patient in order to prescribe effective and appropriate treatment, teachers need to become familiar with the prior knowledge of the students they teach in order to plan effective lessons.

One way to get this information is to create a preassessment instrument. But typical paper-and-pencil tests do not allow for the probing that is necessary to get students to elaborate and reveal the depth of what they know. Therefore, we recommend the one-on-one interview as the most effective means of obtaining the information you need to understand your students' ideas about science.

INTENDED AND ACTUAL OUTCOMES OF INSTRUCTION

Even given a teacher's best intentions and most skillful classroom performances, actual learning outcomes do not always match what the teacher intended (see Activity 3.1). Each student has a unique set of experiences from which personal knowledge is constructed. It is that personal knowledge and the student's unique perspective that are engaged when the student pursues an investigation and creatively constructs personally satisfying explanations. The patterns discovered and relationships perceived are bound to vary from one student to another. After all, learning is a creative endeavor that involves the search for patterns, perspectives, and relationships (Ebert & Ebert, 1993).

Activity 3.1   **Actual Outcomes**

This notion of intended outcomes versus actual outcomes is easy to investigate. Try to observe another teacher's lesson and then complete this activity.

1. Arrange to speak with several students after the lesson is concluded.

2. Before the lesson begins, ask the teacher to tell you what the main concepts of the lesson will be.

3. As the lesson proceeds, write down what you consider to be the major concepts.

4. Finally, talk with several students after the lesson, and ask what they learned that day.

Note: Keep in mind that the teacher may try to do an extra special job of trying to get concepts across because the two of you have arranged this investigation. So try to approach this in a manner that is as nonthreatening possible. The intent is not to evaluate the teacher but to see how his students' preconceptions affect what they learn in the class.

The similarity in students' conceptual development results at least in part from similar learning opportunities provided. Therefore, as teacher you will have control over what is learned. However, knowing that children have personal experiences resulting in unique knowledge and recognizing the differences in their use of language, you can understand, and even predict, that students might achieve different outcomes even after completing the same science activity.

Studies by Osborne and Freyberg (1985) and Wittrock (1974) indicate the following as major differences between the teacher's intentions and the actual learning taking place. Disparities exist because

The *ideas* brought to the lesson by students do not match the assumptions made by the teacher about those ideas.

The *scientific problem* as perceived by the teacher is inconsistent with what the students perceive the problem to be.

The *activity* the teacher proposed is not the actual activity undertaken by the children.

The *conclusions* as stated by the students do not match the teacher's proposed conclusions.

One agreed-upon tenet of constructivism is that the teacher's intentions cannot be directly transferred into student conceptualizations. Language is not a simple conduit carrying information from one mind to another. Through interactions with materials and with their teachers and peers, students construct their own purposes for the lesson, develop their own intentions regarding the activities, and formulate their own conclusions. These constructs may or may not be similar to the teacher's. Therefore, it is important that the teacher attempt to reduce the disparities by recognizing and appreciating the perceptions that the students bring to the lesson.

For example, a sixth-grade teacher designed a lesson to help her students understand that all living things are composed of cells. She wanted them to learn that plant cells have rigid cell walls and that animal cells have membranes that are not rigid. The activity involved having her students prepare and study microscope slides of onion cells and cheek cells.

The following statements from students in the class are in response to the question, "What did you learn today?"

Keysia: You have to be really careful with that stain. It can really make a mess, and it stains your hands and stuff.

Matthew: Each of those little squares have little dots and stuff in them, and there are lots of little square things.

Mikel: I learned that there are these things that are inside my mouth, these cells that grow there, and everybody has them.

Andrea: Onion cells look like blocks, purple blocks, and cells that live in my mouth are pale; they're white, kind of like circles.

Zack: It is hard to see in that microscope. My partner and I had a hard time. We found some stuff, but it was hard.

As you might expect, none of these responses matched the teacher's objectives. That does not mean that the lesson was a failure. It *does* mean that the outcomes are different from what was intended. The teacher was expecting a generalization related to plant and animal cells. The children, on the other hand, were involved in the details of the activity and the specific observations, and that is what they verbalized. It is probable that many experiences will be needed before these students begin to see patterns emerging and therefore are able to generalize. However, this one experience is a starting point and can be built on to facilitate growth and the emergence of the intended concept.

CHILDREN'S SCIENCE VERSUS SCIENTISTS' SCIENCE

The major difference between the scientist's approach to developing explanations or theories and the student's approach is the way observations are used. As they attempt to make sense of the world around them, children do so in terms of personal experiences, their current knowledge, and their facility with language. However, their evidence tends to be limited to directly observable characteristics. Whereas a scientist seeks to anchor her explanations in her observations, the student is inclined to invent explanations only loosely related to the observations, such as in the following examples:

What is thunder?

"Thunder is God bowling."

"Thunder is the clouds clapping."

"Thunder is God yelling at the angels like my mom does at me."

Despite what you might think, the explanations above make sense to each one of the children. The logic is representative of the child's own level of thinking. It is these ideas and explanations about how and why things behave as they do that Osborne and Freyberg (1985) call "children's science." From the child's point of view, these ideas are coherent and sensible. As the child's experiences broaden, their explanations typically change. The following summary generalizations provide insight into students' science:

Students tend to have self-centered or human-centered viewpoints.

Their views are based on everyday experiences and common use of language.

They are interested in specific explanations rather than coherent theories.

They endow inanimate objects with characteristics of humans and other animals.

They consider nonobservables as nonexistent (Osborne & Freyberg, 1985).

We can begin to see how children's science differs from scientists' science. As a way of knowing, children's science succeeds in finding explanations for naturally occurring phenomena. After all, children, like scientists, base their ideas on evidence. However, children construct their versions of science based on their limited experiences and uncritical preconceptions. Adult scientific pursuits also involve preconceptions, but these have been forged through the critical peer review process required to get scientific work published. Moreover, scientists use advanced technologies and often work in teams in environments designed for scientific research, such as laboratories, field-based sites, observatories, and space stations.

Interestingly, it is not just the similarities between children's science and scientists' science or just the differences that are important. Rather, being aware of both is important in teaching science. As a teacher, you will want to arrange opportunities for experiences that will enable your students to understand the science content. Unlike in scientific endeavors, where the results are unknown beforehand, you do know beforehand what you want your students to find out. But as in scientific endeavors, it is your students who will do the knowledge work. Table 3.1 compares the two types of science. As you look over the lists you will find that scientists' science is just a more sophisticated and critical version of what most of us do as a natural attempt to make sense of the world around us.

An important similarity that is not listed in Table 3.1 is that ideas once constructed and accepted as satisfactory, whether by students or by scientists, are difficult to change. Posner, Strike, Hewson, and Gertzog (1982) suggest that children will change their ideas only if their present ones are unsatisfactory in some way. However, dissatisfaction with an idea is not necessarily a sufficient reason for discarding it. Actually, four conditions must be met in order for a student to accommodate a different conceptualization (Table 3.2).

Your goal as teacher is not to colonize your students' minds with scientists' science. Rather, it should be to challenge their naive ideas by providing opportunities for experiences that go beyond what is available in their daily lives and to

Table 3.1   Children's Science Versus Scientists' Science

Children's Science	Scientists' Science
Ideas based on evidence	Ideas based on evidence
Explanations sometimes derived from observations	Explanations derived from prior theory and observations
Explanations sometimes invented to account for observations	Observations used to test explanations
Unassisted senses used to make observations	Sophisticated technologies used to make observations
Nonobservables considered nonexistent	Nonobservables may be detected through instrumentation
Self-centered or human-centered	Objective perspective sought

Table 3.2   Conditions for Conceptual Change

The student must become *dissatisfied* with his or her current understanding.

The student must have available an *intelligible* alternative.

The alternative must seem *plausible* to the student.

The alternative must seem *fruitful* to the student.

Source: Smith (1991).

facilitate a critical consideration of alternative ideas. This is what the constructivist approach to science teaching is all about: allowing for conceptual development generated from experiences that broaden student horizons and from critical consideration of plausible alternatives to the initial understandings.

CONSTRUCTIVISM IN PRACTICE

Piaget (1977) suggests that as a learner strives to organize personal experiences in terms of preexisting mental schemes, knowledge is constructed. We do this by matching new situations to those we already have experienced. A situation that is similar to what we already know is *assimilated* into our understanding. When we assimilate, we make slight changes in a preexisting schema. For example, going to a new restaurant may be a different experience, but it is essentially similar to the overall experience of dining out. Sometimes, however, one has an experience, an encounter with an idea, that is very new or different from anything that has happened before. In that case, the experience requires *accommodation.* Accommodation may involve significantly changing a preexisting schema or perhaps constructing a brand new schema. In their search for understanding, learners look for patterns within their realms of experience, developing personal explanations for natural phenomena and constructing their own versions of reality. Therefore, knowledge is constructed in the minds of the learners. You can see how a constructivist theory of knowledge relates to Piaget's model of cognitive development.

That children learn by the processes of assimilation and accommodation seems easy enough to accept. What we need, however, is a means of instruction that effectively facilitates the construction of concepts identified in the curriculum. In that regard, there are a number of things you can do as a teacher to put your students into situations that will facilitate understanding. The emphasis of such techniques is on having the students actively involved in both the *manipulation of materials* and the *consideration of their own ideas and those of others.* This takes some practice on your part in that it involves challenging student's preinstructional conceptualizations in a nonthreatening manner. Table 3.3 lists techniques teachers can use to help students develop conceptually.

You can see in this list of teaching techniques how important providing for student *thinking* and *activity* is to effective educational planning. What is not as

Table 3.3   Teaching Practices Consistent With Constructivism

Encouraging and accepting student autonomy, initiative, and leadership

Using interactive and physical materials to allow students to collect their own data

Encouraging students to elaborate on their initial responses

Identifying students' preconceptions by asking students for their ideas about concepts before explaining those concepts

Designing subsequent lessons to address any misconceptions identified

Allowing student thinking to drive lessons, differentiating instruction to reach all students, and shifting instructional strategies or modifying content based on student responses

Encouraging students to talk about the topic and get engaged in conversation, both with the teacher and with one another

Using cognitive terms in teaching when framing tasks, such as *classify, analyze,* and *predict*

Challenging students' hypotheses without discouraging their responses, which *requires diplomacy,* challenging ideas but not individuals

Fostering inquiry by including higher-level, open-ended questions and encouraging students to ask questions themselves

Allowing *wait time* after posing questions (a 3- to 5-second pause for students to think before responding)

Providing opportunities for students to perceive relationships and create metaphors for phenomena

Requiring students to reflect on their experiences and actions (e.g., through journaling) and to make predictions

Organizing lesson content around conceptual clusters (problems, questions, discrepant situations, conceptual themes)

Differentiating instruction by aligning the classroom curriculum with the developmental needs of students

Sources: Brooks (1990), Tomlinson (1995, 2003).

obvious is that professional expertise is needed to establish a classroom science program based on a constructivist perspective. You will notice that throughout the list of techniques there is a *dynamic* nature to the conduct of the lesson. This is particularly reflective of Piaget's notion that knowledge is dynamic in that it is ever-expanding, spiraling to encompass more and more experiences and meaning.

STUDENTS' CONCEPTIONS

A *misconception* is a belief expressed by a student that is different from the warranted concepts accepted by the scientific community. An *incomplete understanding,* on the other hand, is a concept that approximates the scientists' science but lacks completeness or coherence. The student has incomplete understanding if he or she doesn't know or comprehend some aspect that is necessary to a full understanding of the concept. For example, a child who believes that the seasons are caused by the distance of the Earth from the Sun during its annual revolution is operating with a misconception. A student who believes that the seasons are caused by how the Earth is tilted on its axis relative to the Sun but is unable to explain how the angle affects the seasonal variations is operating with an incomplete understanding. The teacher should differentiate instruction for the two students because they are in different places cognitively. Do you see how these students have two very different instructional needs? Activity 3.2 includes a list of students' ideas so that you can test your ability to distinguish between misconceptions and incomplete understandings.

Activity 3.2 | Misconceptions Versus Incomplete Understandings

Consider each of the following statements. Indicate whether you think the statement is an example of a misconception or an incomplete understanding. Explain your reasoning.

The Sun rises in the east and sets in the west.

Magnets attract metal objects.

Plants get the food they need to grow through their roots.

You can make a shadow if you have a light source and an object.

Stars do not shine in the day because the Sun is too bright.

If the Sun is shining while it is raining, you can see a rainbow.

THE DYNAMICS OF INTERVIEWING STUDENTS

Eliciting students' understandings can be very challenging. Two factors may help explain why: Students may be receptive or unreceptive to your questions, and the concept or topic with which you are concerned may be quite sophisticated—a difficult idea to grasp. On the plus side, students typically are very receptive to being interviewed and enjoy the opportunity to talk with an adult about their thoughts and ideas. If you are interviewing an introvert, you'll have to be persistent in your probing because he or she won't tend to elaborate or volunteer additional information. With extroverts, their explanations often become quite lengthy. Even students who tend to be reticent in the classroom willingly accept the opportunity to engage individually in a conversation with an adult, especially with the teacher. An environment open to the expression of ideas encourages and allows students to elaborate on their responses, providing much detail. The responses given in this setting are strikingly different from the usual clipped and concise responses so often heard in the traditional subject-centered classroom.

The sophistication of the topic may also make eliciting students' beliefs a difficult challenge. An examination of the distinction between living and nonliving illustrates this point. The distinction between living and nonliving initially appears to be a simple concept. For the past several decades it has typically been addressed a couple of times from kindergarten through sixth grade in the elementary science textbooks. But upon closer examination, the distinction between living and nonliving becomes much more complex. You can find this out for yourself by completing Activity 3.3.

Activity 3.3   Living Versus Nonliving

Write your answers to the following questions.

Is the Sun alive?

Is a candle alive?

Is a fire alive?

Is a horse alive?

Is a bicycle alive?

Is wind alive?

Is a tree alive?

Is a leaf alive?

Is an apple alive?

Is a seed alive?

Is lightning alive?

Is a volcano alive?

Is a bird alive?

Is a feather alive?

Is an egg alive?

Now go back through your answers and ask yourself "why?" or "why not?" for each of them. Finally, consider this: How can you tell whether something is alive? Did you find it difficult to answer some of the questions? Which ones provoked the most thought? Why?

After completing Activity 3.3, you might be more appreciative of the variety of responses that could be elicited by answering each of the questions from the opposite perspective. For instance, if you said that the Sun is not alive, this time say the Sun *is* alive and try to support your answer. Think of different criteria or additional information that, when used, could justify your response. Here's an example:

> *First time:* "No the Sun is not alive. It is a burning ball of gases—a source of energy." *Second time:* "Yes, the Sun is alive. Scientists say it is not a new star nor a really old star, but it is changing and will die someday."

DESIGNING INTERVIEWS

Interviews involve asking a series of questions with varying degrees of difficulty and then probing the student's initial responses. Questions such as "Are all days the same length?" are simple, *information-based questions* and can be answered by a response of *yes* or *no*. Information-based questions are those that elicit responses that provide specific information but do not address causation or relationships. Because an information-based question often can be answered with a "yes" or "no," the student has an equal chance of answering correctly whether or not she knows the answer. You can probe the student's level of understanding by following up an information-based question with the questions "Why?" or "Why not?"

Questions such as "What causes day to change to night?" are more difficult for students and provoke more thought. These *probing questions* require that a student consider cause and effect relationships or justify a response. Probing questions are those that tend to get at the student's *understanding* of a concept rather than simply at his or her knowledge of it.

The following is the transcript of an interview with Thomas L. on the distinction between living and nonliving. It is included here to provide an example of an interview in its entirety. Notice the conversational flow and interchange between Thomas and the interviewer.

The Thomas L. Interview

Thomas, I want to ask you some questions. I want to know what you think about some things. First of all, can you tell me, is the Sun alive?

> *No, I think it is dead. It is just floating. It is dead. The Moon darkens it. . . . Yes, it is alive. I think it knows when to cut on and off. Yes, I think it is alive.*

Is a candle alive?

> *No.*

Why not?

> *It is just made. I just think somebody made it.*

Is fire alive?

> *It is just hot stuff that burns. It is very dangerous.*

Is a dog alive?

Yes, definitely, a dog and a cat are alive.

Why do you say that a dog and a cat are alive?

They move and they talk in their own language. Let me see if I can imitate them (barks like a dog and meows like a cat). *They run and they have got to be alive.*

Is a bicycle alive?

It runs, but it is not alive. It will run. Its wheels are alive. Its steering is alive, but the rest of it isn't. Nothing is alive but the wheels.

Why do you think the wheels are alive?

Because it runs but the rest of it isn't alive.

Do you think the wind is alive?

This is a hard one. Let me think on this one. I am a fast thinker (pauses to think). *The wind goes, but it is not alive. . . . A wind takes another one to blow it. I think that God sends it out of the tip of his little finger and blows it with his middle finger. That is what I think.*

Is water alive?

(chuckles) *This is a hard one; you're getting harder. I'll tell you something about water. When you jump in it, it splashes up to the top. I think that water spouts. It just runs and runs when you take a bath. When you put something in it, it splashes up and is full. Yes, I think.*

Do you think it is alive because of being fuller?

No, I think half of it is real and half is not. There has got to be a difference between it. Some water can do that, and some cannot do that, and some can.

What can it do?

I think that swamp water and sulfur water in West Virginia will not do it, but I think that some water is alive. It is alive because it moves.

Is a tree alive?

Let me tell you a story. Sometimes in commercials they make a tree alive with eyes that can see, and they can talk. The trees outside are dead, but they live. They are asleep every day. They want to walk and move and talk and see, but they cannot because they are stiff. It is a living thing. I would be sad if someone stuck a nail in the tree.

Is a leaf alive?

I think a leaf is dead.

Why?

I think the wind blows it. It is just a leaf you can crush.

Is an apple alive?

Let me start a story. A little boy's mother asked him what is red and has four babies in it. He went for a walk to think about it. He asked the mailman, and he could not tell him what was red and has four, five red things in it. Then he asked a farmer, and he said he didn't know but gave him an apple. The boy went home eating the apple. He told his mother he didn't know the answer to the riddle. She said, "You're eating it." She cut the apple open and inside showed him the five seeds and how they

(Continued)

The Thomas L. Interview (Continued)

looked like a star. It is round and red. The one with seeds is the mother, and the one without the seeds is the daddy. They are parents. A daddy apple and a momma apple were started when the world started, and I guess it just kept going.

Is a seed alive?

Yes, I think God placed a little star with seeds in it in a momma apple.

Is lightning alive?

That is a tough question. I am afraid I can't help you on that, but I know what the noise of it is. The noise is the angels bowling and angels moving furniture.

Is a volcano alive?

That is very easy. I am glad you asked that. Dinosaurs have a place where they lived, and I think the volcano killed the dinosaur. I think the fire killed the dinosaurs. The dinosaurs came form South Carolina, North Carolina, and different parts. The volcano killed the dinosaurs. The volcano is arrested so they can't do nothing. The dinosaur would break the volcano, and if a dinosaur smashes it, it is dead but if it doesn't, it is alive.

Is a bird alive?

Are these all dinosaur questions? Yes, I think the bird is alive.

Why?

He has to be alive because he moves. Some are dangerous, and some are not. If he lies and does not move, he is dead.

Is a feather alive?

They move in action to make them fly. If a dog had feathers on his ears, he could fly. It is moving to an action, so if it is on the wing, it is alive, but if it isn't, it is dead.

What does it mean to be alive?

This is getting tiring. This is the last question. The world spins around real fast, so I think civilization and everything is alive.

What does it mean to be alive?

You're living, you're talking, you're walking, you're feeling. You can do anything you want to do as long as your mother and daddy agree with it.

Although Thomas L. was only 6 years old at the time of the interview and not yet enrolled in first grade, you can see that he has many ideas. He was quite willing to be interviewed and eagerly shared his ideas. Some of these ideas represent explanations he has heard from others and accepted, and others are the result of his synthesis of personal knowledge and experiences. Even the youngest children think and construct their own explanations as they try to understand the world around them. Which of Thomas's ideas would you say are consistent with the scientific distinction between living and nonliving? Consider Thomas's teacher. What kind of instruction would you recommend? And as to living versus nonliving, how would you classify a virus? Why?

CONDUCTING INTERVIEWS

The interviewer should communicate to the student that the interview is not for instruction, nor is it an evaluation for which a grade will be assigned. The purpose of the interview should be communicated in such a way that anxiety is reduced and the interview is seen as a conversation. Try to establish a relaxed, informal atmosphere. Here are some additional suggestions:

• Record the interview with a tape recorder so that you are not preoccupied with writing down the responses. You need to focus all your attention on responding and creating the probing questions.

• Begin your interview by stating your purpose (e.g., "This is not a test. I am not looking for right or wrong answers. I am just interested in your ideas about some things.").

• Be a good listener. Use nonverbal and brief verbal cues to indicate that you are listening and following the person's thoughts. Nod your head, smile, and make simple statements such as, "Hmmm . . . ," "Interesting," and "Okay."

• If you receive the answer, "I don't know," respond by asking, "If you were going to guess, what would you say?" This communicates your willingness to accept any answer and is effective in eliciting a response from the student being interviewed. This response communicates a very different message from your saying, "Take a guess," which we do not recommend.

• When a child gives an answer that does not seem clear to you, use a spontaneous probing question (a probing question that would not have been written in your original list of questions). Instead of restating the explanation in your own words, which may actually influence the child's thinking, ask for clarification, such as, "Tell me more," "Can you explain that to me?" and "What do you mean by . . . ?"

• Remember, this is not an instructional situation. As teachers, we are naturally inclined to "teach," but we recommend that you refrain from pointing out inconsistencies in the student's answers or offering the "correct" answers.

ANALYZING INTERVIEW RESPONSES

Once your interviews are conducted and transcribed, it is time to analyze the responses. Both the specific answers and the pattern of responses that emerge should be examined. Planning instruction for the group will require attention to classwide conceptual tendencies. However, individual needs shouldn't be ignored even though the one student may not reflect the norm for the class. When analyzing the responses, you need to look for individual and group patterns of understanding and categories of responses according to conceptual development. For example, 7-year-old Marie has a unique explanation for day and night:

What is night?
When it gets dark and the stars and moon come out.

Why is it dark at night?
Because you can't go to sleep in the daytime.

Where does the darkness come from?
Black paper.

What is day?
White paper and when the sky is clear, it's blue paper.

What makes the day change to night?
They change the paper.

The differences and similarities that have emerged represent important information for teachers to use in designing instruction for the needs of individuals and for the entire class. However, when we are analyzing interviews, the responses may be classified according to conceptual development. The responses given by students tend to fall into one of three categories:

- *Misconception:* The belief expressed by the student is not supported by evidence. The student's response is unscientific or naive.

- *Incomplete understanding:* The explanation given by the student is partially correct but incomplete. The student understands some aspect of the concept but is not able to apply her understanding in all situations.

- *Scientific understanding:* The student's explanation of the concept is consistent with the accepted, scientific view.

The following steps can be used to guide the process of interviewing students for understanding and designing lessons:

1. Construct the list of questions.

2. Prepare the interview setting.

3. Conduct the interview, using probing questions.

4. Compare the responses to curricular materials (textbook).

5. Design activities to address levels of understanding.

6. Allow students opportunities to use manipulatives and time for exploration.

7. Assess student understanding.

FINDING TIME FOR INTERVIEWING

You might think that interviewing students sounds like a wonderful strategy and agree that it is valuable in designing appropriate instruction, but you think you do not have time to interview all of your students every time you want to start a new unit. And your point is well taken. Time is valuable. However, according to teachers who have used the interviewing technique with their students, the interview questions encouraged higher-level thinking, and the students gave more complex and lengthy responses than are presented during usual class discussions (Kuehn & McKenzie, 1989). Although it may not be possible to interview each student on each topic, a wealth of information can be gained by interviewing a *sample* of students, say four to six. Students with a range of backgrounds and ability levels would be best. This would represent interviewing a fifth or fourth of the class. This many students will give you a reasonable representation of the prior knowledge of the class and provide you a basis from which to plan for all. (See Activity 3.4.)

Activity 3.4   Conducting a Diagnostic Interview

If you have not already done so, we highly recommend that you interview some young people. Select one of the sets of interview questions on various topics found in Chapter 10. Following our suggestions in this chapter, find two or three children or youth to interview. If you select interviewees of approximately the same age, you can get a sense of the diversity of views possible among classmates. However, if you select interviewees of different ages you'll get a sense of how students' views develop with maturity. Either way, you will have the opportunity to collect your own data and experience doing a diagnostic interview. Record your interviews so that you can listen and respond to the students without the distraction of having to take notes and come up with the next question simultaneously. When you listen to the recording, take notes or transcribe key segments. Categorize the responses. Discuss your results with a colleague. We expect that both you and the interviewees will find your conversation interesting, even entertaining, and you'll find that your perspective changes in response to what your students bring to the interview.

CONCLUSION

Incomplete understandings and misconceptions related to the topics of study in science are to be expected. Through our examination of children's science we know that students construct explanations for the world around them based on experiences in formal and informal educational settings. They use their unaided senses to make observations, and their perspectives often are limited by a narrow range of experiences and their own social circle. Explanations will vary from one student to another and are not necessarily in agreement with the explanations espoused by scientists.

The theories or explanations your students construct, whether they are different or like those of others, are personally satisfying. Unless children become *dissatisfied* with their own explanations and find *intelligible alternatives* that are both *plausible* and *fruitful,* conceptual change is not likely to occur. Yet teachers should not be out to colonize students' minds with scientists' science but rather should provide opportunities for students to critically examine their own views and those of the scientists. Your goal for your students should be *epistemological development,* which ultimately means that you will be nurturing social actors with a critical consciousness.

The interview technique is specifically designed to elicit children's science when conducted in a comfortable and accepting environment. The interview is a combination of information-based questions and probing questions and is intended to be nonjudgmental and noninstructional.

By using diagnostic interviews, teachers will be more able to plan and design instruction that enables students to develop critical and sophisticated explanations for natural phenomena. Knowing what your students think and why they think the way they do increases the likelihood that your lessons will have a real impact. Besides that, we think you will find diagnostic interviews fascinating and that your students will astound, startle, and delight you.

PART II

Teaching Children Science

Approaches and Strategies

The four chapters in this section represent methods and techniques that characterize a teacher's interaction with students in the teaching of science. Activities throughout these chapters may be used with students. At the same time, they can serve as exemplars that the teacher can use as a springboard for developing activities, selecting strategies, and determining the best course of instruction for the students in the particular classroom situation. We can make generalizations about students, but as a teacher you do not face generalizations; you face real children. *It is always best to take a topic and fashion a customized lesson to fit your students, adapting rather than adopting an activity written by someone who never met your students.*

Chapter 4, "Developing the Classroom Curriculum," focuses on the increasingly important science-technology-society triad in our increasingly technology-oriented world. Much technology in these times has an almost mystical nature. Yet the mutually beneficial relationship between science and technology, of which scientists and technologists are aware, need not represent mysterious territory to the users of technology. The key lies in helping students see the relationship between science, technology, and their impact on social problems as a regular part of science education in the elementary school. The chapter also provides a look at many of the science education reform programs that that have influenced school science curricula.

Chapter 5, "Engaging Students in Inquiry: Skills and Investigative Techniques," looks at how children enter the classroom with a natural inclination to explain the world around them. This inclination works to the teacher's advantage because the work of the scientist is motivated by this same inquisitive nature. Furthermore, children use many of the same skills to answer their questions that scientists use. Developing these skills to the point of proficiency is a primary focus of a good science program.

The skills discussed in this chapter become the basis for conducting scientific inquiry. A common misconception held by many people, including teachers, is that anything done in science is an experiment. However, experimenting is just one of at least eight investigative approaches that scientists, as well as students, use in their work. Each approach is appropriate for a particular circumstance. Choosing the type of investigation that is best suited to what you want your students to experience is a crucial step in conceptualizing your science lessons.

Taken together, these approaches provide the means to help students formulate questions into something that can be explored, develop the skills necessary for that exploration, and identify the format that would be best for the investigation. In essence, they represent the *tools* with which a teacher constructs a lesson.

Chapter 6, "Designing Science Lessons for All: Differentiating Instruction," will help in selecting and organizing the particular tools and materials needed to meet the demands of the science concepts to be presented and includes lesson formats that provide a dynamic and interactive approach to teaching.

Learning does not end at the close of the school day. In fact, the school day represents only a small portion of the time children spend learning. Chapter 7, "Making Real-World Connections," offers you the opportunity to see that what happens in school makes relevant connections in the minds of students to the world outside school. Some of these experiences bring the world to the classroom, and others extend the classroom to the world. This is a step that is often overlooked in formal systems of education, yet it is the one that makes learning meaningful.

4

Developing the Classroom Curriculum

Teachers and Science in the School Curriculum

Goals for Teaching Science

Reform Efforts of the 1950s–1970s: The Pioneering Alphabet Programs

The Second Wave: End-of-Century Reforms and Contemporary Science Programs

Contemporary Trends: The Science-Technology-Society Approach

Considerations for the Future

Making Room in the Curriculum for Event-Based Science

Your Academic Roadmap

This chapter should help you to understand the following ideas:

- The people who will solve the "people problems" of the future may be the students in your classroom today.
- A science-technology-society approach to education engages students in personal, local, national, and global issues in which science, technology, and society interact.
- Programs developed during the major science education reform movements broke new ground; however, teacher education typically was neglected.
- The professional educator is a multidimensional person who understands the many and varied aspects involved in enacting a high-quality educational curriculum.

"If we always do what we've always done, we'll always get what we've always got."

—Adam Urbanski

TEACHERS AND SCIENCE IN THE SCHOOL CURRICULUM

This chapter is about the science program, that is, the yearlong science component of what will happen in your classroom. The chapter itself is arranged to address some of the goals to be considered in developing your classroom program; familiarize you with both pioneering and contemporary commercial science programs, especially the non-textbook-oriented programs that have resulted from science education research and reform efforts; introduce a major curriculum trend in science education, the science-technology-society (STS) approach; and consider your role as a teacher in program development at your school.

Over the past decade the public school districts across the United State have revised their science programs to be in tune with their state curriculum frameworks and the National Science Education Standards, adopted by the National Research Council in 1996. In addition, individual districts and schools may have adopted a commercial science program, such as a textbook or kit-based series. If that is the case where you teach, your task will be to plan your units and lessons to be compatible with the applicable curriculum frameworks and your primary teaching resource. Yet even with the crutch of a commercial program, you will be continually creating the actual science program to be enacted in your classroom. What's more, you might find yourself in the situation of being part of a school- or districtwide team that makes local decisions about the overall K–5, K–6, or K–8 science program.

Such curriculum work is important and demanding. For one thing, the curriculum operates on several levels, from the daily lesson in your classroom all the way up to your school district's multigrade scope and sequence framework of concepts, skills, and habits of mind to be taught each year. Doing curriculum work requires not only a good grasp of subject matter but also a vision of what schooling is about as a whole: its purposes and roles in the community and consideration of alternative possibilities.

Like the curriculum as a whole, the science program can be thought of as the *intended* or *explicit* curriculum. This is the curriculum that is written down in scope and sequence charts and in lesson and unit plans. From the student's point of view, curriculum also can be thought of as that which is actually experienced or learned. The experienced curriculum consists of aspects of the explicit curriculum and, in addition, the *implicit* or *hidden* curriculum. Regardless of teachers' best intentions, what is learned always involves some things that cannot be anticipated, let alone planned. For instance, two young boys that we know of were on a field trip one day. While they were riding on the bus an argument broke out. There was no violence, just a difference of opinion. The question was, "In a fight between a whale and a bear, which would win?" Both animals had been discussed in class in a lesson on mammals, but the teacher did not include a discussion of relative strength. Yet to these boys it was an issue of great interest.

There is at least one more aspect of curriculum, that of the *null* curriculum. The null curriculum tells you what is left out of the curriculum, either intentionally or unintentionally. In a politically sensitive society such as ours the null curriculum is an important concern. In past years, examples of the null curriculum have included such content as evolution and sex education. Can you think of some science topics that were left out of your own school experience?

In the real world the intended or explicit curriculum of the school rarely, if ever, matches the learned curriculum. Nevertheless, because we believe the school is a public trust, we believe our intentions as educators should be made as explicit as possible. Educators must be prepared to be reasonably accountable for their curriculum decisions. Furthermore, it is important to understand that curriculum development is never really completed. Rather, it is a *continual* process that entails individual and group deliberation.

GOALS FOR TEACHING SCIENCE

Think about this for a moment before you read further: What do you think should be the purpose of science education? Program goals or intended outcomes are a good place to begin thinking about science in the school curriculum. The *goals* of a program provide a framework and a focus for the content and learning activities for the classroom curriculum. In the United States, there seems to be broad agreement that the overall purpose of the school science program is to foster *scientific literacy*. This purpose is advocated in the National Science Education Standards (National Research Council, 1996) and is explained as follows:

> An essential aspect of scientific literacy is greater knowledge and understanding of science subject matter, that is, the knowledge specifically associated with the physical, life, and earth sciences. Scientific literacy also includes understanding the nature of science, the scientific enterprise, and the role of science in society and personal life. (p. 21)

Professor Jon Miller (2004) of Northwestern University has become an expert on the public understanding of science. He claims that scientific literacy has three constitutive dimensions: the nature of science, science content knowledge, and the impact of science and technology on society. His definition emphasizes the need for an understanding of the vocabulary, concepts, and processes of science. Miller and others agree that U.S. scientific literacy is low, with less than 20% of adults qualifying as even being attentive to science issues. His research found that the scientifically literate were mostly males, people older than 35, and college graduates.

Research such as Miller's is often cited as a criticism of the way science is taught in the schools and as part of the rationale for reforming science education. However, consider the fact that many accomplished scientists are knowledgeable only in the areas related to their own field. There are physicists who cannot articulate a Darwinian argument for evolution and geneticists who are unable to explain the standard model for quantum theory. Some scientists may indeed have broader scientific knowledge, but many others are narrowly focused in their specialty fields. Regardless, nobody knows it all these days; science is constantly changing, and being on top of more than a few scientific fields is very challenging.

Science Appreciation

Not everyone agrees that scientific literacy is an appropriate goal for the school science program. Physicist Morris Shamos of New York University argues that the American public doesn't actually have a greater capacity for scientific literacy. He doesn't think people are *incapable* of understanding more science; they simply have no incentive to learn more. After all, learning science takes some mental effort. Instead of science literacy as a goal for school science, Shamos and others suggest *science appreciation* (Hively, 1988). He contends that the best we can do is to educate a public that is not antiscience.

Professor Watson Laetsch of the University of California and former director of the Lawrence Hall of Science is also a critic of the concept of scientific literacy. Laetsch claims that there is no convincing evidence for the utilitarian argument for scientific literacy (i.e., that increasing scientific literacy will produce better workers or make industry more competitive). Most people, he claims, can lead useful and happy lives without being informed about science. But Laetsch does endorse what he calls the *humanistic argument* for science education, that the purpose for learning science is the *enjoyment of science.* According to Laetsch, teaching science can be defended solely on the grounds that scientific knowledge gives pleasure and enriches people's lives (Hively, 1988).

In its *Science for All Americans* the American Association for the Advancement of Science (AAAS, 1989), though drawing on the idea of scientific literacy, ultimately falls back on the case for enrichment, stating, "The most powerful argument for improving the science education of all students may be its role in liberating the human intellect" (p. 153). Our own view is that the notion of scientific literacy is difficult to grasp and even more difficult to assess, and so attaining scientific literacy as Miller defines it may be too lofty a goal for school science.

Citizen Formation

Other goals for science education should also be considered. We agree that learning science can be intellectually liberating, and we believe learning science can contribute to our students' formation as citizens in a democratic society. Thus an aim of the school science program should be to enable students to become *competent social actors* (Geelan, Larochelle, & Lemke, 2002). With *citizen formation* as a goal, the science program would need to go beyond the content of the traditional physical, life, and earth and space science of programs of the past. Programs addressing this goal would include attention to *knowledge of science* (nature of science) and scientific knowledge (subject matter, or disciplinary, knowledge). Thus, as discussed in Chapter 1, a recent focus of the K–8 science program has become the nature of science, which is based on the history, philosophy, and sociology of science.

Figure 4.1 The Domains of Science Education

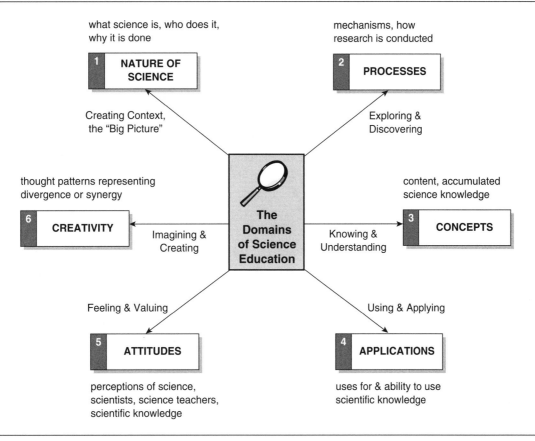

Source: Enger & Yager (1998).

The goal of citizen formation would also mean a focus on what science says about our relationship to the environment, including such things as pollution, global climate change, resource depletion, wildlife habitat destruction, and the loss of biodiversity. Here, science education overlaps and integrates with environmental education and social studies education (as can be seen in the Geography Education Standards Project [1994] and the Curriculum Standards for Social Studies of the National Council for the Social Studies [1994]). For students to become competent social actors, the science program must be multidimensional, addressing all six domains of science education as identified by Enger and Yager (1998) and illustrated in Figure 4.1: the nature of science, knowing and understanding, exploring and discovering, imagining and creating, feeling and valuing, and using and applying.

Summary

It should be obvious to you by this point that science is a subject area like no other. There are many perspectives on its goals, content, and scope. We cannot tell you that any one perspective on the purpose of school science is *the* right one. What we do want to tell you is that deciding on the goals for your classroom science program is the best place to begin planning a sound curriculum. With that in mind, let's consider some of the commercial programs that have been produced by science education reform efforts over the past half century or so.

REFORM EFFORTS OF THE 1950s–1970s: THE PIONEERING ALPHABET PROGRAMS

After World War II science got much more attention in U.S. education at all levels. Figure 4.2 graphically depicts the period after the war and the various influences on science education. Two major waves of effort to change the teaching of science have occurred, with the first just after the war, from the mid-1950s to the early 1970s. During this first reform effort the political motivation for change was the Cold War, the perceived threat to U.S. security and hegemony from the former Soviet Union. Many educators associate this reform movement with the launch of the Soviet satellite *Sputnik* in 1957, but it was actually spurred more by the low scores U.S. troops made on their military enlistment exams.

The projects of the 1950s to the 1970s focused on creating new science teaching materials and broke new ground by introducing multidimensional, non-textbook-based science programs. Through the National Science Foundation millions of federal dollars were spent to fund curriculum-writing projects at universities and for pilot testing. The project directors typically were academic scientists rather than science educators. The first programs to be published were secondary science programs, including the Physical Science Study Committee's physics (PSSC, 1959), the Chemical Education Material Study (CHEM Study, 1963), the Earth Science Curriculum Project (ESCP, 1967), and the biology series of the Biological Science Curriculum Study (BSCS, 1960). These programs emphasized processes of science and higher-order thinking and also contained new content. Being developed by academics, they also emphasized pure science and left out the applications of science in everyday life.

In a similar way, university-based teams developed a number of elementary and middle school science programs. Among the most widely used of what came to be called the "alphabet soup programs" were the Science Curriculum Improvement Study (SCIS, 1963), the Elementary Science Study (ESS, 1960), the Conceptually Oriented Program in Elementary Science (COPES, 1971), and Science: A Process Approach (SAPA, 1965). Two others were particularly noteworthy: the Intermediate Science Curriculum Study (ISCS, 1970) and Man: A Course of Study (MACOS, 1968).

Hands-on science and discovery learning were the hallmarks of these new programs. The assumption underlying the hands-on approach was that if students became directly involved with materials and phenomena, they would experience the flavor and excitement of science and would discover important science concepts for themselves.

The ESS, developed by the Education Development Center of Newton, Massachusetts, a private nonprofit organization, was one of the first K–6 programs of this period. There were no student textbooks, but for the first time

Figure 4.2 Postwar History of Science Education in the United States

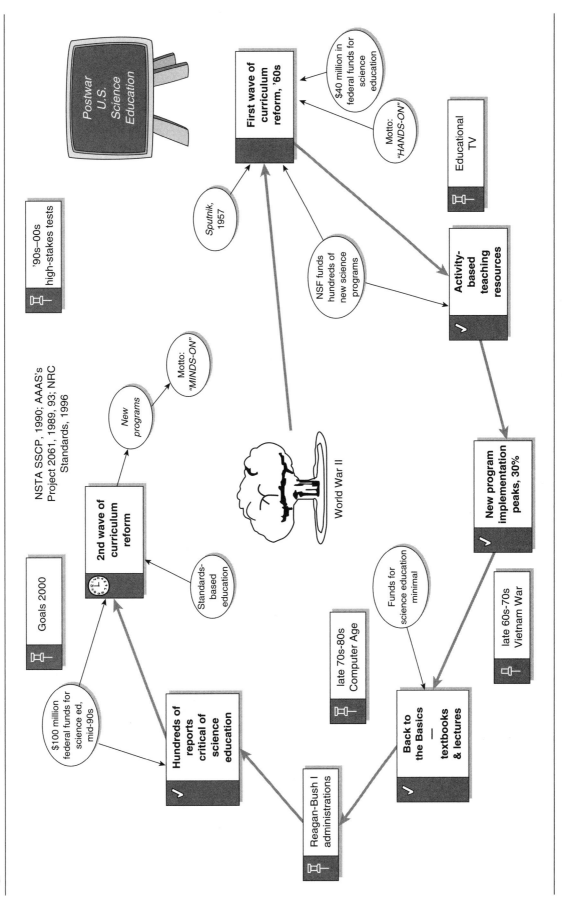

teachers were provided science lessons that addressed important science content, engaged with hands-on learning backed by established psychological principles, and had been tested in diverse classrooms. Eighty units were developed in the form of teachers' guides containing science content background and suggested student activities that could be the core program or could be used to enrich the existing program. Classic ESS units include "Kitchen Physics" for Grades 5–8, "The Behavior of Mealworms" for Grade 6, "Mystery Powders" for Grades 3 and 4, "Growing Seeds" for grades K–3, "Gases and Airs" for Grades 5–8, and "Batteries and Bulbs" for Grades 4–6.

Competing with ESS was SAPA, developed by the American Association for the Advancement of Science. SAPA designers claimed that the ability to do the *processes* of science is retained longer by students than *information* and therefore focused on developing specific skills and competencies (e.g., for K–3, observation, classification, recognition of space-time relations, measurement, communication, inference, and prediction, and for Grades 4–6, defining terms operationally, interpreting data, controlling variables, experimenting, and forming hypotheses and models). Activities were individualized and sequenced, each skill mastered in turn.

The SCIS, developed by the Lawrence Hall of Science, Berkeley, California, was a K–6 program organized by key concepts. Key concepts included matter, interaction, relativity, ecosystems, energy, equilibrium, and evolution. This program introduced the three-phase learning cycle model that has now evolved to a seven-phase model, discussed later in this chapter.

Among the most prominent programs targeting the upper elementary and junior high school grades (this period was before the middle school movement) was the ISCS. ISCS was unique among the programs of the era in that besides being entirely hands-on and laboratory based, it was individualized and self-paced. The ISCS teacher guide specified a limited role for the teacher, making this program the best example of the so-called teacher-proof curricula of the period.

Perhaps the most innovative of the alphabet programs of the period was MACOS, created specifically for sixth grade. It was designed by Harvard anthropologist Irven DeVore and psychologist Jerome Bruner and their colleagues, and the intellectual underpinning for the project was Bruner's (1960) classic, *The Process of Education.* Pedagogically, MACOS was one of the most powerful of the reform programs: Students worked with real anthropological data in cooperative group activities to make and test hypotheses about adaptive behaviors. The program combined methods and perspectives of anthropology, sociology, psychology, and biology and was initially viewed as an original and engaging way to promote scientific literacy and to help students learn to think like social scientists. However, MACOS was attacked on the floor of Congress in the mid-1970s for its underlying premise of the theory of evolution and its explicit videos of animal and human behaviors. Because of protests from religious conservatives and the political right, it was removed from many American schools and used to justify a total ban on the use of federal funds for curriculum development.

Was federal support for curriculum development a failure? How did these reform programs compare with traditional programs in terms of results? Studies conducted by educational researchers of the outcomes of the alphabet programs generally supported their efficacy in terms of students learning and in developing more positive attitudes toward science (Atkin & Black, 2003). The programs of this period did succeed in moving science education away from the "read-about-science," textbook-centered programs they were intended to replace. Yet researchers also found shortcomings. One criticism was that the content was too limited. Programs of this period tended to focus on basic science concepts—pure science—with little or no attention to applications and technology, the history and nature of science, and science-society issues. In general, not enough attention was given to assessment, and there were few provisions for variations in learners or for special needs students. Some of the programs were inflexible in design and were not teacher-friendly. There was no articulation between elementary and secondary programs, and some programs, such as MACOS, were designed for only a single academic year.

Summary

Despite widespread support in the science and science education communities for the reform alphabet programs, they were never widely adopted by U.S. schools. In fact, only a quarter of schools ever used any of them (Weiss, 1987). Even so, many of the schools that did adopt them retreated back to earlier practices in the late 1970s and early 1980s, when the back-to-the-basics movement put science education on the back burner. The reform effort might have been more successful if policymakers had put more emphasis on teacher education and professional development. To implement one of the new programs in the classroom, a teacher needed both subject matter mastery and competence in conducting an activity-based, discovery-oriented program. Despite opportunities provided by government-subsidized summer institutes for educators, few teachers of that period were appropriately supported in making the transition to the new programs' content and methods.

By the end of the 1980s the traditional science textbook once again dominated school science. Most teachers today have never used anything but a textbook to structure their classroom science programs. Despite their shortcomings, the 1950s–1970s reform projects are still excellent sources of hands-on activities, and many can still be found in schools. More than 1,000 field-tested activities from these classic programs are also available on *Enhanced Science Helper K–8* (University of Florida, 1996), a CD-ROM developed by Mary Budd Rowe and the University of Florida.

THE SECOND WAVE: END-OF-CENTURY REFORMS AND CONTEMPORARY SCIENCE PROGRAMS

After the MACOS flap and the cutoff of National Science Foundation curriculum development funding, science education entered a period of neglect in U.S. schools. Then a second wave of reform effort gathered steam in the 1980s as hundreds of studies and reports in that decade proclaimed the importance of science in the curriculum and decried American students' lack of science literacy. International comparisons found that our students' performance was behind that of students of many Asian and European nations. The most influential of these studies is the Trends in International Mathematics and Sciences Study (TIMSS), which regularly assesses student achievement in science and math in 42 countries in Grades 4, 8, and 12 (for the latest results see http://nces.ed.gov/timss/). As a result of this second call for action to improve science education, all state governors and President George H. W. Bush met in Charlottesville, Virginia, in 1989 and ratified six national goals for education, one of which specifically addressed science education. Consequently, the place of science as a core subject in the K–8 curriculum has gained widespread public acceptance and a number of new reform initiatives have been undertaken in the last decade.

These newest curriculum projects purposefully avoided the shortcomings of the 1960s projects. Unlike the first wave reforms, which were developed primarily by academic scientists, the new projects represent the curriculum work of teams that included scientists, teachers, university science educators, school district curriculum supervisors, and commercial publishers. These projects differ in a number of ways from both from textbook-based programs and from the 1960s discovery learning programs.

One difference is in science content. New content has been incorporated, such as computer technology and environmental issues. At the same time the program developers tried to follow the dictum "less is more," a notion advanced by Theodore Sizer (1984) in his book *Horace's Compromise*, which addressed secondary school reforms. In the second wave programs *depth of understanding* was the aim and thus "big ideas" have been emphasized and content has been focused on conceptual themes, with fewer topics treated in greater depth.

One of the new programs is Science and Technology for Children (STC), now in its second edition and a joint project of the Smithsonian Institution's National Science Resources Center and the Carolina Biological Supply Company for Grades 1–6 (see http://www.carolina.com/stc/). The 24 eight-week units include activity books and materials for students to learn science concepts and reasoning skills through investigation, discovery, and application. The integration of science with mathematics, language arts, social studies, and art is encouraged. This project later added a middle school program, Science and Technology Concepts for Middle Schools (STC/MC), with eight modules.

Another of the new programs is Full Option Science System (FOSS), a K–8 program created by the University of California's Lawrence Hall of Science and marketed by Delta Education (see http://lhsfoss.org/). This program has 33 kits containing the materials needed for all hands-on and collaborative group activities. Each module includes a teacher preparation video, a teacher's guide, and an equipment kit. The videos show how to prepare for the activities. The teacher's guide contains an overview, a set of activity folios, and duplication masters. Units are correlated to *Encyclopedia Britannica* media offerings and interactive computer software.

Another new program is BSCS T.R.A.C.S. (Teaching Relevant Activities for Concepts and Skills, K–5, 1999) and BSCS Science & Technology (Grades 6–8, third edition, 2005), both developed by the Biological Science Curriculum Study and Kendall/Hunt Publishing Company (see http://www.bscs.org/). At each grade level in T.R.A.C.S. there are four modules, one each in physical science, earth and space science, life science, and science and technology. A full-year kindergarten program is integrated in one *Teacher's Guide.* The kit-based program is based on a learning cycle instructional model and includes many hands-on and cooperative group activities. BSCS Science & Technology is a multilevel, thematic program that integrates life, earth and space, and physical sciences in the context of themes and issues. With hands-on activities and use of the 5E learning cycle model in a cooperative learning environment, BSCS Science & Technology encourages an inquiry approach.

Insights is the final new program we will consider. It is a K–6 program created by the Education Development Center, Inc. (the producer of the ESS in the 1960s) and Optical Data Corporation and marketed by Kendall/Hunt Publishing Company (see http://www.kendallhunt.com/). Each of the 21 modules contains up to 20 hands-on learning activities. Six major science themes are represented: systems, change, structure and function, diversity, cause and effect, and energy. The program also uses a learning cycle approach and can be used at more than one grade level. Kits rather than textbooks are the core resources, and there is an optional student notebook. A feature of this program and others is the literacy connection, promoting language development and emphasizing writing, such as through the science notebooks.

Also still available are updated versions of the ESS and SCIS programs of the 1960s, both published by Delta Education (publisher of FOSS). SCIS 3+ is a comprehensive, activity-based science curriculum that provides a full year of science for K–6. Delta Science Modules represent 57 topic-based units that can be sequenced to provide a comprehensive K–8 science program (see http://www.delta-education.com/).

Many contemporary science programs incorporate technology both as new content and as a new learning tool. The rapid development of computer technologies in the past decade, in access speed and quality, and especially the growth of the Internet, have made available a wide range of teaching resources in the form of texts, sound recordings, and visual images. You'll be able to enrich your classroom science program with all kinds of electronic media: DVDs of educational TV programs such as *NOVA* and *Animal Planet* (also available on videocassette), recorded books on tape, computer software, and so on. Students may use these technologies to conduct investigations and communicate their results in multimedia reports, thus linking learning science to literacy development.

However, it is important to note that there is growing concern about what many perceive to be the overuse of technology. The Internet is a repository of both information and misinformation, yet many students are inclined to believe that if it's on the Net it must be true. Even more disturbing, writers such as Richard Louv (2005) have noted that along with the loss of an appreciation of nature (he calls it *nature-deficit disorder*) the constant barrage of electronic media that children are exposed to has already been linked to conditions such as attention deficit hyperactivity disorder. Technology is a valuable new tool for both teaching and learning, but some argue that their fascination with technology is robbing children of a broader base of experience, emotionally, intellectually, and sensorially (Oppenheimer, 2004). Science and technology are inexorably linked, but it remains the teacher's responsibility to understand the difference between the appropriate and inappropriate uses of technology in the classroom.

And let's not forget the classic teaching resources: manipulatives, trade books, posters, big books, the school community (the frequently overlooked relatives of the students and neighbors around the school), and the school grounds and nearby natural areas. Moreover, many professionally prepared science instructional materials are commercially available to supplement the core science curriculum, such as the TOPS Learning Systems *Science with Simple Things*, with more than 100 topic teacher guide booklets (see http://www.topscience.org/index.html) and the Lawrence Hall of Science *Great Explorations in Math and Science* (GEMS), with 70 teacher guides and handbooks for K–8 (http://www.lhsgems.org/gems.html). Many of these teaching resources are illustrated in Figure 4.3.

Figure 4.3   Today's Science Programs Draw on Multiple Instructional Resources

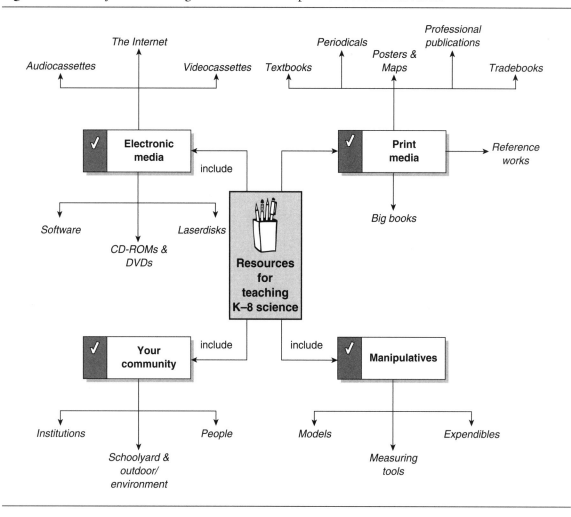

Summary

The contemporary curriculum projects developed since the 1990s tend to be similar in several ways:

- Use of more open-ended investigations and cooperative group methods, especially for problem solving
- Inclusion of content about the nature of science and the values and social connections of science
- A more humanistic approach, with examples from everyday life to increase relevance
- More emphasis on environmental and ecological issues
- Integration of science across the curriculum
- More flexibility to provide for the needs of different students (Carin, 1993, pp. 221, 231)

We recommend that you investigate the current crop of commercially available science programs and supplementary materials at professional conferences and in science education journals to determine whether any are a good match for you and your students.

CONTEMPORARY TRENDS: THE SCIENCE-TECHNOLOGY-SOCIETY APPROACH

For the teacher of science, *science-technology-society* (STS) refers to particular curriculum content: the nature of science and technology and the connection of science and technology to our lives as social beings. STS also refers to an approach to teaching science that includes problem-solving and decision-making activities set in real-world contexts. STS is interdisciplinary and equally belongs in the social studies program. STS also connects with environmental education because many environmental concerns often are STS issues. STS provides a natural structure for integrating your classroom curriculum because there are also many opportunities to link science with the language arts and mathematics.

An emphasis on STS also offers a valuable mechanism for the development of critical thinking (Penick, 2002). The proliferation of information via the Internet and the media gives rise to the need to develop skills in distinguishing fact from fiction. As it is, students tend to believe that if it's on the Net, it must be true. By the same token, the media—for instance, movies and television programs—take license when it comes to accurately representing issues in science. Well-designed STS activities can help students develop critical thinking skills that enable them to analyze information before accepting it as true (Miller, 2006).

In the National Social Studies Standards (National Council for the Social Studies, 1994), "science, technology, and society" and "global connections" are 2 of 10 themes identified as social studies content (p. 28). The National Geography Standards identify "physical and human systems" and "environment and society" as three of six content clusters for geography (Geography

Education Standards Project, 1994). A "geographically informed person" is said to be one who understands how human actions modify the physical environment, how physical systems affect human systems, and how changes occur in the meaning, use, distribution, and importance of resources.

An STS approach to science education has been favored by science educators since the 1970s, and recent studies indicate that students taught through an STS approach learn the concepts as well as students who study from textbooks, but the STS students applied concepts better in new situations and at home and in their communities, developed more positive attitudes about science, and exhibited more creativity (Yager & Yager, 2006, p. 248). STS addresses two distinct goals in the curriculum:

• Teaching about the nature and culture of science and technology, both as experienced by practitioners and as understood through sociology, history, psychology, anthropology, and philosophy

• Addressing personal, local, national, and global issues that interface between science, technology, and society that entail personal decision making and informed, premeditated action (Cheek, 1992, p. 199)

An STS approach to science education is also supported in the National Science Education Standards (National Research Council, 1996). You will recall that the standards divide K–8 content into eight areas, and two of these are

• Science and technology
• Science in personal and social perspectives

"Science and technology" refers to the first STS education goal, and "science in personal and social perspectives" refers to the second. In the National Science Education Standards, "science in personal and social perspectives" is subdivided into

• Personal health (for Grades K–4 and 5–8)
• Characteristics and changes in populations (Grades K–4)
• Types of resources (Grades K–4)
• Changes in environments (Grades K–4)
• Science and technology in local challenges (Grades K–4)
• Populations, resources, and environments (Grades 5–8)
• Natural hazards (Grades 5–8)
• Risks and benefits (Grades 5–8)
• Science and technology in society (Grades 5–8) (National Research Council, 1996, pp. 138, 166)

A long list of problems and issues can be related to these topics (Table 4.1). To which of the categories just listed can you link the items in Table 4.1?

STS issues connect to many human endeavors. One of your goals should be to promote students' awareness of their natural environment from an ecological perspective. They should understand how human activities interact with

Table 4.1   A Few STS Topics Related to Science in Personal and Social Perspectives

Population growth and ecological carrying capacity	Desalinization of sea water
Population demographics in different areas	Aquifer management
Consumption of resources, use of resource reserves, and resource depletion (fossil fuels, fresh water, mineral resources)	Solid waste and toxic waste disposal
	Nuclear waste containment
Air and water pollution	Radiation exposure (e.g., ultraviolet, microwave, power-plant leaks, high-voltage power lines)
Soil contamination and mineralization	
Climate change	Ozone depletion
Sustainability	Acid rain
Food and agricultural policies	Land use policies
The oceans as a commons	Surface mining
Diseases, disease prevention, epidemiology, and medical policies	Forestry management, clearcutting, deforestation, wildlife habitat destruction, and desertification
World hunger and poverty	Housing and commercial development building policies
Aquaculture	
Bioaccumulation of toxins in food chains	Soil erosion
Energy policies (geothermal energy, nuclear energy, energy from biomass, solar energy, energy from oceanic currents and times, wind energy, and dam construction for hydroelectric power)	Conservation and preservation policies
	Loss of biodiversity
	Use of animals in research
	Health care policies
Resource exploration and exploitation (offshore drilling, Arctic National Wildlife Refuge)	Biotechnology policies (cloning, stem cell research, genetically engineered crops, eugenics)
Environmental impact of extracting minerals (mountaintop removal in coal mining)	Forensic science
Renewable and nonrenewable resources	Transportation policies

and change the environment. Your students should study environmental conditions in their locality and region and develop an awareness of the global environment, because everything is connected. They should learn how conditions such as climate have varied over time, what changes are occurring now, and what is causing them. As a teacher you should always promote responsible citizenship to your students.

Some scientists have not always been responsible citizens—Hitler's scientists come to mind—but science and technology are major agents of change in our day. Had it not been for the work of physicists and engineers there would have been no atomic weapons but also none of the benefits of nuclear technologies. Even if science and technology are the source of a social problem, they can be among the solutions as scientists strive to understand and address such problems.

The opening decade of the twenty-first century has been particularly unsettled in the United States, especially since the attack of September 11, 2001. National security has come to the forefront as the United States and its allies have reacted to terrorist threats. But there have also been other major social changes recently. For one thing, there has been a rapid development of new technologies of communication and information processing. These technologies have expanded in dimensions few people ever imagined. For better or for worse, the new technologies have facilitated a process of *globalization* of society. Changes in the economic system have also occurred during this period. International competition for markets has led to a concentration of wealth. Also, multinational corporations with great power control a large share of commerce and trade. International rather than national political institutions now regulate most trade.

A final dimension of change in this period is the deterioration of many measures of environmental quality and a concomitant rise in the public's environmental consciousness. People have become increasingly aware of the environmental impacts of both industrial production and communal and personal lifestyle choices (Waks, 1995). These and other social changes cumulatively have led to what is called *postindustrial society.* The nature of citizenship in postindustrial society is evolving in our times. Social polarization is part of this, and so is a change in the character of citizenship compared with how it was understood in the past. Another part of current trends is a diminishing of social, political, and even civil rights. If our job as educators is to help students come to understand the world situation and their options as social actors, then today's national and global situation clearly presents a significant challenge.

Carrying Capacity: The Crunch Is Here, Now

Understanding the world situation today and our own situation *as a species* involves grasping several ecological and economic concepts. One of these is *carrying capacity,* basic to understanding the idea of a *sustainable* society. A sustainable society is one that "satisfies its needs without jeopardizing the prospects of future generations" (Brown, Flavin, & Postel, 1990, p. 173). Carrying capacity, given a set of environmental conditions, is the maximum number of organisms that a particular ecosystem can sustain indefinitely. Ecologists can accurately estimate the carrying capacity of, say, a hectare of woodland, for a species such as the white-tailed deer or wild turkey.

Unfortunately, no one really knows for sure what the Earth's carrying capacity is for us, *Homo sapiens.* As this is being written the world population has now surpassed 6.5 billion (for an up-to-the-minute count see http://www .census .gov). The last billion was added in only about 11 years (whereas the first billion wasn't reached until the 1800s). Population is projected to grow to between 8 and 11 billion by midcentury (United Nations Population Division, 2004; see http://www .un.org). When the first author was a child the U.S. population was 150 million, but now, just over five decades later, it is more than 300 million. How will this change in population affect the planet, and how will it affect people's lives in the United States and in undeveloped parts of the world?

Unfortunately, there are no existing models of sustainable societies. The world's industrial societies have created automobile-centered, fossil fuel–driven economies that are clearly unsustainable, yet most developing nations are aspiring to the same resource-consumptive systems. However, a sustainable society cannot overshoot the carrying capacity of the ecosystem.

Land availability is just one of many factors involved in calculating carrying capacity. In Table 4.2, an apple is used as a model representing the Earth. The activity with the apple demonstrates the finite nature of the Earth's arable land resources. The carrying capacity for our species also is dependent on resources such as fresh water, minerals, and energy resources. The rate at which these resources are being consumed can be used to gauge changes in the carrying capacity. Carrying capacity changes when the environment is degraded by pollution. Experts may disagree on how much of any given resource remains, but everyone recognizes that as resources are consumed and environmental quality declines, the carrying capacity is decreased, meaning that the environment is able to support fewer inhabitants in the long run.

With a fixed land resource base and a growing population, each person's portion gets smaller. The bottom line is that the Earth's remaining resources simply are not sufficient to indefinitely sustain the level of

Table 4.2   A Concrete Demonstration of the Finite Nature of Earth's Land Resources

Consider the Earth as an apple. Slice the apple into quarters. Set aside three of the quarters; these represent the oceans of the world. The remaining 1/4 represents, roughly, the Earth's land area. Slice this land quarter in half, which yields two 1/8 sections. Set aside one of these pieces; it represents land inhospitable to people and to agriculture (polar areas, deserts, wetlands, and very high or rocky mountainous areas). The other 1/8 piece is the land area where people live but not necessarily where they grow the foods needed for life. Slice this 1/8 piece crosswise into four fairly equal sections, yielding four 1/32 pieces. Set aside three pieces, which represent areas too rocky, too wet, too cold, too steep, or with soil too poor to actually produce food. This piece represents also the areas of land that could produce food but are buried under cities, highways and roads, shopping centers, and other human-made structures. This leaves only one remaining 1/32 piece. Carefully peel the skin off this piece, only about 3% of the Earth's surface. This small apple peel represents the soil layer, the very thin skin of the Earth's crust on which humankind depends for food. Soil depth varies according to the bedrock and other factors, but on average it is less than 2 meters to consolidated material (rock). The arable land area and soil quality limit the amount of food-producing land available to humanity. In many places around the globe soil is being lost through erosion, and in other places it is degraded by processes such as mineralization.

consumption to which we in the developed countries have become accustomed. Yet our economic system depends on consumption, and advertisements urge us to buy what we don't need. In the words of Robert Louis Stevenson, "Sooner or later, every man must sit down to a banquet of consequences." There is a relationship between our ultimate ability to create a sustainable society and the beneficial environmental functions of an unpolluted, biologically diverse global ecosystem.

Most species in a good portion of the biosphere are too tiny to see without aid. Ecologists recognize a phenomenon called the pyramid of diversity. The pyramid of diversity tells us that species that consist of very small individuals have greater diversity. The reason for this is that small organisms can divide the environment into smaller niches than large organisms can. Because there are so many species of small individuals, such as bacteria, most species on the Earth remain unknown to science.

There is evidence that we are in the midst of a major extinction event. Over the last 10,000 years, and particularly the past 500, the rate of species extinction has increased hundreds of times over what it was before humans arrived (Ward, 1994). Noted biologist E. O. Wilson of Harvard University claims that the one thing the children of the future will have the hardest time forgiving us for is the loss of species that we allowed to happen. An impoverishment of the planetary gene pool has been occurring on our watch. The culprits? HIPPO! HIPPO is an acronym for *habitat destruction, invasive species, pollution, overpopulation, and overharvesting of resources.* Because so many species have yet to be identified, Wilson points out that we don't even know what we're losing (Wilson, 2005).

The message from Wilson and other scientists is that biological diversity contributes to the health of the global ecosystem and that human activities are harmful to other species. One responsible reaction is to work to reduce one's own impact on the biosphere by reducing consumption, reusing, and recycling (the 3Rs); see Figure 4.4. Another is to work for the preservation of significantly large areas as wilderness. As teachers, there is much we can do to educate others to value species diversity.

CONSIDERATIONS FOR THE FUTURE

Without doubt, the situation in which we humans find ourselves in the twenty-first century has been exacerbated by our neglect of the consequences of our enterprise. Of course, we cannot simply shut down, clean things up, and proceed in a more responsible manner. A *transition* is needed, and science and technology will be part of whatever solutions emerge as we look for alternatives to our current practices. Where and when will the paradigm shift to sustainability begin? The shift is taking place here and now, which should give you some sense of the responsibility teachers bear.

Most environmental scientists are very concerned about our present situation, but few consider it hopeless. Younger students should be spared the picture of doom and gloom we have been considering here. They need the empowerment of believing that they can make a difference. The good news is that people are intelligent enough to face and resolve the problems that have been created (with the caveat that solutions come with consequences). Significant changes in lifestyle may be needed. One of the people who will some day be at the forefront of change may well be a student in your classroom.

Infusing STS Education Into the Curriculum

As a teacher, you can engage children in learning about ecosystems and their components through activities such as creating a classroom terrarium and conducting field studies in the neighborhoods, fields, forests, streams, and ponds of your locality. You can help students assess environmental quality and identify local and regional problems and needs. With experience and knowledge of their locale, students can compare different ecosystems and seek patterns of similarity and difference. By the end of their middle school years, students can understand most ecological concepts and principles involved in environmental problems and can learn much about the role human actions play in the environment. They also can develop an appreciation for nature and a commitment to environmental values.

Students also can learn to judge the relative importance of various environmental issues. Public perceptions of the seriousness of problems can be very different from the perceptions of knowledgeable scientists. In one study, two thirds of adult respondents ranked hazardous waste sites as the most serious problem but ranked the climate alteration due to the greenhouse effect as 23rd. In contrast, Environmental Protection Agency scientists ranked the greenhouse effect much higher and hazardous waste sites as low to medium in health risk (Smith, 1989).

Find out what children in your own classroom think is most serious. Do a "think-pair-share" (TPS) activity with the class. Make a list of environmental problems (see Table 4.3 for ideas), and ask the class to rank them in order, with "1" being the most serious. Next, have each child compare his or her responses with those of a classmate. Finally, ask children to share their observations and the results of their discussion with the class. The TPS format is a good way to conduct STS discussions because every student gets involved. Your students' thoughts about a problem or issue can become more systematic and focused if you have them address the following six questions (Enright, 1993, p. 4):

- What is happening?
- Why did it start?
- Why does it continue?
- Why don't we hear more about it?
- Why should we care?
- What can we do?

Table 4.3   Conserving Planetary Resources: What You Can Do

Use compact fluorescent light bulbs (six times more energy efficient than regular bulbs).

Set the water heater thermostat no higher than 120°F and wrap the tank with insulation.

Fill unused parts of the refrigerator with water jugs.

Keep refrigerator gaskets clean, and make sure they seal tightly.

When power gadgets wear out, revert to hand-powered substitutes (e.g., alarm clock, food mill, lawn mower, snow blower).

Get a solar recharger for rechargeable battery devices.

Think about what you can live without.

Simulations and role-playing activities enable students to interact with each other and discuss issues related to the environment and society. Playing a role helps one take another's perspective and gain insight into a situation. Students can be creative in interpreting their roles as long as they don't violate the assigned "givens." Be sure to follow the activity with a debriefing; your observations and questions can challenge further thought. Students can compare the make-believe to real-world situations and do follow-up research.

Another way to make students think about the consequences of human activities is the "futures wheel" activity (Puls & O'Brien, 1994, p. 8). In the center of a blank page, students draw an oval and fill in the name of an invention or event, such as genetic engineering, an internal combustion engine, or the repeal of the Clean Water Act. Now draw ovals around the center and fill in some of the potential outcomes of the invention or event and add lines connecting to the center. Next, have students think of some of the possible consequences of the surrounding changes or outcomes. Follow the same process for tertiary outcomes, and continue the process as far as you can imagine possible outcomes, adding additional ovals if necessary.

Many STS issues can lead to group or class projects. An example is habitat restoration. Whatever the type of habitat (e.g., woodland, pond, prairie, desert), such a project would require students to learn how to identify both native and alien plant species. One possibility is to stake out parcels that can be assigned to small groups of students, each led by a parent or community volunteer. Groups might record their progress on a bulletin board or class Web page with photographs of the "before" conditions so changes can be chronicled. Helpful resources might be your local 4-H or county extension agent or state or national forester. Depending on the size of the habitat, this project might involve your classes over several years. See Table 4.4 for additional project ideas.

Table 4.4   STS Project Ideas

Inventory street trees in the neighborhood. Plant trees in historic districts, in parking lots, and around public buildings, plant a living snow fence or windbreak, or plant bulbs, annuals, wildflowers, or shrubs on traffic islands, in vacant lots, and in other public spaces.
Create an arboretum of native trees on the school grounds.
Create a garden in a park with raised beds and accessible walkways for people who are elderly or have disabilities, or a scent or touch garden for the blind.
Plant a heritage garden of traditional varieties of fruits, vegetables, and flowers to preserve genetic diversity, or, if your community has a strong ethnic heritage, plant an ethnic garden.
Restore or preserve an old cemetery or adopt a neglected urban park.
Preserve an important natural area such as a wetland, a grove of virgin timber, or habitat for an endangered species, or preserve a remnant of native prairie.
Use media and communication outlets to publicize your project.

Summary

Infusing STS into the curriculum is a great way to integrate the subjects and make learning both active and relevant. STS education also tends to provide students with better application skills and better attitudes toward science (because it is relevant) and engages them in higher levels of thinking.

MAKING ROOM IN THE CURRICULUM FOR EVENT-BASED SCIENCE

In the popular movie *Dead Poets Society*, the teacher played by Robin Williams captivated his students with the notion of *carpe diem*, or "seize the day." To the science teacher, seizing the day means creatively modifying your lesson on the spot in response to a question, an expressed interest, or a current event, such as a storm, earthquake, volcanic eruption, or environmental disaster—such as an oil spill or industrial accident. A student may bring to class something he or she found, such as a snake skin or an unusual-looking beetle. These situations represent valuable *teachable moments*, and they can occur at any time. Taking pedagogical advantage of such happenings requires sensitivity and flexibility, but there are few better ways of engaging students and demonstrating the relevance of science to their lives.

One potentially productive response to an event or special object is to invite children to express what they already know about it. Expression can be oral, but an event also is an opportunity for children to write or draw. By providing diverse contexts for expression, teachers help children more easily connect new information and the relevant concepts to their prior knowledge and experience. You might also have your students construct a semantic web, or concept map, showing relationships between the event and the science, as well as the science-society connections. Figure 4.4 is an example of a concept map based on Hurricane Katrina's devastating passage over the U.S. Gulf Coast in 2005. Such a web could be used to organize a study of weather. Concept maps can be constructed both before and after studying a topic. The postlesson map can be compared to the initial map for assessment purposes. Stop and think what you could include on a concept map of the 2004 Indian Ocean earthquake and tsunami.

Another way students can investigate an event or phenomenon is to interview relatives and community residents about their recollections. Older children could use tape recorders and transcribe and summarize their research findings. The production of such oral histories is what led to the success of the famous *Foxfire* book project (Wiggington, 1972), which now numbers 14 volumes.

CONCLUSION

The development of the school science program takes place on many levels and is influenced by many views of science education, as summarized in Table 4.5.

Figure 4.4   Concept Map Based on the 2005 Gulf Coast Hurricane Katrina

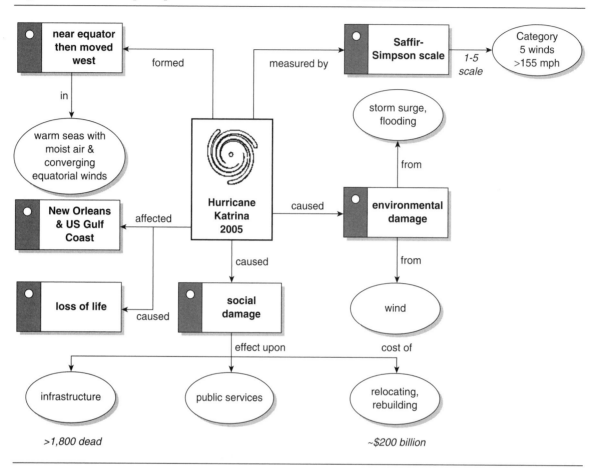

Table 4.5   Views of Science Education and Reform

View	*Focus*	*Desired Outcome of Reform*
Core knowledge	Content	Knowledge of key science concepts and practice in answering the questions of science
Constructivism	Learning	Experiential understanding of science and practice in thinking like scientists
STS	Critique	Critical perspective on science and practice in evaluating pros and cons of science
Culturally relevant, community based	Compatibility	Understanding of science in context and practice in using science to do important things

New research-based curriculum materials and new technologies have opened up even more possibilities for the classroom teacher. Curriculum development grows out of a foundation of science background knowledge, understanding of students' development and learning theory, and a familiarity with a range of resources. Also essential are sensitivity to students' interests, awareness of current events, and an ability to be flexible in acting out a variety of teaching roles. Taken together, these are the characteristics of a professional educator.

An STS approach to curriculum facilitates personal decision making and encourages informed and reflective action. STS education is a part of the more comprehensive changes in education and society occurring globally in the transition to postindustrial societies. As Neil Postman has said, "The new education has as its purpose the development of a new kind of person, one who . . . is an actively inquiring, flexible, creative, innovative, tolerant, liberal personality who can face uncertainty and ambiguity without disorientation, who can formulate viable new meanings to meet changes in the environment which threaten individual and mutual survival" (Postman & Weingartner, 1969, p. 218).

5

Engaging Students in Inquiry

Skills and Investigative Techniques

Children's Questions

Inquiry

Science Process Skills

Investigations Come in Different Forms

Your Academic Roadmap

This chapter should help you to understand the following ideas:

- Children are born investigators who naturally ask questions about the world around them.
- The inquiry approach is the planned use of questions to initiate activity.
- Children who know how to conduct investigations and who understand the value of the inquiry process are well prepared to find answers to their own questions in the future.
- Science lessons that draw on multiple process skills are more effective.
- There is more than one approach to scientific investigation; eight investigative techniques are appropriate for elementary and middle school science.
- Knowing how to conduct an investigation and when to use which form of investigation are fundamental understandings.

"What I wonder about is why sometimes dogs are wild and some not. And why do dogs chase cats?"

—Ashley, 6 years old

CHILDREN'S QUESTIONS

The young are fascinated by the world around them. They are curious about crawling things, creatures that hop and fly, unusual rocks, stars and planets, and much more. They want to make sense of it all. And they don't have to be told to be curious. They are naturally curious, natural investigators. Your task in teaching science is to nurture those natural inclinations.

Most of us are familiar with the phase that children go through at about 4 years of age when curiosity blossoms into questioning. Some questions they ask are interesting or cute because of the child's naiveté or because the questions are the same ones we thought about ourselves as children and haven't thought about since. "Why do dogs chase cats?" "Why do balls bounce?" "Why don't chickens fly?" Questions such as "Why do we have to go to Aunt Jane's house?" reflect a child's social-emotional personality development. In early childhood, children are working to establish their own identity and a sense of autonomy, so many of their questions test the limits of that autonomy (Erikson, 1950). Questions such as "Why do worms wiggle?" reflect cognitive development. Children seek to make sense of their world by constructing plausible explanations based on their observations (Piaget, 1929). Because of their limited experiences, children often seek missing information by asking questions of others. Typically these are "why" questions, expecting the person asked to supply the needed information. Such questions present opportunities for teachers to channel this natural curiosity into systematic investigations.

As teachers, we need to eschew the stereotype that science is a collection of facts that answer questions and instead promote the view that science is the *search for understanding* (National Research Council, 2000). Science, properly understood, can be used by students to answer many of their own questions. Students can be guided to make observations that refute or support their personal theorizing. Therefore, the classroom science program must be rich in opportunities for investigations and "science talk" (Gallas, 1995).

Science talk can develop out of a student's question, but science talk can also be prompted by your own questions to your students. Karen Gallas argues that during such a talk students should not have to raise their hands to speak, because if hands have to be raised and a student called upon, the class might feel that the teacher is controlling the conversation. Instead, the teacher's role in science talk is that of a model and a coach. You have to pay attention to what the students are saying rather than calling on the next one to speak. The teacher can then use what she has heard to plan instruction that targets the student's *zone of proximal development* (Vygotsky, 1978). The zone of proximal development (ZPD, pronounced *zo-ped*) is what the student can do or understand with the assistance of others and is more indicative of mental development than what he or she can do alone (Vygotsky, 1978, p. 85). The ZPD characterizes mental development *prospectively,* describing what might be achieved given the appropriate interactions with the facilitating other.

INQUIRY

Inquiry is the process of seeking information by questioning. An inquiry may be initiated by a student. A student's question usually is expressed with the expectation of an immediate oral response. For example, a student might ask, "What kind of bird is that?" or "What do bluebirds eat?" The student wants an answer from someone perceived to be knowledgeable. Inquiry can also be initiated by the teacher. For example, to elicit what your class already knows about a topic, you may ask, "What do you know about bluebirds?" Channeling the power of questions for instructional purposes is known as the *inquiry approach,* a process that is "driven by one's own curiosity, wonder, interests or passion to understand an observation or solve a problem" (Llewellyn, 2002, p. 5).

The inquiry approach is more developmentally appropriate for K–8 students than the traditional "chalk 'n' talk" and textbook read-about approach and much more in tune with the nature of science. The traditional approach is characterized by didacticism, the teacher *telling* the students what they need to know, *listing* information on the board, and *providing verification* by having students read their textbooks and write definitions of vocabulary terms. Essentially, in the traditional approach the teacher decides what is important, provides all of the needed information, and controls when one topic is completed and the next one addressed.

The inquiry approach, on the other hand, emphasizes *experience before explanation.* Initially the teacher may guide an inquiry. However, the ultimate goal is to move your students toward directing their own inquiries. Thus the inquiry approach spans a spectrum from providing scaffolding and structure to allowing independent investigation. Through practice you will be able to judge when your students can handle more independence.

An important goal is to teach students to phrase their questions in a way that can be investigated. These questions will be used to initiate activities that in turn will provide new information and generate new questions.

The "I Wonder . . ." Model

One of the best ways to facilitate information seeking is to model the process. You can create opportunities for yourself to verbalize some of the thinking that takes place and is not otherwise observable to your students. For example, you can use the following sentence starters:

"I've been thinking about . . . (what you said about . . .)"

"I've noticed (or observed) something just now . . ."

"I wonder about . . ."

The following conversation is an example of how this process could be verbalized in front of the class.

This morning I looked outside and noticed that it wasn't very sunny. I observed lots of gray clouds. I wondered whether it was going to rain today. I could have just carried an umbrella in case it did rain and not thought about it any more. However, I was planning to wear my new shoes, and I really didn't want to get them wet and dirty the first time I wore them. So I checked the newspaper and the Weather Channel. The paper predicted. . . .

By listening to you thinking out loud, verbalizing the sequence of your thoughts, your students are exposed to the strategy called *wondering*. Wonderings arise as people become aware that there is a gap between a particular experience and their ability to explain it. As we get older, these gaps often seem to appear when we are challenged to explain something we thought we knew. (See Activity 5.1.)

As you model and repeat this process in the classroom, your students may begin to recognize the pattern and begin to imitate it (Table 5.1). More important, they may learn that it is worthwhile to verbalize a question and systematically come up with ways to answer it.

Activity 5.1   Using the "I Wonder..." Strategy

Create a scenario you could use to model the "I Wonder . . ." information-seeking process. After writing the scenario, identify the vital components: observations, questions, and possible answer sources.

1. List observations.

2. Formulate questions.

3. Identify possible sources of information.

The possibilities for inquiry are only as limited as one's imagination. Topics might reflect personal experiences or hobbies, such as travel, fishing, or gardening, or might be related to students' problems and interests, such as bicycling, pets, or a visit to the dentist. After experiencing the "I Wonder . . ." process several times, students can begin to participate by suggesting possible sources of information and then collecting that information. With additional practice and encouragement, students will generate their own investigations by identifying situations for the application of the "I Wonder . . ." model. Why not do Activity 5.1 and give this inquiry strategy a try for yourself?

SCIENCE PROCESS SKILLS

We have established that children and youth are naturally curious and that they tend to engage in many of the processes scientists use as they attempt to answer questions. In fact, throughout our daily lives we all use the skills described here. As you read about inferences, predictions, classification, and so forth, you will see that they are skills for life and living. The educational challenge is to help your students develop and refine these skills.

This set of intellectual abilities or skills is known as the *science process skills.* In the 1960s, when much effort went into science education curriculum development, as described in Chapter 4, the science process skills were generated as a way of describing what scientists do. The basic science process skills are *observation, inference, classification, communication, measurement,* and *prediction.*

Observation

Observation is the use of one's senses to perceive objects and events, their properties, and their behavior. Impressions from the senses of sight, touch, taste, smell, and hearing can be collected and interpreted based on prior knowledge and experience. Observation feeds the process of meaning making. Most people tend to emphasize *visual* observations and depend less on their other senses. Students must be encouraged to attend also to their senses of hearing, smell, and touch. However, you may want to establish a class rule that says the sense of taste is not to be used for making observations unless it is specifically permitted.

Qualitative Observations

Most observations made by students are qualitative ones, such as "It is green on the outside" or "The inside part of the peel is white and mushy." Students observing the same object would be likely to use the same color descriptions (*green* and *white*) but would be less likely to use the same texture description (*mushy*). Because of the nature of our language, people use different descriptive terms. This reflects the many ways people perceive things, but it can lead to confusing descriptions when we communicate our observations. For instance, if a friend were to say that she bought a blue car, the car one imagines may not match the shade of blue of the actual automobile.

Quantitative Observations

Quantitative observations are those that include numbers and use a unit of measure. Quantitative observations usually are more precise than qualitative observations. If a student reports that a lemon has six seeds, it is likely that other children observing the same piece of fruit would make the same quantitative observation. Observations using comparisons, such as "an arm's length" or "as big as my fist," are considered quantitative because a unit (an arm or a fist) has been used as a standard to which something is compared.

Providing children with magnifying lenses, rulers, thermometers, and other tools enhances their ability to make observations. Even these simple tools enable students to make more precise observations and become better investigators.

Inference

Inference is the act of making statements that attempt to explain or interpret objects or events that are based on observations. Your students may need help in distinguishing between observations and inferences. Suppose that while observing a plant, a student reported, "Two leaves are dying." The student may think that he was making an observation, but he was actually making an inference. He is *interpreting* the difference in the conditions of the leaves he observed on the plant. The associated observation would simply be that two leaves are mostly yellow and brown and the other leaves are green. The inference is that the nongreen leaves are dying. Other attempts to explain the difference in leaf color might be "Part of the plant doesn't get any sunshine" or "This type of plant has a mixture of leaves" (variegated leaf color). Each of these explanations is a plausible inference.

Students should be able to recognize that more than one reasonable inference could be given for a set of observations. (See Activity 5.2.) Although an inference is an attempt to interpret observations, it may be based on the evidence of past experiences. Because every individual has a unique set of past experiences, you are likely to find your students capable of generating diverse inferences for their observations. You may stimulate higher-level thinking by engaging your students in metacognition about the distinction between observation and inference and encouraging them to make more than one plausible inference from a set of observations. Metacognition is thinking about thinking, and we all engage in metacognitive activities all the time. The ability to think metacognitively is associated with intelligence and higher-order thinking that involves active control over one's thinking (Martinez, 2006).

Activity 5.2   Observation and Inference

This activity has four parts. Be sure to complete all four.

1. Select an object to observe. Choose something that is common because it is used occasionally but something you have not paid much attention to, such as a peanut in the shell, a safety pin, or nail clippers. Generate a list of at least six observations.

2. Read through your list of observations. Decide which of the senses you used to make each observation. Also indicate whether each observation is qualitative or quantitative. Now go back to your object and make more observations using the senses you had previously used the least and also add more quantitative observations. Add these new observations to your list.

3. Next, try observing an event rather than an object. Select an event that takes a brief period of time to occur. A candle burning, an ice cube melting, or a seltzer tablet dissolving in water are examples of simple events appropriate for this activity. Make a list of four observations at each of these times: before, during, and after the changes occur.

4. Finally, write two inferences that interpret what happened in the event you observed.

Copyright © 2007 by Corwin Press. All rights reserved. Reprinted from *Teaching Constructivist Science, K–8: Nurturing Natural Investigators in the Standards-Based Classroom* by Michael L. Bentley, Edward S. Ebert II, and Christine Ebert. Thousand Oaks, CA: Corwin Press, www.corwinpress.com. Reproduction authorized only for the local school site or nonprofit organization that has purchased this book.

Classification

Classification is the act of grouping objects or events into categories based on specified characteristics or attributes. When objects and events are grouped, the numbers and the diversity become more mentally manageable. By studying the characteristics and attributes of groups, looking for similarities, differences, and patterns, we can make generalizations that serve as the basis of concept development. A student's ability to classify can be developed with practice and appropriate coaching. For example, intermediate-level students can learn to use and create dichotomous keys for identifying leaves, rocks, and even everyday artifacts such as jar lids. In the life sciences, the classification system for living things is based on the work of the "father of taxonomy," Swedish natural philosopher Carolus Linnaeus (also called Carl von Linné) invented the binary system of *binomial nomenclature* (genus and species) that is still used today.

Binary Classification

Binary classification is the classification of all objects in a set into two groups, or subsets, based on a given characteristic. Asking students to get into two lines, one for boys and one for girls, is a form of binary classification. One group would be "boys" and the other group would be "not boys" (labeling the second group as "girls" obscures the logical procedure). Your students also could be separated into two groups based on characteristics such as eye color (those with brown eyes and those with eyes that are not brown) or the type of clothing worn (those wearing shoes with shoestrings and those wearing shoes without strings). Binary classification is the most basic and appropriate form of classification for young children to be taught.

Multistage Classification

Multistage classification is a succession of binary classifications (Figure 5.1). Suppose that a set of blocks is separated into two groups based on a characteristic of shape; some are rectangular and others are not. The group of blocks that are rectangular can be subdivided into those that are square (cubic) and those that are not square. Other characteristics, such as color and size, can be used to continue the subdividing (e.g., "red," "not red"). Each time, the

Figure 5.1 Multistage Classification

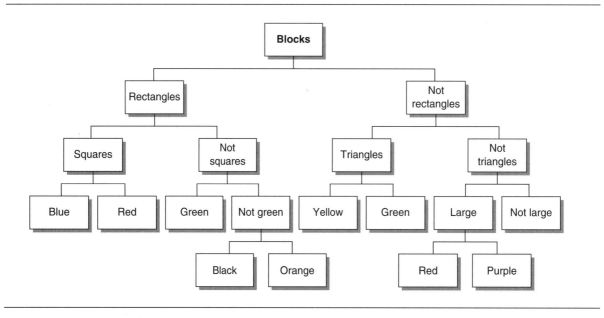

Figure 5.2 Multistage Classification Scheme Numbered

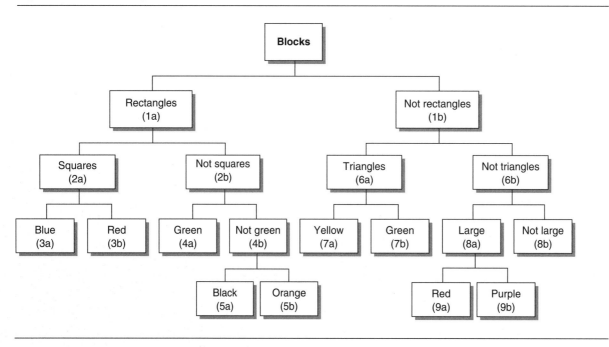

remaining objects are placed into two categories until all objects in each group have the same characteristic.

Dichotomous Keys

A taxonomic or dichotomous key is a multistage classification system that is written out in a format that involves answering questions that lead to an identification. Figure 5.2 demonstrates how each level of the classification scheme is numbered. Note that for each level there is an A and a B. The "A" side represents the particular attribute (e.g., "red"), and the "B" side represents the absence of that attribute ("not red").

Table 5.1   Taxonomic Key for Colored Blocks

1a	Rectangle	Go to 2
1b	Not a rectangle	Go to 6
2a	Square	Go to 3
2b	Not a square	Go to 4
3a	Blue	Blue square
3b	Not blue	Red square
4a	Green	Green rectangle
4b	Not green	Go to 5
5a	Black	Black rectangle
5b	Not black	Orange rectangle
6a	Triangle	Go to 7
6b	Not triangle	Go to 8
7a	Yellow	Yellow triangle
7b	Not yellow	Green triangle
8a	Large	Go to 9
8b	Not large	Small trapezoid
9a	Red	Red trapezoid
9b	Not red	Purple trapezoid

The multistage classification scheme we have just described would be written out as a taxonomic key, as in Table 5.1.

By selecting an object and then reading down the taxonomic key, you can identify what that object is named. Of course, this might be easy when we are talking about colored blocks. However, taxonomic keys often are used for field guides. So when you are out collecting leaves, you can read down the key, answer questions (e.g., about the shape of the leaf), and ultimately find that indeed it is poison ivy that you are holding. (See Activity 5.3.)

Activity 5.3   Classification

This activity has three parts. Begin by selecting a group of items to classify. You might choose your CD collection, your wardrobe, a pile of laundry, a collection of action figures, or a collection of jar lids. Whatever you decide upon, choose something that will have at least 15 different items.

1. This particular activity would work best if you had a classmate or friend with whom to work. Begin by classifying all of the objects into just two groups. Then have your friend look at the two groups and try to identify the characteristic or attribute you had used to separate the two groups. Try it again using a different set of characteristics.

2. Now take your 15 or so objects and classify them using a multistage system. Keep in mind that a multistage system simply begins as a binary classification (one group possesses the characteristic and the other does not) and then continues subdividing the remaining groups of objects until only one item is left in each category (assuming that there are no two identical items in your initial group of stuff).

3. With item 2 completed, write out your multistage classification scheme as a dichotomous key. Use the numbering scheme in Table 5.1 as a guide to numbering your classification scheme. When you are finished, you should be able to select an item from the group and identify it by reading through your key.

Copyright © 2007 by Corwin Press. All rights reserved. Reprinted from *Teaching Constructivist Science, K–8: Nurturing Natural Investigators in the Standards-Based Classroom* by Michael L. Bentley, Edward S. Ebert II, and Christine Ebert. Thousand Oaks, CA: Corwin Press, www.corwinpress.com. Reproduction authorized only for the local school site or nonprofit organization that has purchased this book.

Communication

Communication is the transmission of information from one person to another by verbal or nonverbal means. (See Activity 5.4.) People interact and share ideas by communicating. In the earlier classification example using blocks, the completed diagram would be an example of a communication, or an *inscription.* If a child had classified the blocks by describing the characteristics to another child, they would be using oral communication. Nonoral forms of communication that are especially important in science include charts, graphs, maps, and drawings. Charts are a means of organizing information, such as temperature observations made over a period of time (Figure 5.3) or the number of seeds that germinated under various conditions. The various nonoral forms of communication depict data in different ways and scaffold learning.

Graphs are used to visually show patterns that may exist in the collected data. For instance, a line graph may be used to show how the temperature of a closed container of water placed in sunlight increased over a period of time (Figure 5.4). There are different types of graphs (e.g., line, bar, pie). Some types are inappropriate for depicting particular kinds of data. For example, *only* line graphs are used to display the change in a single variable over time.

Maps and drawings are used to indicate important components and the relative position of the components (Figure 5.5). Maps are used when distance is

Figure 5.3 Temperature Chart

Daily High and Low Temperatures (degrees Fahrenheit)

	Monday	Tuesday	Wednesday	Thursday	Friday
High Temperature	63	62	55	50	42
Low Temperature	47	49	48	32	26

Figure 5.4   Graph of Water Temperature Inside a Glass Jar

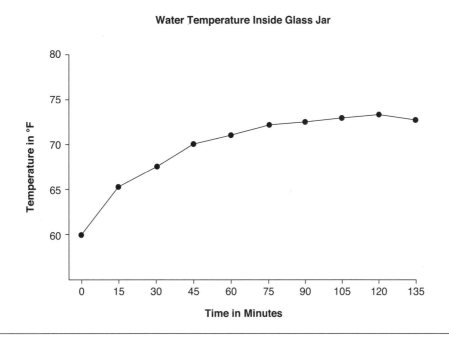

Water Temperature Inside Glass Jar

Figure 5.5   Sample Map

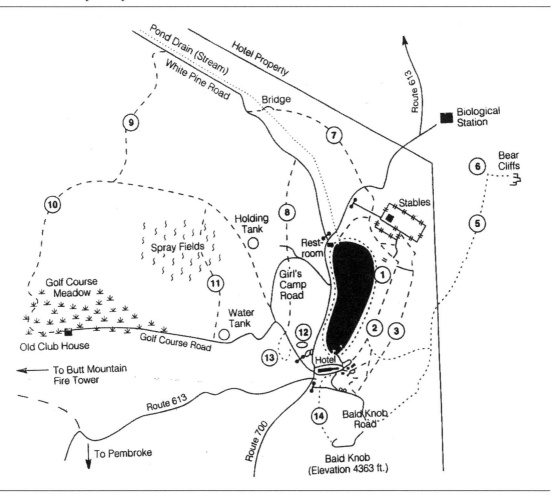

an important factor. Drawings usually are used to provide details of objects. Scientific illustration is a field where science and art overlap.

| Activity 5.4 | Communication |

Try out your skill in communicating with this activity. Choose a location some distance from where you live. It could be the college or university, the school where you are doing observations, a friend's house, or another location of your choosing. Prepare two sets of directions that explain how to get from the one place to the other. One set of directions is to be written in a narrative format. The other is to be a map. Give both forms of communication to a friend or classmate without any additional comment. Which form of communication does he or she prefer? Which do you prefer? Why?

Measurement

Measurement is the act of using numbers to describe objects or events. Measurement involves a specific form of observation called *quantitative* observation. To you as an adult, the value of the use of numbers for precision is obvious. For children, this is not so obvious. For students to understand measurement as a process, they must learn to recognize attributes that are measurable, such as temperature, length, area, mass, and volume. They need to get firsthand experience through a variety of activities to develop an understanding of and appreciation for standardization of measurement, estimation, and the use of tools for collecting precise observations.

Young children in particular need to be taught about the value of standardization of units. (See Activity 5.5.) Any unit could be invented and used as a standard, as long as we all agree on it. At some point in the past, the standard measures of today were someone's new idea. Horses are measured in hands, the speed of ships in knots, and computer operations in nanoseconds. So a good place to begin is to allow your students to invent their own nonstandard units of measure, such as pencils or shoes, and let them practice using their units to measure things. When that has been done, it will be easier to introduce standard measures, such as the metric system, and to discuss the merits of a system based on 10 as compared with American customary units. Be sure to mention that the metric system is the only official system of measurement in the United States. We were one of the original signers of the Treaty of the Meter in 1875, which established the International Bureau of Weights and Measures (BIPM, acronym for French translation), the agency that administers the International System of Units (SI). In 1893, Congress adopted the metric standards, the official meter and kilogram bars supplied by BIPM, as the standards for all measurement in the United States. Since that time our customary units have been defined officially in terms of metric standards. American scientists and engineers have always used and promoted the metric system, but the public has lagged far behind (Rowlett, 2000).

Activity 5.5   Standard and Nonstandard Units of Measure

Rulers and meter bars represent standard units of measure rather than the concept of measurement. For you, and your students, to understand the concept of measurement, it is helpful to measure objects using nonstandard units. Although you can measure time, distance, volume, weight, or speed, you will probably find it easiest to confine this activity to distance (or length).

1. Select three items to use as your nonstandard unit of measure and one standard unit. For instance, you might select a watchband, a page of notebook paper, and a convenient stick as your nonstandard units and a metric ruler as the standard unit. In order to make this activity more interesting, select three very creative nonstandard units. Now go out and measure 10 objects using each of the four units of measure. Avoid confining yourself to small items. Accept the challenge.

2. Construct a data table for this activity. Across the top of your table, list the four different units of measure. Down the left side, list the 10 objects you will measure.

3. After you have completed the measurements, consider each of the units you used. What were the advantages and disadvantages of each?

Prediction

Prediction is the act of forecasting future events based on a previously developed model. (See Activity 5.6.) The models used to make predictions are based on experience. A model is a visual or cognitive representation that relates various aspects to one another. In this situation, a *guess*, compared with a prediction, is not backed up by experience or by a model. A well-developed model allows one to be more confident in making predictions related to a situation. A good example is a meteorological model that allows forecasters to make accurate predictions of future weather conditions in a locale.

Of course, students make predictions all the time. If they enter the classroom and see seeds, bags of potting soil, and containers on the tables, they might predict that they will be planting seeds during science class. If they are entering art class and see seeds, glue, and construction paper, they may predict that they will be making collages. Students are able to make these predictions because they have past experience with similar materials and have formulated a model concerning how the materials are used in a classroom setting.

Predictions, unlike inferences, are verifiable. Children can be asked to predict which pendulum will swing more slowly, which plant will grow to be the tallest, or what color will result from the combination of given pigments. After their predictions are made, your students can test them through appropriate actions, such as the mixing of pigments or the swinging of pendulums. The testing of some predictions, such as plant growth, may take an extended period of time but can eventually be verified. Verification of predictions contributes to the conceptual model by strengthening or modifying it and therefore is an important part of the process.

Activity 5.6   Prediction

Practice your prediction skills with one of the following:

1. Fill a glass with water. Fill it as full as you can without flowing over. Now predict how many paper clips you can place carefully into the glass of water before the water spills over the edge. After you have written down that number, gently drop paper clips into the water. Compare your prediction with the results. Explain any differences.

2. Gather a collection of a dozen objects that are metal or partially metal, such as various coins, pens, tableware, rulers, candlesticks, nails, or screws. Make a list of your objects and indicate which ones you think will be attracted to a magnet. Test each object by placing a magnet near it. Record your results. Explain any differences between your predictions and the results. Write one sentence that explains what type of objects are attracted to magnets. Next, collect half a dozen different objects that are metal or partially metal. List the objects and indicate your predictions. Test each prediction and record the results. Were your predictions more accurate the second time? Why? How does one improve in making predictions?

We have just looked at the basic process skills. The *integrated science process skills* incorporate the basic process skills *in combination* to facilitate various investigative activities. The most commonly listed integrated science process skills are listed in Table 5.2.

Table 5.2   The Integrated Science Process Skills

Identifying and controlling variables
Defining terms operationally
Formulating hypotheses
Collecting and recording data
Interpreting data

The integrated skills are more sophisticated. In addition, they tend to be organized for particular investigative pursuits. Elementary school science focuses on the basic skills, whereas science instruction in the intermediate and middle grades addresses the integrated skills.

INVESTIGATIONS COME IN DIFFERENT FORMS

Science process skills do help students as they pursue understanding, but science is more than a set of skills, however highly developed. As a way of knowing, a means for understanding the world around us, the heart of science is *investigation.* Many people think this means using "the scientific method"; many think that *experimentation* is synonymous with the scientific method. These notions may have come from out-of-date textbooks or science fair–type projects with specific steps and rules.

Indeed, experimentation *is* a form of investigation that is critical to scientific endeavors. However, experimentation is not the *only* form of scientific investigation, and not all scientists or sciences depend on it. Scientists investigate nature in a variety of ways that are suited to different purposes. Here we introduce eight types of investigations (Table 5.3), each appropriate for the K–8 science curriculum. Although the goals of some of types are similar, each uses a distinctive strategy and meets a particular need.

Trial and Error

Trial and error is the least sophisticated form of investigation. It is somewhat like the way very young children try to deal with a situation. Consider how a young child tries to solve a problem, such as how to pack things into a lunchbox or how to retrieve an object that has fallen into a hole beyond the child's reach. One attempt to solve the problem seems to be followed by another without any particular logic involved. However, there is a difference between children's trial and error and scientists' trial and error.

As used by scientists, trial and error is *systematic.* One attempt to solve the problem is followed by another, but a record is kept and the search for the necessary or desired pattern gradually narrowed. An example of this investigative method is the work of Thomas Edison. In looking for the best filament for his light bulb he tried nearly 600 different possibilities before reaching the desired solution.

Table 5.3   Types of Investigations

Trial and error	Experimenting
Documenting	Reflecting
Prediction testing	Generating models
Product testing	Inventing

Students can be taught to systematize their own trial-and-error procedure so that it becomes a more efficient form of investigation. (See Activity 5.7.) You can facilitate this by asking questions and encouraging good record keeping. In addition, you can model how the feedback from one trial is used in a logical way by thinking out loud as you and the students process the information and decide what to try next and what to avoid.

| Activity 5.7 | Trying Out Trial and Error: The Egg Drop Activity |

Packaging a raw egg to withstand a drop of 3–4 meters is a good activity for trial and error.

1. Each team is given an egg and asked to package it using common, available materials. The only rule is that the total package can be no larger than 20 cm in any direction. Before dropping the packages from, say, a second story window or from the top of a playground slide, ask the teams to share what type of packaging they used and why. *Caution:* Choose your drop site with care because some eggs may break and need to be cleaned up.

2. After the egg packages have been dropped, ask each team to report its result, including the fate of the egg and what about the packaging succeeded or failed. Those whose eggs did not survive may be given a second opportunity to package and drop an egg. The sharing of the results is very important because it mirrors the communication of scientists and hence the nature of science.

Documenting

Observations systematically recorded over a period of time represent a form of scientific investigation that we call *documenting.* Scientists conduct extended observations while studying things such as volcanoes, rain forests, and endangered animals, making and recording their observations to document their research. Administering surveys in the social sciences is also an example of the investigative method of documenting.

Many classroom activities are naturals for documenting. Having an animal in the room can be fascinating for students. Many enjoy caring for animals. Students can be taught to make and record observations on a chart, in a class journal, or in individual journals. The information can then be reviewed periodically to identify patterns of behavior and changes in growth, if they exist.

Documenting plant growth also can be interesting and informative. Indoors or outdoors, gardening activities provide rich opportunities for documenting. Or teams can select a particular tree on the school grounds and begin documenting their observations in September and carry on until May. Such changes over 8 months typically go unnoticed when there is no purposeful plan of observation, but changes will be quite noticeable to those who document their observations and review the evidence they collected.

Other activities that are appropriate for documenting include constructing and maintaining bird feeders, charting local weather conditions, and monitoring changes in the neighborhoods around the school. *Phenology charting* can be carried out by intermediate-level students and up. By plotting the dates of the first appearance in the spring of common flora and fauna (through the last sighting in the autumn), students document the change of seasons and the consistency of events from year to year. Over the long term, the data of these charts can reveal trends such as climate change.

Creating and administering surveys also fall into this category of investigative methods. Students can pick any topic they deem relevant, compose survey items, and poll their peers, school staff or faculty, families, or neighbors. Survey results might even be useful to share with the community, such as those documenting public perceptions and beliefs on science-technology-society issues pertinent to the students' locality. Once students have participated in a few documenting investigations, they can easily be encouraged to identify their own topics of interest and conduct documenting activities independently.

Prediction Testing

Prediction testing is similar to experimenting: Both involve statements that focus the direction of the investigation. However, prediction testing is a much less complex form of investigation than experimenting. Rather than controlling variables and identifying cause-and-effect relationships, prediction testing emphasizes developing a *model* that is based on accumulated observations. Whereas predictions are statements based on models that forecast future events, *prediction testing* includes an additional step of verifying the prediction. Whether or not the prediction turns out to be accurate, the information gained through the verification process is used to further develop the model, which is what makes this method so useful in science.

Scientists often use prediction testing as a form of investigation and continue the development of models by finding evidence to support or modify existing models. Astronomy provides many historic examples of prediction testing. Einstein's Theory of Relativity received a big boost when, during the total eclipse in May 1919, British astrophysicist Sir Arthur Eddington confirmed by observation his prediction that light from a star appearing from behind the Sun would be bent slightly by that massive body's gravitational field.

Another example of the use of prediction testing in science is found in the field of meteorology. For decades, scientists have collected and recorded daily weather observations. Based on those observations, meteorologists have identified numerous patterns related to the movement of air masses and the sequence of weather phenomena. The weather forecasts we hear on the news are actually predictions based on highly sophisticated and well-developed scientific models of atmospheric processes (even if the occasional missed forecast makes that hard to believe).

Classroom investigations that use prediction testing begin with questions or challenges such as "Which pendulum will swing faster?" or "Where in the room do you think the temperature will be the highest or the lowest?" or "Which objects will sink, and which will float?" (See Activity 5.8.) Ask your students to make predictions *before* observing the actual events, such as the swinging of pendulums, the measurement of air temperature, or the placement of objects in water. The predictions can be written down by individuals on their own papers, or you can record a class tally of predictions on a flipchart or overhead transparency or on the chalkboard. Data collection sheets can be used to help children systematize this form of investigation.

Activity 5.8   Sink or Float

1. The teacher provides each group of students with a set of common objects, a container of water, and a data sheet, such as the one in Figure 5.6. The challenge is then presented: "Which of the objects will sink in water, and which will float?"

2. The teacher directs students to follow the directions on the data sheet: "Be sure that a prediction is listed and a reason provided before the item is placed in the water. Remember, this is an investigation, not a test of knowledge."

Product Testing

At first, product testing may seem to be an unfamiliar form of investigation. (See Activity 5.9.) However, it is easily recognized when considered in the context of commercial advertising. For instance, suppose we want to determine which paper towel is more absorbent. We could listen to the television commercial and accept the claims that it makes. Another option would be to perform our own test on a selection of paper towel brands. This second option is called product testing, the process of identifying and using criteria to make decisions about quality.

Suppose we really do want to determine which of the brands is the best paper towel. We would not want to limit the investigation to the time it takes to absorb water because absorption is just one characteristic of paper towels. We would want to test many factors. The first step of product testing, then, is to generate a list of criteria that might affect the final rating of quality. Possible criteria for deciding which is the best paper towel might include size, thickness, absorbency, color, smell, and type of paper (made from recycled versus raw materials).

Figure 5.6   Sink or Float Data Sheet

Sink and Float

Directions:

1. For each item listed, predict whether the object will sink or float in water. *Give a reason for each of your predictions.*

Object	Prediction: Sink or Float	Reason for Prediction	Observation: Sink or Float	Explanation
Plastic pen	_____	_____	_____	_____
Pencil	_____	_____	_____	_____
Straight pin	_____	_____	_____	_____
Aluminum foil	_____	_____	_____	_____
Clay ball	_____	_____	_____	_____
Jar lid	_____	_____	_____	_____
Orange	_____	_____	_____	_____

2. After writing your predictions and reasons for predictions, test the predictions and record your observations on the chart. If your observations do not match your predictions, write your explanations for the discrepancy.

3. Summarize your findings on what makes some objects sink and others float.

Copyright © 2007 by Corwin Press. All rights reserved. Reprinted from *Teaching Constructivist Science, K–8: Nurturing Natural Investigators in the Standards-Based Classroom* by Michael L. Bentley, Edward S. Ebert II, and Christine Ebert. Thousand Oaks, CA: Corwin Press, www.corwinpress.com. Reproduction authorized only for the local school site or nonprofit organization that has purchased this book.

Activity 5.9   Product Testing: Cookies

The data collection sheet in Figure 5.7 is based on four criteria that provide a good introduction to product testing.

1. Provide a copy of the data collection sheet to each student. Although you can use the full-size cookies, it is handy to buy three different brands of mini–chocolate chip cookies.

2. Label three paper plates A, B, and C, respectively. Because the students are not to know which brand is represented, be sure that you label the boxes as A, B, and C so that you will know which cookie was which brand later on. Place a quantity of cookies on the respective plates; these will be presented to the class.

3. Provide each student with three paper towels and have them label the towels as A, B, and C. When they select two or three cookies from plate A, they should place them on towel A, and so on. Now let them conduct the test in accordance with the steps on the data collection sheet.

4. Tally the ratings after each test so that students can see how changing the criteria can change the rankings of the cookies.

5. After conducting the product test, the class should discuss the results and what the impact would be if different criteria were used. For example, the cost of the cookies might make a

difference in selection at the time of purchase. The brand name, trans fat content, or calorie content also makes a difference to some people. Key concepts that students should learn as a result of this form of investigation are that conducting product tests determines personal and group preferences and that the criteria selected for testing affect the results of the test. The decisions made as a result of product testing vary as the criteria change.

Figure 5.7   Data Collection Sheet for Product Testing Activity

THE MINI-CHOCOLATE CHIP COOKIE TASTE TEST

Directions: Cookies should be on coded trays. Take two cookies from each tray. Be sure to label each cookie's code so that the brands don't get confused. Test each brand doing the test in order from 1 to 4.

Test 1: Appearance of the cookie
Award 1st place to the cookie that looks the most delicious and 3rd place to the one that looks least appetizing. Explain why the cookie looks good or bad under "Reason."

	Cookie Code	Reason
1st place (3 points)	_____	_____
2nd place (2 points)	_____	_____
3rd place (1 point)	_____	_____

Test 2: Number of Chips
Carefully break up one cookie of each brand and count the number of chips found. Award 1st place to the cookie with the most chips and 3rd place to the cookie with the fewest chips. Save the chips for the next test.

	Cookie Code
1st place (3 points)	_____
2nd place (2 points)	_____
3rd place (1 point)	_____

Test 3: Taste of the Chocolate
Taste the chocolate chips you separated from each of the cookies. Award 1st place to the cookie that has the best-tasting chips and 3rd place to the cookie whose chips you least like.

	Cookie Code	Reason
1st place (3 points)	_____	_____
2nd place (2 points)	_____	_____
3rd place (1 point)	_____	_____

Test 4: Taste of the Cookie
Now taste the second cookie of each brand. Think about the texture. Is it chewy or crispy enough? Do you like the flavor of the cookie? Is it sweet enough? Award 1st place to the cookie you like the best and 3rd place to the cookie you like the least.

MY PREFERENCE IS . . .
This is it! It is time to determine which of the three brands you liked the best. Total the number of points each cookie received in tests 1, 2, 3, and 4. Put the total points in the Total Score column.

	Cookie Code	Reason	Cookie Code	Total Score
1st place (6 points)	_____	_____	A	_____
2nd place (4 points)	_____	_____	B	_____
3rd place (2 points)	_____	_____	C	_____

Copyright © 2007 by Corwin Press. All rights reserved. Reprinted from *Teaching Constructivist Science, K–8: Nurturing Natural Investigators in the Standards-Based Classroom* by Michael L. Bentley, Edward S. Ebert II, and Christine Ebert. Thousand Oaks, CA: Corwin Press, www.corwinpress.com. Reproduction authorized only for the local school site or nonprofit organization that has purchased this book.

Experimenting

Experimentation probably is the best-known investigative form associated with science. In fact, the science process skills were originally generated by science educators through a process of analyzing experimentation to identify its discrete components. Today, most textbooks and science curriculum guidelines include a list of integrated science process skills in addition to the basic science process skills. Sometimes experimenting itself is included on the list. However, as we will see, experimenting is not so much a skill as an investigative form that involves all of the integrated science process skills. In terms of its procedures, the sequence of steps, and the precision involved, experimenting is the most rigorous of all investigative forms.

Usually, the purpose of an experiment is to find out what factors affect a particular natural phenomenon. When an experiment is conducted, the experimenter manipulates or operates on some variable, and one or more other responding variables are measured. The former variable—the one you operate on—is called the independent variable, and the latter, those that change as a result of the manipulation, are called responding or dependent variables. Table 5.4 is a list of the typical steps experimenters go through. Activity 5.10 provides an opportunity for you to try your hand at conducting a simple experiment.

Table 5.4   Steps for Experimenting

Designing an Experiment

1. Phrase a general question related to a topic or phenomenon (e.g., "How does x affect y?").

2. List the variables involved.

3. Identify the manipulated (independent) variable.

4. Identify the responding (dependent) variable.

5. Plan how to control all the other variables.

6. Write a hypothesis of what you think the answer is (e.g., how x affects y).

7. Define terms operationally.

8. Write procedures.

9. Prepare data table (optional).

Conducting an Experiment

10. Collect and record data.

11. Analyze data (usually after graphing results).

12. Draw conclusion.

13. Compare conclusion and hypothesis.

Activity 5.10   Paper Helicopter

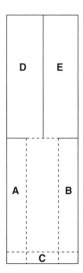

1. Make a duplicate of the drawing on the right.

2. Cut on all the solid lines and fold on the dotted lines.

3. Fold A away from you. Fold B away from you.

4. Fold C up and away from you.

5. Fold D toward you but do not bend it more than 90°; and fold E away from you, also not more than 90°.

6. Stand on a chair and drop your folded paper.

   Your observation?

   Try it again. Of what does it remind you?

   We call it a paper helicopter, with rotors and a long, skinny fuselage hanging down.

Copyright © 2007 by Corwin Press. All rights reserved. Reprinted from *Teaching Constructivist Science, K–8: Nurturing Natural Investigators in the Standards-Based Classroom* by Michael L. Bentley, Edward S. Ebert II, and Christine Ebert. Thousand Oaks, CA: Corwin Press, www.corwinpress.com. Reproduction authorized only for the local school site or nonprofit organization that has purchased this book.

Let's use the paper helicopters from Activity 5.10 as an example for designing and conducting an experiment. The first step is to state the problem in the form of a general question.

1. Phrase the question.

   Suppose our question is, "What factors affect the flight of paper helicopters?"

2. List the variables.

   Our list could be much longer, but it might include the following variables:

Length of rotors	Length of fuselage
Angle of rotors	Weight of helicopter

3. Identify the manipulated or independent variable.

   From the list generated in step 2, select one item to be the manipulated or independent variable, the one we will deliberately change to see whether it affects the flight of the helicopter. For this example we will choose the length of the rotors. The most basic rule of any experiment is that there can be only one manipulated variable. There can be many experiments, so that multiple variables can be tested, but in each individual experiment there is just one manipulated variable. In this case, make five helicopters, each with different rotor lengths: 2 cm, 4 cm, 6 cm, 8 cm, and 10 cm. Use three or more variations of the one manipulated variable so that the data will be more likely to reflect an existing pattern.

4. Identify the responding or dependent variable.

   How will we observe the differences, if they exist? We could see whether the helicopter flies in a straighter line, or flies faster, or flies for a longer period of time. Suppose we select the length of time it stays aloft as our responding or dependent variable because it can be quantitatively measured using a stopwatch.

5. Control all other variables.

   All the other variables that we listed in step 2 must be controlled. For instance, we can say all five helicopters will be constructed out of the same paper, having the same overall shape and size, except for the length of the rotors. The helicopters will be launched from the same place, out of any draft or wind, and from the same height.

6. Write a hypothesis.

   A hypothesis is a statement that indicates an anticipated relationship between the manipulated and responding variables and the direction of that relationship. The hypothesis is a statement that we can test. In this experiment the hypothesis could be as follows:

   > As the **length of the rotors** *increases,* the **length of time aloft** *increases.*

7. Define terms operationally.

   This is not the same as using definitions that are found in a dictionary. Defining a term operationally means explaining how the term is used in the context of the experiment. The dependent variable and all ambiguous terms must be defined. The definition must include how the dependent variable will be measured and in what units. The following would be an operational definition of "length of flight time":

   > *The time aloft will be the time from the release of the helicopter to the time it touches the floor. Time will be measured to the nearest tenth of a second using a stopwatch.*

8. Write procedures.

   The procedures explain in writing how the experiment is to be conducted. The procedures communicate to others how they could replicate the experiment, should they choose to do so.

9. Prepare a data table.

   A table is a helpful way of organizing the collected observations. For our helicopter experiment the table in Figure 5.8 would be adequate for recording the data. With the data table prepared, the *design* phase of the experiment is completed.

10. Collect data.

    We are now ready to conduct the investigation and have some fun. One member of the team can launch the helicopters while other members observe and record the flight times. The information collected can be entered into the table in Figure 5.9.

Figure 5.8 Flight Time in Seconds

| | Length of Rotors | | | | |
	2 cm	4 cm	6 cm	8 cm	10 cm
Time in Seconds					

Copyright © 2007 by Corwin Press. All rights reserved. Reprinted from *Teaching Constructivist Science, K–8: Nurturing Natural Investigators in the Standards-Based Classroom* by Michael L. Bentley, Edward S. Ebert II, and Christine Ebert. Thousand Oaks, CA: Corwin Press, www.corwinpress.com. Reproduction authorized only for the local school site or nonprofit organization that has purchased this book.

Figure 5.9 Flight Time in Seconds for Each Trial

| | Length of Rotors | | | | |
	2 cm	4 cm	6 cm	8 cm	10 cm
Flight 1					
Flight 2					
Flight 3					
Flight 4					

Copyright © 2007 by Corwin Press. All rights reserved. Reprinted from *Teaching Constructivist Science, K–8: Nurturing Natural Investigators in the Standards-Based Classroom* by Michael L. Bentley, Edward S. Ebert II, and Christine Ebert. Thousand Oaks, CA: Corwin Press, www.corwinpress.com. Reproduction authorized only for the local school site or nonprofit organization that has purchased this book.

11. Analyze the data.

    The data are analyzed for patterns that may help answer the initial research question. Examination of the data can be facilitated by using graphs to represent the data.

12. Draw the conclusion.

    The conclusion is a statement, based on analysis of the data, that indicates the *observed* relationship between the independent and dependent variable. In this experiment the conclusion might be "Helicopters with longer rotors fly for longer periods of time than helicopters with shorter rotors" or "The longer the rotor, the longer the time aloft."

13. Compare the conclusion and hypothesis.

The conclusion may support the hypothesis or not support the hypothesis. In our example the conclusion does support the hypothesis. It is a mistake to say that the conclusion of an experiment *proves* a hypothesis. The conclusion is an expression of the results of just one experiment. Replicating an experiment (i.e., collecting additional data by repeating the same experiment) adds support to the hypothesis and strengthens the conclusion. As the number of replications increases, support for the hypothesis increases, but there is always the chance that the results of a future trial would be different (a consequence of the inductive logic involved in scientific reasoning). Although a hypothesis can never be *proven,* extensive experimentation supporting the hypothesis leads to its acceptance by the scientific community, and it may even become a scientific principle. This is a characteristic of the nature of science: *tentativeness.*

Reflecting

You are probably familiar with the process of reflecting but may have not associated it with a method of science. However, reflecting is an important element of the scientific endeavor. It is different as an investigative form in that reflecting is not really product or information driven. Instead, scientists use this method as a means of synthesizing their thoughts about a topic or concern. The synthesis includes the scientist's own thinking about the findings of the research studies and the theorizing of her peer community.

Reflection can be a solitary process but also occurs when scientists meet to work on a project or get together and talk at conferences. Science progresses very much through social processes, so professional organizations, meetings, and conferences all play an important role. The conversation also occurs through publishing in journals and through communication with others via telephone or e-mail. Online technologies such as Listservs and blogs foster reflection and are widely used communication tools in the scientific community. The result of reflection often is a question for extending the study or clarification of the direction of the current pursuit.

Students can participate in their own forms of reflection and should be encouraged to do so. Students can write reflectively in their science logs or journals, which can be digital or paper. Journaling also is a way to integrate subjects across the curriculum. (See Activity 5.11.) Unlike assessment, reflection provides students an opportunity to consider what they have done and to organize it in a manner that facilitates synthesizing. Near the end of a unit, you might ask your students to share what they know about the topic, such as by completing the last column of a KWL chart. You can help them consolidate what they learned and formulate additional questions to guide future studies.

A journal can be a bound book of blank pages accompanied by specific instructions for formatting, it can be a collection of pages in a looseleaf notebook, or it can be a computer file. The important thing is that it provides the student with a way of recording his or her thinking about a topic.

For field activities you will want a paper journal. A useful one can be made from several sheets of folded 8.5 × 11 paper. You might want to get fancy and print cover pages that students can decorate or label as they like. With five pages folded in half and stapled along the crease, the journal will contain nine two-page entry areas. On the top of each left-hand page, have students write the heading "Observations." On the right-hand page have them write the heading "Reflections." After an activity or investigation, have your students write what happened on one side and then on the "Reflections" page have them write their reactions and questions. Here are some "stems" to provoke your students' thinking:

The purpose of today's science investigation (activity) was . . .

I learned . . .

The question that I have is . . .

Copyright © 2007 by Corwin Press. All rights reserved. Reprinted from *Teaching Constructivist Science, K–8: Nurturing Natural Investigators in the Standards-Based Classroom* by Michael L. Bentley, Edward S. Ebert II, and Christine Ebert. Thousand Oaks, CA: Corwin Press, www.corwinpress.com. Reproduction authorized only for the local school site or nonprofit organization that has purchased this book.

Generating Models

Models are visual, mental, or mathematical representations of a system. Models include all the essential components of the system and help us understand how the parts relate and interact with one another. Examples are a model of the atom or of DNA, the Solar System, a cross-section of a flower, or a three-dimensional torso of the human body's musculature. Two-dimensional diagrams found in books are also models that attempt to clarify complex phenomena, such as biogeochemical cycles, food webs, and energy transformations in a plant cell. In chemistry the equations of the ideal gas laws are models of how gases behave under various conditions.

Models themselves are not a form of investigation but are the products of investigations conducted by others. But *modeling* or *generating models* is indeed an important form of investigation. The purpose of modeling is to create a product that represents what is known and that is *heuristic*, that is, enables further investigations. The process of generating a model facilitates understanding. It allows students to apply what they have learned in an active way. And you will have your students' various inscriptions as concrete evidence of what they know and can apply.

A "mystery box" activity is a good example of an activity that leads to generating models and is a way to stimulate students' creative thinking (Activity 5.12). Because the object involved is unknown, there are few preconceptions associated with the investigation. Students feel less inhibited in trying to explain something that does not have a predetermined value. Mystery boxes are simply closed boxes whose contents cannot be seen. You can make one from a shoebox. Inside you can place a marble and create obstacles for the marble (such as a simple maze) out of cardboard that you can glue or tape in place. Of course, with the top off it is easy to see the marble in the maze, but if you've never seen inside the box and the top is on, visualizing what's inside becomes quite a test of imagination. Allow your students to manipulate the box and make observations from their senses of touch and hearing about the movement of the marble. Then challenge them to sketch what they think the inside looks like. This sketch is the model of what they predict is inside. This activity mirrors the nature of science in that many aspects of nature are like black boxes that cannot be visually observed. This was the case when scientists first proposed how atoms were structured.

| Activity 5.12 | Mystery Boxes |

You will need a shoebox, some cardboard, glue or tape, and a marble. Cut the cardboard into strips that are about 2 cm taller than the inside of the shoebox. Fold the strips along the long edge so that there is a 2-cm base on each strip. Arrange the cardboard strips inside the box to form a simple maze. Use glue or tape on the 2-cm base in order to fasten it to the box. If you make several mystery boxes you may want to make the mazes increasingly sophisticated to challenge your students. Remember to put a marble, ball bearing, or BB inside the box before taping or gluing the top in place.

You need not limit yourself to mazes in the box. Make cardboard ramps or barriers. Add a bell that the marble could strike. When your students investigate the mystery box, ask them to sketch what they think is the structure inside. Resist the temptation to let them see inside. The point of mystery boxes is to provide opportunities to generate models, not to know what happens to be in a particular box.

Copyright © 2007 by Corwin Press. All rights reserved. Reprinted from *Teaching Constructivist Science, K–8: Nurturing Natural Investigators in the Standards-Based Classroom* by Michael L. Bentley, Edward S. Ebert II, and Christine Ebert. Thousand Oaks, CA: Corwin Press, www.corwinpress.com. Reproduction authorized only for the local school site or nonprofit organization that has purchased this book.

Inventing

A mutually beneficial relationship exists between science and technology. Science is a way of generating knowledge. Inventing, the active process of technology, is a way of solving problems and often involves applying the knowledge generated through science. Allowing students opportunities to invent demystifies the world of technology. At the same time, students become actively engaged in understanding how things work and the underlying science (Ebert & Ebert, 1998). Inventing is a form of investigation that is product driven rather than being a search for information. It is the process of selecting and

Table 5.5 The Process of Investigating Through Inventing

Foundation Steps

 1. Identifying a problem or need

 2. Researching former solutions to the problem

Process Steps

 3. Generating ideas toward a new solution

 4. Designing the invention

 5. Constructing the invention

Concluding Step

 6. Patenting the invention

combining previously existing ideas or objects to form new and unique entities. The inventing process is described in Table 5.5.

The *foundation steps* contribute the background work for inventing. The inventing process begins with identifying a problem or a specific need, which may come from personal experience or, in a classroom setting, may be provided by the teacher. Researching former solutions provides information for the investigator. This information may reference the science involved and identify advantages and disadvantages of the solutions.

The *process steps* are the exciting part of inventing, the steps that actually develop the product. Creative thinking is emphasized during these steps, especially when generating ideas. Although designing a model for the invention is a cognitive process resulting in a mental image, students should be encouraged to sketch their designs on paper (creating a model), a process that helps clarify their ideas. Constructing the invention begins with collecting and assembling parts. As the invention is being designed or constructed, sometimes using a trial-and-error approach, difficulties may occur that were not apparent during the generation of the idea. The inventor may return to the first of the process steps and generate additional possibilities. The three process steps may be repeated multiple times before the inventor is satisfied with the invention.

The *concluding step,* patenting, is conducted as a means of claiming ownership of the invention. This step is quite involved, requires the assistance of attorneys, and can be expensive. Yet it is the safeguard of creative enterprise. Patenting is even a provision in the U.S. Constitution, and students should have some understanding of patents.

CONCLUSION

Too often, children who have entered school as question marks finish school as periods, as Neil Postman once noted. By the middle school and high school years students have become conditioned to wait to be told what they are supposed to know and have not developed the skills that would allow them to keep asking questions and finding ways to solve problems. The inquiry approach is a perspective on science education that provides an antidote to this situation.

The basic science process skills enable the inquisitive mind to find answers. Whenever you fashion a lesson for your class, you should ask yourself which of the process skills you can involve. Rarely is it the case that only one of the skills would apply to a given investigation. So challenge yourself to incorporate as many as possible. The result will be a classroom of actively engaged students who are developing valuable skills while learning science. Can you ask for anything more?

An investigation is a systematic study. Table 5.6 compares the forms of investigation discussed in this chapter. Each form of investigation uses particular strategies and serves a specific purpose. Results can be in the form of information, products, or questions that guide additional inquiry.

Table 5.6   Forms of Investigation

Type	Strategy	Result
Trial and error	Arbitrary search for solutions	Product or information
Documenting	Making and recording observations	Information
Prediction testing	Making and testing predictions	Information
Product testing	Identifying and using criteria	Information
Experimenting	Identifying and controlling variables	Information
Reflecting	Contemplating ideas	Questions, guide for future pursuits, or synthesis of what has been accomplished
Generating models	Creating visual constructs	Product
Inventing	Selecting and combining	Product ideas or objects

6

Designing Science Lessons for All

Differentiating Instruction

What Is a Differentiated Classroom?

Inquiry and Learning Models

Your Academic Roadmap

This chapter should help you to understand the following ideas:

- A product of science is knowledge gained through having a curious attitude and using an investigative approach.
- Differentiated instruction is a way of planning and teaching in which you can address standards while also providing motivating, challenging, and meaningful activities for all students.
- Inquiry science is a way to zero in on the zone of proximal development of your students as they come to understand standards-based content.
- The Planning for Conceptual Change model makes students aware of their own level of conceptual understanding before instruction and provides experiences that prompt them to question their initial beliefs, test those beliefs, and grow to a new level of understanding.

"Science is different things for different people. Science, for me, is learning about rocks and minerals and different kinds of scientific facts."

—Jamie, 12 years old

WHAT IS A DIFFERENTIATED CLASSROOM?

If you are like us, you can remember science classes you experienced as a student that were anything but engaging. If students do not engage with science in school, it is probably a result of the way science and students are brought together. In this chapter we consider *differentiated instruction* as a way for teachers who are faced with a heterogeneously grouped classroom to design science lessons and to teach in a way that engages all students and meets their educational needs. We will also consider the value of lesson planning using two instructional approaches or models for the organization and presentation of science: the learning cycle and conceptual change models.

Differentiated instruction is an approach to planning and teaching in which each student's individual needs are addressed. It is not *individualized instruction,* in which separate lessons are created for each student. In differentiated instruction lessons are planned for the whole class but through the use of teaching strategies that address a wide range of student variations, such as their ability levels, learning styles, and interests.

There are many reasons why differentiated instruction is needed in American classrooms. Differentiation

- Encourages inclusion of all students
- Addresses different learning styles and particular learning needs
- Allows the teacher to reach all of the students some of the time
- Recognizes diversity among students
- Fosters social relations and self-worth
- Meets social, emotional, and academic needs
- Is supported by multiple research studies (Eaton, 1996)

In differentiating, you as the teacher recognize the differences between your students and hold different expectations for performance in the same class. You provide choices as to how students will demonstrate their competencies and understanding of the content. The teacher of yesteryear in the one-room schoolhouse with its multiaged student body did not use the term *differentiating* but probably practiced some form of it in instruction.

In contemporary times student diversity is so great that many of today's classrooms are analogous to the one-room schoolhouse. With rising immigration, public school enrollment has increased steadily and is projected to peak at some 50 million K–12 students in 2014. *The Condition of Education 2005* indicated that 42% of public school students were racial or ethnic minorities (National Center for Educational Statistics, 2005). In 1972 this figure was 22%—quite a demographic change in just over three decades. In 2002 the number of Hispanic students in the United States surpassed that of African

Americans, and in 2003 in the West, enrollment of minority students exceeded that of Whites.

So your heterogeneous classroom today might include a mix of second-language learners and mainstreamed special needs students (students with learning disabilities or with behavioral or emotional problems) and intellectually gifted students, not to mention "average" students. This increasingly diverse student population in American classrooms presents a challenge to teachers as to how to respond with curriculum and pedagogy that meets all their needs. Teachers have had to become more culturally sensitive in enacting curricula that integrate multicultural viewpoints. Teachers have also been challenged to increase their pedagogical repertoires and skills and to differentiate instruction to address the varied learner needs.

Stop and think for a minute about your own school and the students in your community. Which students are being served most effectively? Which students are being least well served?

Being culturally sensitive has a knowledge component: knowing about the customs and cultures and the variety of religious faiths of different students. But the main component of being culturally sensitive is *affect.* The *affective dimensions* of learning include feelings, emotions, self-esteem, attitudes, motivation, willingness to participate, and valuing what is being learned: "We now know it is mandatory to incorporate the body, the feelings, and the social and intuitive dimensions of the human in the educational process" (Campbell, 1988, p. 6). Therefore, your planning should consciously include the affective domain, focusing on getting students more fully engaged and keeping their success level high.

Although the affective domain is critical for learning, many teachers do not give it much attention in their planning. However, attending to affect can make all the difference in the world in terms of what students learn and their attitudes toward school and toward science itself (Zembylas, 2005). There is a strong link between the *emotional climate* established in the classroom and student cognitive development:

> Teachers need to understand that students' feelings and attitudes will be involved and will determine future learning. Because it is impossible to isolate the cognitive from the affective domain, the emotional climate in the school and classroom must be monitored on a consistent basis, using effective communication strategies and allowing for student and teacher reflection and metacognitive processes. In general, the entire environment needs to be supportive and marked by mutual respect and acceptance both within and beyond the classroom. (Caine & Caine, 1991, p. 82)

When students think that their teacher cares and they feel good about themselves as learners, they are willing to take risks and put forth the effort necessary to learn. They are more willing to tackle tough tasks if they believe they can succeed. Projecting that you care for and respect your students and communicating your confidence that they can learn can motivate them to do their best.

The heart of differentiated instruction is the recognition that one student's best result may not be of the same caliber as another student's best. For the teacher the key thing is to know each student and to be a good judge of what you will recall Vygotsky called the *zone of proximal development* (see p. 78): what, with effort and support, a student is capable of learning.

Again, consider your own school and the students in your school. What do you see in terms of the range of student variation in interests, perspectives, and strengths? What do you already do to help a student realize that he or she belongs and contributes to the success of the class as a whole? In your school and community, what different cultures, ethnic groups, and socioeconomic levels are present, and how do students from these groups see their worlds represented in your classroom? Are the different needs of girls and boys equally addressed?

Tomlinson (2003) argues that all students need affirmation, contribution, power, purpose, and challenge. She suggests five teacher responses to the needs of students: *invitation, opportunity, investment, persistence,* and *reflection.*

One way to contribute to your students' sense of power is to provide choices for them in your classroom. Students grow when they see themselves as partners in the classroom agenda. They grow when they are given opportunities to make contributions that move their imaginations toward new possibilities for themselves. Can you think of students in your school community who need such opportunities? What difference might it make if teachers were more adept at communicating to their students that they really cared for them and their continuing growth?

Differentiating Instruction in Your Science Classroom

For more than 40 years, researchers in the cognitive sciences have been accumulating findings about the nature of thinking and learning. Cognitive science studies and other lines of scholarship have led to the social constructivist model of learning. The predominant view of educators today is that people of all ages, beginning with what they already know, construct their own understandings by processing and acting on their experiences of the people and things around them. The older view, the transmission model of learning, which holds that students simply accept and retain the explanations presented to them by authority figures, has been discredited. Thus we now recognize that learning depends on prior knowledge and processes of both assimilation and accommodation and is not just a process of recording inputs on a blank mental tape.

These research findings and the constructivist perspective require educators to rethink instruction, to move beyond the familiar "chalk 'n' talk" methods and the "one-size-fits-all" curriculum and toward active learning strategies and differentiated instruction. Differentiated instruction is a planning model and can be considered as a way to address inclusion and a range of student abilities and talents. When we think about differentiating, we think about teaching that addresses the learning needs of all students. This is achieved by focusing on what the students *can* do rather than what they *cannot* do.

So how is it done? The following five steps oversimplify what is a very complex and intellectually demanding process but are consistent with the literature and will help you conceptualize the process. It is important to note that there is not just one stepwise process for differentiating. For example, Kathie Nunley (2003, 2004) has developed a differentiation model that she calls layered curriculum. In her method, three levels of activity or task options are provided to the class for every lesson, keyed to the traditional A–F grading scheme. Nunley suggests a five-step process for layering curriculum and provides free sample differentiated lessons on her Web site (http://help4teachers.com):

1. *Identify what you want to happen* as a result of your lessons, or your desired outcomes: what students are to understand or be able to do as a result of instruction. In other words, determine your learning objectives, and don't forget to consider multiple domains (see Chapter 4, Figure 4.1).

2. *Know your students.* Consider students' past records of performance to determine their capabilities, prior knowledge, and relevant past experiences. Get to know your students informally; have regular conversations with individuals about ideas. Depending on your students' ages, use an interest inventory, hold a parent-student-teacher conference, conduct an interview, or invite students to respond to an open-ended questionnaire asking about their learning preferences. Use problem-posing preassessments to become aware of student learning needs (their prior knowledge of the content and readiness to learn the new content and skills). A good preassessment identifies what must be learned and what has already been achieved. A good preassessment also stimulates students' curiosity about the content and allows them to explore their own ideas.

3. Plan *tiered* (or layered) instruction. This involves creating options for learning the content that are at different levels of abstraction and application. It involves using a variety of teaching strategies to address different expectations for students, different learning styles, interests, and levels of ability and development. You may need to adapt the environment, the materials, or the mode of presenting the information. Bloom's taxonomy (Table 6.1) may be a useful guide to creating assignments and assessments.

Table 6.1   Bloom's Taxonomy

Knowledge: Requires memory recall in order to repeat information

Comprehension: Requires rephrasing or explaining information

Application: Requires the application of knowledge to determine an answer

Analysis: Requires identifying motives or causes, drawing conclusions, or determining evidence

Synthesis: Requires making predictions, producing original communications, or problem solving with more than one possible solution

Evaluation: Requires making judgments or offering supported opinions

---

Source: Eaton (1996).

4. *Provide for student practice and reflection.* Create assignments based on students' needs, levels of ability, and cognitive development (not all students must do the same assignments).

5. Link assessment and evaluation *to the student.* Compare a student's performance with his or her ability and cognitive development rather than with the performance of other students. Use a variety of assessment techniques (e.g., classroom observations and checklists, portfolios, rubrics, performance-based assessments, knowledge mapping).

Tiered instruction is a way to teach a particular content and meet the different learning needs in the class. The tasks you assign and the texts, materials, and process chosen will vary according to interest, readiness, and learning profile of the students. You adjust the activity to provide different levels of difficulty and scaffolding. Of course, it is most important to accurately assess the different levels of students (the tiers). Preassessment is a way to determine what students know before teaching begins and should be used regularly to make instructional decisions about student strengths and needs, to help determine groups, and to help determine which students are ready for more advanced instruction. See Table 6.2 for examples of preassessment strategies. Tiered instruction is a strategy that can be used at the assignment level or embedded in a lesson or unit.

In designing differentiated lessons today's teachers have an advantage over their peers of past decades in terms of the availabilities of many new computer technologies. Teachers now have a range of hardware and software at their disposal and all kinds of educational Internet sites only a mouse click away. Such technologies can be used for remediation, additional practice, extension, and acceleration. Many other teaching strategies are useful in differentiating science instruction (see Harmin & Toth, 2006, for the latest edition of our favorite source for teaching strategies). Here is a sample of strategies that can be implemented in differentiated instruction:

Advanced organizers represent information presented at the beginning of a lesson that the student can use as a frame to organize and interpret incoming information (Mayer, 2003). Advanced organizers include graphics such as Venn diagrams and concept maps and strategies such as KWL charts. Advanced organizers provide a "heads-up" for students, help clarify the ideas they will be exploring, and develop links between what they already know and what they are expected to learn.

Allowing multiple right answers in open-ended assignments gives your students opportunities to do investigations that engage their problem-solving skills and critical thinking in ways that lead to more than a single answer. This models the nature of science.

Anchor activities are ongoing assignments that students can work on independently, such as journals or learning logs. These activities can keep students occupied productively while you work with one group at a time.

Science can be connected to social issues, real-world experiences, and community projects via performance assessment tasks, role plays, simulations, and so forth, based on situations of interest to students.

Table 6.2   Examples of Preassessment Strategies

Teacher-prepared pretests

KWL chart

Writing prompts and samples

Questioning

Guess box

Picture interpretation

Prediction

Teacher observation and checklists

Student demonstrations and discussions

Initiating activities

Informational surveys, questionnaires, and inventories

Student interviews

Student products and work samples

Self-evaluations

Portfolio analysis

Game activities

Show of hands to determine understanding ("every-pupil response")

Drawing related to topic or content

Anticipation journals

Standardized test scores

Chunking is breaking content, assignments, or activities up into smaller, more manageable parts and providing directions for each part. This process is especially helpful for students who may become overwhelmed with too much to do or too much material to digest at once.

Compacting works for your best students. It involves eliminating repetition for students who have already mastered particular content by streamlining lessons. Begin by preassessing students and crediting them for what they already know; then provide acceleration and enrichment options that allow them to move ahead. Compacting also helps teachers with assessment as student proficiency and enrichment activities offered in place of regular class work are documented. Compacting is especially recommended for more intellectually talented students, but "average" students often are advanced in particular content in which they have an interest.

Emphasizing thinking skills means giving students the opportunity to think aloud, discuss their thinking with peers, and reflect, such as through science talks and journal writing.

Developing student responsibility entails allowing students to contribute to evaluation criteria, write project proposals, and complete self- and group evaluations.

Flexible grouping is about matching students by readiness and not assuming that all students need to do the same work. Flexible grouping involves allowing movement between groups based on readiness and growth.

Flexible pacing allows for differences in students' abilities to master the curriculum content.

Goal setting and planning means involving your students in their own individual goal setting and in planning their own learning activities.

Group investigations engage students in cooperative mixed-ability groups on open-ended tasks or in cooperative like-ability groups working on appropriately challenging tasks.

Hands-on projects and activities involve students in using manipulatives and the natural environment in appropriate ways to make science more relevant and to foster interest.

High-level questioning means using questions that draw on advanced levels of information, questions that require leaps of understanding and challenge student thinking. Questioning strategies are discussed in more detail in Chapter 3.

Independent study involves providing opportunities for students to work on their own or with a classmate to investigate topics of interest.

Integrating curricula around a theme means creating interdisciplinary units that make connections across subjects by exploring a conceptual theme. For example, themes such as "living in the future" link student concerns to the larger world and connect science to social studies and health. You can find lists of major conceptual themes in the *Benchmarks for Science Literacy* (American Association for the Advancement of Science, 1993) and the *National Science Education Standards* (National Research Council, 1996).

Interest centers are stations situated off the beaten path in the classroom and used for activities that may be completed by students independently or in teams and at their own pace.

Learning contracts are proposals negotiated between students or student teams and the teacher before projects in which the resources, steps toward completion, and evaluation criteria are mutually agreed upon.

Long-term projects provide opportunities for students to investigate events, topics, or issues, as individuals or in teams.

Mentorships and apprenticeships provide opportunities for students to work with a knowledgeable and skilled adult to carry out a project or task. These strategies are good for career awareness and help students develop the skills of production in a field.

Multiple texts are available in a classroom library with books that accommodate differences in student reading levels. You should have on hand books at different levels to enable you to match a range of reading levels in a class. Increasingly trade books and other resources can be downloaded from the Internet in text or audio versions.

Shared inquiry involves cooperative learning and opportunities for students to collaborate in searching for answers to questions.

Student choice means opportunities for students to select the content, process, or product of an assignment that most interests them and that is most appropriate for their level.

Student-generated criteria for tasks and products of work allow students to help determine grading criteria and rubrics.

Tasks and products designed for multiple intelligences and learning styles allow all students to tap into their own strengths and preferences for class credit. This strategy is motivating and encourages students' engagement with the lesson content.

Obstacles to Differentiating

Differentiating instruction takes more time and effort than planning for traditional whole class instruction. Differentiating instruction also requires the teacher to have strong subject matter knowledge and perhaps a more extensive repertoire of teaching strategies than would be typical for K–8 teachers. Differentiating instruction entails knowing which strategies can address student variations.

Differentiating instruction is not a simple process, so if you are new to this concept, don't expect to master it right away. Of course, you will already have mastered some teaching strategies, and those will form your base. Plan to start slowly and build. For a more extensive consideration of differentiation we recommend the work of Carol Ann Tomlinson (see bibliography).

Summary

If your students enjoy science class and experience success in learning, their self-confidence and positive attitudes toward science will naturally follow. As a teacher you can foster a positive attitude in your students by exhibiting positive feelings and sharing scientific interests of your own. If you are curious about something in the natural world and demonstrate to students your own pleasure in pursuing the answers to questions and solving problems, then your students will be more likely to enjoy the same pursuits themselves. On the other hand, if you have a negative attitude toward science, then everyone in your class is more likely to perceive science as an unpleasant part of the curriculum.

Differentiation is an approach to instruction in which the teacher plans for the diverse needs of students. The ultimate goal of differentiated instruction is to provide a learning environment that optimizes the potential for student success.

In differentiating instruction, teachers use active instructional strategies that lead students to positive learning outcomes. Teachers make many adjustments of assignments and assessments when necessary, aiming to hit the zone of proximal development of every learner. "In an appropriately differentiated classroom, all learners should . . . have consistent opportunities to be active learners by working on interesting tasks, . . . and all should continually be involved with learning that is new to them" (Kiernan & Tomlinson, 1997, p. 7).

Differentiated instruction is a way to plan for teaching in which you can address standards while also providing motivating, challenging, and meaningful activities for your students. However, differentiation is a complex undertaking that takes time and resources and demands teacher flexibility and openness to change. Moving beyond traditional teaching means taking risks such as trying out unfamiliar strategies, but you are likely to find the learning outcomes for your students worth every effort.

INQUIRY AND LEARNING MODELS

The increasing diversity of the nation's student body truly challenges the teachers of today to think about how to be more successful in meeting both the state and national science education standards and the learning needs of everyone in the class. *Inquiry teaching* is an approach that is required by standards-based education, and it also works well in a differentiated classroom. Inquiry science connects to two of the eight content areas identified in the *National Science Education Standards* (see Table 2.1 in Chapter 2).

We saw in Chapter 1 that scientists use a variety of investigative approaches to explain the natural world, but it is important to note that all scientific approaches are *systematic.* Though naturally inquisitive, most students lack a systematic approach in their everyday pursuits. Inquiry teaching can make available to these students the kinds of experiences that will add a systematic perspective to their science class work.

Inquiry teaching is an *inductivist* approach to instruction that mirrors the inductivist nature of science. Inquiry science teaching is an approach that emphasizes students' personal experiences with information and materials as a foundation for conceptual development and thus taps into the student's naturally inquisitive nature. The science process skills, which are used in systematic investigations, are emphasized. Having materials to manipulate adds a tactile modality to the learning. Students make firsthand observations rather than depending only on reports in textbooks or other sources. Students are encouraged to ask their own questions and are given problems to solve rather than answers to memorize.

The Learning Cycle is one model for inquiry science teaching. The 7-E model (Eisenkraft, 2003) is a template for planning and getting the most out of the inquiry activities that you lead in your classroom science program. Models such as the 7-E Learning Cycle should be used in a differentiated classroom. Inquiry learning models also draw on preassessments you've conducted. Inquiry science is a way of hitting the zone of proximal development of your students as they come to understand the standards-based content. The two models for designing and presenting science lessons each capitalize on the process of science and build positive attitudes toward science.

The 7-E Learning Cycle

The Learning Cycle is a model for designing science lessons to foster successful, positive experiences for students. The Learning Cycle idea in science education can be traced back to the 1920s, but Atkins and Karplus (1962) at the University of California at Berkeley developed a three-stage model that was incorporated into the 1960s Science Curriculum Improvement Study (SCIS) program. The SCIS learning cycle's steps were *exploration, invention,* and *discovery.* Since that time the Learning Cycle has been used and modified by many science educators. The Biological Science Curriculum Study program uses a five-step learning cycle called the 5-E model, consisting of *engagement, exploration, explanation, elaboration,* and *evaluation* (Bybee, 1977). The model we suggest is the most recent modification of the 5-E model and is presented in Table 6.3 in chart format and in Figure 6.1 in graphic form.

Table 6.3   The 7-E Learning Cycle

Phase 1: Elicit

Determining prior conceptions: "What do you know about . . . ?"

Phase 2: Engage

Arouse student interest by using a discrepant event, telling a story, or showing an object or picture.

Phase 3: Explore

Have students work with manipulatives (e.g., natural objects, models) to investigate a question or phenomenon. Have students make predictions, develop hypotheses, design experiments, collect data, draw conclusions, and so forth.

Phase 4: Explain

Introduce concepts and terms; verbalize the concept, and summarize the results of the exploration phase.

Phase 5: Elaborate

Have students apply the newly learned concepts to new domains. Pose a different (but similar) question and have students explore it using the concept.

Phase 6: Evaluate

Use the formative assessment from the *Elicit* phase and assess, for example, the design of the investigation, the interpretation of the data, or follow-through on questions, looking for student growth. Growth is the desired change in the differentiated classroom and can occur in any of the domains. Expectations vary according to the student's beginning point.

Phase 7: Extend

Lead students to connect the concept to different contexts.

Source: Eisenkraft (2003).

Figure 6.1   The 7-E Learning Cycle in Graphic Format

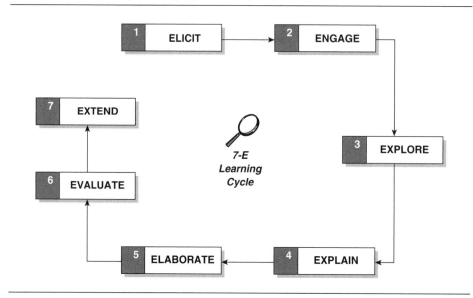

Elicit

The purpose of the *Elicit* phase is for you to access your students' knowledge of the content at hand before the start of instruction. This phase might involve the familiar KWL strategy mentioned earlier, or could involve a "student talk" discussion of some aspect of the content. This phase might be addressed through the process of interviewing selected students about their background knowledge of the key ideas of the lesson.

Engage

The *Engage* phase is intended to motivate students, to capture their interest in the topic. Interest can be captured in many ways, for example through a *discrepant event* demonstration, an interesting natural or human-made object, a challenging question, or a problem to solve. Discrepant events are situations in which something does not happen as one would expect it to happen. For example, what would you expect to happen if a needle were stuck through a balloon? Well, if the needle passes through without a pop, then you have a discrepant event.

Explore

The *Explore* phase may be the most active phase for the students. Independently or in small groups, students investigate the concept to be learned using their science process skills. There is a social dimension as students talk and share with one another as they work. The teacher's role is to provide support and scaffolding as needed, challenging students and encouraging independent thinking during the investigation. The purpose of the exploration phase therefore is to provide students with opportunities for experiences to construct their own understanding of the concept.

Explain

In this phase students report their findings and discoveries to the class. While eliciting information and ideas generated by the students during the *Explain* phase, the teacher directs the discussion, provides appropriate terminology, and, as necessary, helps students resolve differences in their findings. All the while, the teacher is guiding the students as they develop a deeper understanding of the content from the scientific perspective. The purpose of the *Explain* phase is to allow opportunities for verbalizing and clarifying the concept. Here is where teacher explanations, texts, and media typically are used to help clarify the content.

Elaborate

If the students understand the new content, they will be able to see applications to a new but closely related situation. In this phase opportunities are provided for students to practice transferring their learning to other contexts or domains. Applying the content to other situations may include numerical problem solving or posing and exploring a different (but similar) question (Eisenkraft, 2003).

Evaluate

The purpose of this phase of the learning cycle is to assess student understanding of the content. Kiernan and Tomlinson (1997) argue, "In an appropriately differentiated classroom, all learners focus much of their time and attention on the key concepts, principles, and skills identified by the teacher as essential to growth and development in the subject—but at varying degrees of abstractness, complexity, open-endedness, problem clarity, and structure" (p. 6).

Extend

The purpose of this phase is to provide for the transfer of the new concepts to different contexts (e.g., after a study of force and motion, including momentum, have students investigate the use of safety belts or airbags in cars and how they work) (Eisenkraft, 2003). This phase challenges students' understanding to apply what they have learned. Figure 6.2 is a planning worksheet you might find useful in working with the 7-E Learning Cycle instructional model.

The Learning Cycle is not a linear progression but a cyclic one, as the name implies. You may choose to extend the study of the topic by using the *Extend* phase, for example, to begin a new cycle. The question or challenge of the *Extend* phase becomes the topic for a new *Elicit* phase to tap student background for further study of the topic.

Teaching for Conceptual Change

Teaching for conceptual change is a different approach to lesson design but has some familiar elements. Like the learning cycle models, the conceptual change model makes students aware of their own understandings before instruction and provides experiences for individuals to question their initial beliefs, test

Figure 6.2   A 7-E Planning Worksheet

Topic: _____   Date: _____

Standards: _____

Elicit: Find out what the students already know or think about the topic. Phrase an interesting opening question.

_____
_____

Engage: Use a follow-up question or an appropriate discrepant event to arouse their interest. For example, based on their first responses, pose a what-if question or use a brief demonstration that exemplifies the question but not the answer.

_____
_____
_____

Explore: Identify an investigative technique and the science process skills to be used in the exploration. Describe the exploration activity the students will complete.

Investigative Technique_____   Process Skills: _____

_____
_____
_____

Explain: List the terms to be introduced and concepts to be explained. Summarize the results of the *Explore* phase using the terms introduced during this discussion.

_____
_____
_____
_____

Elaborate: Pose a similar but different question or provide another activity in which the students can apply what was done in the *Explore* and *Explain* phases to a new situation.

_____
_____
_____

Evaluate: Indicate whether you will use a formative or summative assessment. Formative evaluations enable you to make instructional decisions about whether to provide additional clarification, reteach, or move on. Summative evaluations are used to measure achievement and assign a grade. Briefly describe your evaluation plan.

_____ Formative Assessment _____ Summative Assessment

_____
_____
_____

Extend: Provide an example or opportunity for students to explore the concept outside the classroom. What applications of this concept might they look for? In what situations might they find evidence of this concept or principle at work?

_____
_____

Copyright © 2007 by Corwin Press. All rights reserved. Reprinted from *Teaching Constructivist Science, K–8: Nurturing Natural Investigators in the Standards-Based Classroom* by Michael L. Bentley, Edward S. Ebert II, and Christine Ebert. Thousand Oaks, CA: Corwin Press, www.corwinpress.com. Reproduction authorized only for the local school site or nonprofit organization that has purchased this book.

Table 6.4   Model for Planning for Conceptual Change

Step 1: Being Challenged
 Students become aware of their own understanding of the topic.

Step 2: Sharing Ideas
 Students expose their personal beliefs by sharing them with others in the class.

Step 3: Exploring Concepts
 Students work with manipulatives, testing ideas and exploring the content.

Step 4: Resolving Conflicts
 Students work to resolve conflicts between what they found during
 exploration and their previous beliefs.

Step 5: Making Connections
 Students make connections between the newly learned concepts and other
 parts of their lives.

Step 6: Pursuing Questions
 Students raise and pursue their own questions reflecting individual interests.

Source: Adapted from Stepans, J. (1994). *Targeting students' misconceptions: Physical science activities using the conceptual change model.* Riverview, Fla.: Idea Factory, Inc.

those beliefs, and grow to a new level of understanding. The Planning for Conceptual Change model presented in Table 6.4 is a modification of Stepans's Teaching for Conceptual Change (Stepans, 1994).

What is the teacher's role in the conceptual change teaching model? The most obvious task is to facilitate the process. This is accomplished by sensitive listening and observing and then asking questions or making suggestions at appropriate times. In the *Being Challenged* step, the teacher might ask students to predict what will happen if something else is done in an activity, for example. In the *Sharing Ideas* step students are encouraged to think about the content or question first and then share their own ideas with others in small groups (the "think-pair-share" [TPS] strategy). Students are encouraged to give reasons for their predictions. The teacher may then ask for an oral report of the prediction by a group spokesperson. The teacher may write the prediction statements on the board or on an overhead transparency without rewording. If two or more students give the same explanation, tally marks can be used to indicate the frequency of responses. Everybody's ideas are shared, although not necessarily individually.

In the *Exploring Concepts* step, students are provided materials for investigating the content and may be provided with a data collection sheet or allowed to design their own way to record observations. Data are recorded and manipulated for analysis, such as by graphing.

In the *Resolving Conflicts* step, the class as a whole discusses the information discovered during the exploration. If some groups have different results or additional information, this is shared with everyone. Your role as the teacher is to help your students resolve any discrepancies or conflicts between what was predicted and the results and to facilitate their verbalization of the concept (rather than presenting the scientific explanation yourself).

In the *Making Connections* step, you extend the lesson by asking students how the concept is important to them or how what they have learned is connected to their daily lives. Too often teachers fail to make the new information relevant for the students, as if the students will simply accept it as so. Sometimes connections make sense to students and sometimes not. It is better if the students themselves ponder and recognize the relevance of the content. If you have your students make their own connections, then you can be assured that the content is relevant from the students' perspective.

By the *Pursuing Questions* step, your students have achieved some ownership of the new content as they have made connections between what they learned and their lives. The ownership becomes more personal if students are then encouraged to raise and pursue their own content-related questions. Not everyone will have the same interest in the content or the same question, so not everyone will want to pursue the topic. Some students will be satisfied with what they have already learned, and this is okay. To allow for individual differences, you should create opportunities for open-ended investigations and provide guidance only as requested or needed. Your students should also be encouraged to pursue further questions on their own time. Not everyone should be expected to pursue the concept further.

As you can see, both learning cycle and conceptual change models are dynamic lesson planning formats because student thinking is integrally involved in the progress of the lesson. The inherent dynamism of the lesson models is enhanced when the teacher incorporates strategies that facilitate the inductivist or discovery approach. Strategies for sharing information can take many forms. Each one has advantages and limitations. Three such strategies are discussed further: discussion, demonstration, and the Socratic method.

Discussion

Discussions are used to promote the verbal exchange of ideas. Both teacher and students are verbally active. The advantages of discussions extend beyond simply sharing ideas. In participating in a discussion individuals hear about different perspectives related to the topic as others share their own points of view. The consideration of multiple perspectives, along with seeking patterns and relationships, is at the heart of creative thinking (Ebert, 1994).

Depending on the position of the discussion relative to the overall lesson, the "science talk" can serve different purposes. Discussion that occurs at the start of a study may engage students' interest and reveal their preconceptions about the content. Students can contribute what they already know about the topic and be encouraged to identify what they would like to find out as a result of the study (the KWL strategy). Discussion can also *follow* an investigation or activity. Besides facilitating the sharing of observations and inferences, discussions enhance social interaction skills and often help clarify thinking. In addition, discussions are useful in drawing closure to a topic of study. The whole class can participate as the lesson or unit content is summarized. However, discussions alone do not contribute to conceptual change. Discussions are most effective when used as one complementary component in your instruction.

Demonstration

Occasionally it is more appropriate for you to be the one who manipulates the objects while your students observe. Sometimes things happen so quickly or subtly that students would miss the key observations unless the teacher did the demonstration, stopping at the appropriate times and telling them what to watch for. You should also conduct demonstrations when safety hazards are involved. Depending on their age, you might not want your students to handle burning or toxic materials, for example. It is also appropriate for you to demonstrate the correct use of delicate or expensive equipment. Once students become familiar with the proper use of such equipment, however, it should not be necessary to confine your teaching approach to demonstration.

Socratic or Maieutic Method

What is typically called the Socratic method is actually the *maieutic* method, a particular approach to teaching based on the famous questioning techniques by which Socrates educated his students and the citizens of Athens. *Maieutic* refers to midwifery. In the context of education, it refers to the notion that people often already know more than they think they know and that such knowledge can be brought to awareness by questioning. Socrates believed that people were "pregnant with knowledge" and that his task was to assist in the birth of that knowledge by having them answer his questions. Don't let the fact that Socrates was executed for asking so many pesky questions intimidate you. The situation with your students will be quite different.

In the classroom, the teacher uses questions to draw from students what they already know about the content and to guide their thinking as they share and synthesize new ideas. The teacher uses questions that will lead students' thinking in the direction of a desired outcome. However, the teacher must also be prepared to make adjustments. Even with much forethought anticipating what students might think and say, the teacher needs to be flexible in order to accommodate spontaneous and unexpected responses generated by the class.

Questioning, when used correctly, is an effective teaching technique that encourages students to think more critically for themselves. As a teacher you should be aware of the level of the questions you formulate, being sure to vary the level and include some higher-level questions (according to Bloom's cognitive domain taxonomy; Table 6.1). By asking many *divergent* questions, rather than the more typical convergent questions, you will encourage your students to consider more than one perspective before responding and to seek multiple solutions to problems. Divergent questions are especially appropriate for encouraging creative thinking. Students may not be accustomed to this sort of questioning at first but will soon contribute enthusiastically if you are able to create a nonjudgmental and accepting environment. Questions that require reflection may be useful for summarizing and personalizing learning at the end of a lesson or a unit of study.

Summary

As we have already noted, there is no one scientific method. Also discussed earlier, science is a way of pursuing knowledge involving many forms of investigation and a variety of perspectives. No single teaching strategy can facilitate that kind of pursuit. Do not try to look at all that has been presented in this or other chapters and try to find the one best approach or strategy. What will lead to your success is the appropriate *combination* of strategies that supports your teaching style and the needs of your students. Select strategies and use them when and where they are appropriate to the situation rather than deciding to use one for one lesson and a different one for another lesson.

The approaches to teaching science suggested in this chapter may require more work and take more time for the teacher than the traditional textbook approach, but the results will be worth the time and effort. The primary result will be that your students will construct their own understanding of the science content and make connections between their prior knowledge and the new information.

As you consider the teaching models, we hope you will distinguish between the *teaching* process and the *learning* process. You cannot learn for the student, but each student comes to you with an inclination to learn. You can arrange opportunities for experiences that will capitalize on that inclination.

The Learning Cycle model and the Planning for Conceptual Change model are both formats that recognize the nature of the learner *as an inquirer*. The Planning for Conceptual Change model can be integrated and used with the Learning Cycle model in designing science lessons.

Some children may be unwilling to give up their previous beliefs even though there are good reasons for doing so. Forcing children to repeat scientific explanations does not make for meaningful growth in understanding. Instead, it often results in students developing dual perspectives: a school explanation and a personal belief for outside school. Some students simply need time and additional experiences, opportunities to struggle with the concept, before adopting a more sophisticated scientific understanding.

CONCLUSION

Most science textbooks and curriculum guides are crammed with information. The phrase aptly used by Project 2061 is "over stuffed and under nourished" (American Association for the Advancement of Science, 1989). Covering too much may actually hinder effective learning. High-quality learning takes time: time for doing and time for thinking. Rushing the process results in inferior learning.

The level of understanding and the retention of science learning are greatly increased if science lessons capitalize on the natural curiosity of students and encourage a positive attitude toward science and learning, emphasize the science process skills as students conduct investigations, and involve the use of manipulatives so that students are physically active and have firsthand experiences while learning the concept. With this in mind, you can design science lessons that give students a pleasant and educative experience. A science program that accomplishes this incorporates a variety of teaching strategies, including differentiation, discussion, demonstration, and the maieutic method. The basic science process skills are essential to that process and include observation, inference, classification, communication, measurement, and prediction.

The two complementary lesson formats discussed in this chapter represent a student-centered approach to science education. The Learning Cycle model is a heuristic for designing science lessons that encourage a positive attitude toward science and foster success for all students. Planning for Conceptual Change is a way of planning instruction that emphasizes conceptual understanding. In either case, planning a science lesson is focused squarely on the matter of what the *students* will do rather than what the *teacher* will do. If you find yourself writing lesson plans that include a lot of "the teacher will," then you are probably losing the dynamic opportunities that a discovery approach would afford you and your students.

Scholars have suggested many purposes for schooling in our times. We believe schools exist to prepare each young person to contribute to democratic society as an informed and thoughtful citizen. What's your vision for the ideal science classroom, the ideal school? What's north on your compass? In education, what matters most to *you?*

7

Making Real-World Connections

Relevance and the Teaching of Science

Approaches for Relevant Connections

Nontraditional Educational Opportunities

Your Academic Roadmap

This chapter should help you to understand the following ideas:

- Children need opportunities to use science to investigate questions in the context of their own lives.
- Real-world demonstrations, relevant documentation, and individual investigations are three techniques for helping children understand science beyond the classroom.
- Opportunities for making real-world connections abound if the teacher is willing to coordinate the efforts of valuable community resources.

Imagination is more important than knowledge. Knowledge is limited, whereas imagination embraces the entire world—stimulating progress, giving birth to evolution.

—Albert Einstein

RELEVANCE AND THE TEACHING OF SCIENCE

Making learning relevant is a goal of science educators. Teachers and textbook writers have made accommodations just for this purpose, providing examples or stories that capitalize on experiences common to the lives of today's young people. School-to-work transition, a more recent concern, focuses on drawing attention to connections between science content and possible occupations.

The various attempts to make learning relevant for students have had an impact on many classrooms. Yet the teacher cannot make the learning relevant. The student is the only one who can do that. Just as each student constructs his or her own reality, relevance is something one must establish for oneself. The teacher can only *create opportunities for experiences* that are more or less likely to be regarded by a student as relevant to his or her life.

Thus far in this text our approach to the teaching of science has been directed toward what can be done in the classroom setting. We have described science very broadly as a way of finding answers to questions or solutions to problems. We have suggested that it is a *search* that leads to an understanding of the world around us through *investigation.* Investigations come in many forms: trial and error, documenting, prediction testing, product testing, experimenting, modeling, inventing, and reflecting. Each of these investigative forms has its appropriate place in the search for understanding, and the science process skills are the mental tools we use to do the investigation.

Regarding how to teach science, in Chapter 6 we recommended the 7-E Learning Cycle model (Eisenkraft, 2003) as a template for designing inquiry-oriented lessons. This planning model uses a hands-on approach, promotes a positive attitude toward science by eliciting and respecting student ideas, and encourages learning by providing exploration activities before concept verbalization. We also discussed the merits of another instructional planning model, the Teaching for Conceptual Change model. In both models students are encouraged to pursue more detailed studies of topics that are of particular interest to them.

With appropriate teacher preparation and communication of the science through instructional models such as these, students are more likely to perceive the connections between school science and the world in which they live. However, through our own studies, in which we have interviewed many students about their content understandings, we have found that students do not always learn what teachers intend but instead construct their own explanations at different levels of understanding of the pertinent concepts. To address this shortcoming of instruction, teachers can provide opportunities for students to examine the science content in real-world situations that make explicit connections between the science and the students' lives.

Homework characteristically has been used to provide practice of new learning, especially vocabulary. However, typical homework assignments involve contrived situations that do not relate to the world outside school. To be consistent with an investigative approach to teaching and to promote the use science as a process for understanding the natural world, homework must involve investigative opportunities outside the school walls and in the context of their homes, communities, and lives.

APPROACHES FOR RELEVANT CONNECTIONS

Three strategies can be used to foster the making of relevant connections: real-world demonstrations, relevant documenting, and individual investigations. In using *real-world demonstrations* the teacher brings something commonly found in the home or community environment into the classroom for the purpose of investigation. The second strategy would require the teacher to challenge students to use documenting of specified observations for the purpose of collecting data that students themselves deem relevant. This *relevant documentation* might take the form of listing the frequency of specified occurrences in the home environment, such as surveying the number of home appliances that use electricity. It could also take the form of maintaining individual journals that record observations in a home or community setting. An example might be keeping a record of all the food personally consumed in 24 hours or the names of TV programs viewed during a specific period of time. In using the third strategy, a teacher would ask students to conduct investigations at home and then report the results to the class. These *individual investigations* might take the form of experiments, inventions, product tests, family member or neighbor interviews, or any of the other investigative forms described in Chapter 5.

Each of the strategies has advantages and limitations. The strategy of real-world demonstration is the most teacher centered, whereas the strategy of individual investigation offers the most input and direction from individual students. It is the latter alternative that should become the most frequently used strategy because it fosters the highest degree of relevance. But let's consider each strategy in more detail.

Real-World Demonstrations

Real-world demonstration is the most teacher centered of the three strategies for making lessons relevant because the teacher is the only one typically involved in manipulating the materials. Generally there are three situations in which we advise that the teacher do a demonstration. One is when the activity involves special precautions or when hazardous materials are used. The teacher conducts the demonstration to ensure everyone's safety. A second situation involves the use of expensive pieces of equipment. The teacher demonstrates in order to give special directions and illustrate appropriate equipment handling before or instead of student use. An example would be the first time students use their microscopes. The final situation has to do with the outcome desired.

Sometimes students are likely to miss important observations during an event. The teacher can facilitate learning by conducting a demonstration in order to stop to ask students pertinent questions and focus their observations during the process.

In the case of real-world demonstrations, an additional limitation exists that is beyond the control of the teacher. The teacher may choose to demonstrate an activity because of limitations in the home setting. For example, to illustrate the often overlooked occurrences of chemical and physical changes in the home, the teacher might want students to bake a cake. In some home environments, that request would be met with support and encouragement. However, some home settings may not have the necessary materials, equipment, or adult support to conduct such an investigation. To avoid problems, the teacher may decide to bake a cake at school. Opportunities for student interaction exist, and at the same time, the teacher can use questioning to facilitate student observations.

Here is an example. Let's suppose that you are fortunate enough to have access to an oven in your school, perhaps in the cafeteria. The purpose of the demonstration would be to examine physical and chemical changes in events that are common in the home environment. You'll need the following materials (in addition to the oven, of course):

- Cake recipe or cake mix (note: recipes using metric measurements can be found on the Internet)
- Ingredients (eggs, milk or water, as listed)
- Metric measuring cups and spoons
- Mixing spoons and spatula (or electric mixer)
- Bowl
- Baking pan, pot holders, cooling rack
- Toothpicks
- Measuring stick (metric, if possible)
- Many tasting spoons or forks (to be used for individual observations)

Whether you choose to use a commercial cake mix or a recipe, there will be many opportunities for observing chemical and physical changes. For example, leavening is what causes the cake to rise, and it is based on the production of carbon dioxide. Students may better understand this process by conducting an isolated examination of the reaction of baking powder. See Table 7.1 for an investigation of a variety of baking powders. This examination may provide a greater appreciation of the chemical reaction.

While following the directions for making a cake, the teacher can provide opportunities for students to make observations of each ingredient before and after it is combined with others. Transparent bowls would enable students to see changes through the sides. While students are observing you may help them focus by asking questions such as "How does it feel? Taste? Smell? Look?" (Safety note: The raw egg and the batter with the raw egg should not be tasted because of the possibility of bacterial contamination.) Students can measure the volume of batter before and after beating with an electric mixer.

Table 7.1   Baking Powder Investigation

Materials needed: 3 egg whites, 3 types of baking powder (double acting with phosphate, double acting with alum, and a combination of baking soda and cream of tartar), 3 beakers, metric ruler, equal-arm balance with standard metric masses, and stopwatch.

Procedure:

1. Measure out and place 4 grams of each of the baking powders in separate dry beakers. Note the time and then add the white of one egg to each of the dry mixtures. Stir gently until powder is moistened, and then stop.

2. At the end of every minute for 5 minutes, measure the height of the foam in the beaker.

3. At the end of 5 minutes, place the beaker in a pan containing very hot water (near boiling), and for the next 5 minutes again measure the rate of rise.

4. Record your results.

5. Answer the following questions:
   Which type of baking powder produced the most carbon dioxide (foam)?
   What did you notice when the beakers were placed in hot water?

Because it has not always been convenient for bakers to bake cake batter immediately, double-acting baking powder was developed. Alum (sodium aluminum sulfate) is the acidic ingredient. It will not react with the baking powder ingredient until it is heated, and so the leavening does not begin until the batter is in the oven. The double-acting powders with alum initially had the disadvantage of leaving a bitter taste and making the baked product heavier. Consequently, double-acting powders with two acid ingredients were developed. Cream of tartar, a fast-acting ingredient, starts forming carbon dioxide as soon as it mixes with liquids. It begins to change the texture of the cake before being placed in the oven and therefore overcomes the heaviness. Alum, a slow-acting ingredient, does not react until placed in the heat of the oven. It can be used in lesser amounts now that two leavening ingredients are used, thereby avoiding the bitter taste.

Source: Adapted from Eby and Tatum (1977).

Depending on your circumstances at school, the baking may have to take place elsewhere and at another time. The alternative is to do what the TV chefs do: Set aside the batter you have just mixed (and observed) and take out the cake you baked ahead of time. Making observations of the baked cake involves everyone. And although the comparison of observations before and after baking is vital to the lesson, from the students' perspective the observations made after baking are more tasty.

Figure 7.1 is a sample observation form for use in the cake baking activity. Response forms such as this often are helpful when students are conducting documentation activities. The forms are meant to facilitate the learning by directing the students' observations. Having made their observations, students

Figure 7.1 Observation Form for the Cake Baking Activity

Cake Baking Activity

Ingredient	Amount	Observations
Flour		
Salt		
Baking soda		
Sugar		
Butter		
Egg		
Milk		
Vanilla extract		
Cake batter		
Baked cake		

Identify changes. (Note whether you think the change is chemical or physical.)

1. _____

2. _____

3. _____

4. _____

5. _____

Copyright © 2007 by Corwin Press. All rights reserved. Reprinted from *Teaching Constructivist Science, K–8: Nurturing Natural Investigators in the Standards-Based Classroom* by Michael L. Bentley, Edward S. Ebert II, and Christine Ebert. Thousand Oaks, CA: Corwin Press, www.corwinpress.com. Reproduction authorized only for the local school site or nonprofit organization that has purchased this book.

then have sufficient information from which to construct their own inferences and explanations related to the demonstration. This approach transforms the demonstration technique into a discovery learning experience rather than the direct information transmission approach of more typical demonstrations.

Relevant Documentation

Content in the curriculum may be relevant to students in a general sense, but the teacher may need to provide opportunities for more personal connections. An example might be nutritional studies that address the need to consume a variety of foods within specific groups. In fact, the U.S. Department of Agriculture has recently completely revised its classroom icon, the Food Guide Pyramid (see http://www.mypyramid.gov/). Your school lunch menu might be examined as a science investigation, although what students eat outside school probably is more reflective of their personal choices and would be more relevant to them. Students could maintain records of what they actually consumed in a period of hours, as in Figure 7.2.

Figure 7.2   A Documentation Journal

My Science Journal

Sara

The Things I Eat – Day 1

Breakfast –

Lunch –

Snack –

Supper –

Snack –

On another topic, perhaps you are familiar with the following investigation associated with the study of heat energy, air, or weather. Students are given thermometers to predict and measure air temperature in various locations around the room or outside on the school grounds. From investigating they may learn that the outside temperature when taken in the sunshine is greater than when taken in the shade, or they may learn that the air near the ceiling of the classroom is warmer than the air near the floor. The activity is a good one, and the information acquired is useful. However, through relevant documentation, the students can make connections between what they learned at school and their lives at home. The teacher might send the same thermometers home with students with directions to measure the temperature of different locations in their homes. Record sheets such as the one in Figure 7.3 can be sent with them to facilitate documentation. Because students have actually collected data in personal settings, the real-world connections are explicit. The teacher's questions are no longer contrived or hypothetical but instead address the individual decisions students make in their personal surroundings.

Many topics like this in the science curriculum have connections to the home environments of the students and consequently may involve relevant documentation. In studying sound, for example, students can document examples in the home where sounds are enhanced (stereo speakers and door-bells) and where sounds are suppressed (headphones and closed doors). In studying energy, they can document the various types or frequencies used in the home. Other things that can be documented include living things (e.g., plants, animals, and fungi), the applications of magnets (e.g., latches on cabinet doors, stereo speakers, and note holders), or examples of the controlled use of light (e.g., lamps, cameras, TV).

Individual Investigations

Individual investigation is the most student centered of the three strategies to make activities relevant. You will want students to gain experience designing

Figure 7.3   Temperature Measuring Activity

Temperatures in My Home

1. Place the thermometer on your bed. After several minutes, measure the temperature of the air in the room where you sleep.
   The temperature of the air over my bed is _____.

2. Predict what the temperature will be in other parts of your room. Do you think it will be warmer (W) or cooler (C) than the air just above your bed? Record your prediction by placing a W or a C in the space next to each location. Use the thermometer to measure the temperature (in °C) in each location. Leave the thermometer in place for several minutes to allow the thermometer to register the new temperature. Use the following table to record your predictions and measurements.

Temperatures in My Home

Location	Prediction	Measurement
Bedroom floor	_____	_____
Bedroom window	_____	_____
Bedroom ceiling	_____	_____
Bedroom door	_____	_____

3. Identify other areas of your home, such as the kitchen, stairways, and TV area, to measure the temperature and record the data in the following table.

More Temperatures in My Home

Location	Prediction	Measurement
_____	_____	_____
_____	_____	_____

Based on the information you collected about temperature variations in your home, answer the following questions.

A. Where in your home is the temperature the warmest?

B. Where in your home is the temperature the coldest?

C. In the summer, would it be more comfortable, temperature-wise, to watch TV sitting on the floor or on the furniture? Why?

D. In the winter, would it be more comfortable, temperature-wise, to watch TV sitting on the floor or on the furniture? Why?

Copyright © 2007 by Corwin Press. All rights reserved. Reprinted from *Teaching Constructivist Science, K–8: Nurturing Natural Investigators in the Standards-Based Classroom* by Michael L. Bentley, Edward S. Ebert II, and Christine Ebert. Thousand Oaks, CA: Corwin Press, www.corwinpress.com. Reproduction authorized only for the local school site or nonprofit organization that has purchased this book.

Figure 7.4   An Example of an Individual Investigation Form

Individual Investigation Form

Name: _____   Date: _____

Type of Investigation (circle):   Trial and error   Prediction testing

                                            Inventing   Experimenting

                                            Reflecting   Documenting

                                            Modeling   Product testing

Outcome (circle):   Information   Product   Question

Procedures: _____

Results: _____

Copyright © 2007 by Corwin Press. All rights reserved. Reprinted from *Teaching Constructivist Science, K–8: Nurturing Natural Investigators in the Standards-Based Classroom* by Michael L. Bentley, Edward S. Ebert II, and Christine Ebert. Thousand Oaks, CA: Corwin Press, www.corwinpress.com. Reproduction authorized only for the local school site or nonprofit organization that has purchased this book.

and carrying out their own investigations in the context of their personal interests. Having honed their science process skills, with a little encouragement, students are capable of conducting their own investigations. The teacher's role in the process is to be available for guidance and support. The students are given the freedom to choose a question that they find relevant. For example, they may choose to conduct a product test to evaluate paper towel absorbency or determine the best cat litter.

This kind of assignment might span a range of open-endedness and of the types of investigation. This is a useful strategy in the differentiated classroom. A form such as the one in Figure 7.4 might be used to facilitate the documentation of an investigation. It provides opportunities to identify the type of investigation selected by the student. By having students identify the intended outcome in terms of information, product, or question, the teacher can monitor the students' understanding of the purpose of each investigative process.

An example of a completed form, Figure 7.5, shows how a student kept a record of a personally relevant individual investigation conducted at home. The form is designed to provide guidance without dictating the investigative type or the plan and conduct of the study. However, the teacher should approve investigations before they are begun in order to ensure that the proposal is appropriate and safe and that the student has identified an appropriate investigative technique and plan of action. The teacher may also want to monitor more closely the investigations of particular students or provide special encouragement to those who need it.

Summary

The three strategies for helping students make real-world connections can be implemented in several ways. Each of the techniques can stand alone as a lesson

Figure 7.5   Example of a Completed Individual Investigation Form

Individual Investigation Form

Name: *Alex*   **Date**: *10/24/2006*

Type of Investigation: *Prediction testing*

Desired Outcome: *Information*

Procedures:

I predict that when ice cubes are added to a refrigerated soft drink it will get colder faster than when ice cubes are added to a soft drink stored at room temperature.

I got 2 glasses just alike and put 4 ice cubes in each one. Next I poured the cold soda in one and the room-temperature soda in the other. I put thermometers in each glass and recorded the temperatures in degrees Fahrenheit. I measured the temperatures every 2 minutes.

Temperature Measurements (°F)

Minutes:	0	2	4	6	8	10	12	14		18
Refrigerated:	42	39	39	36	32	32	32	32 . . .		
Room temperature:	62	46	44	40	40	40	39	39 . . .		

Results: The cold soda did get colder, but the warmer soda got cold faster.

Copyright © 2007 by Corwin Press. All rights reserved. Reprinted from *Teaching Constructivist Science, K–8: Nurturing Natural Investigators in the Standards-Based Classroom* by Michael L. Bentley, Edward S. Ebert II, and Christine Ebert. Thousand Oaks, CA: Corwin Press, www.corwinpress.com. Reproduction authorized only for the local school site or nonprofit organization that has purchased this book.

or an assignment. It is also possible to combine approaches such as doing a demonstration in class and challenging students to design individual investigations to apply or extend what has been learned from the demonstration. Relevant documentation is a technique that can be started early in a lesson sequence (or school year) and continued for an appropriate period of time to collect data for subsequent use. For example, a brief discussion of weather patterns in September could start data collection that would provide the basis for meteorology lessons in March or April. Keep in mind that if you do engage students in long-term projects such as this, you will need to provide encouragement to sustain their motivation. An occasional review of what has been collected, talk about a particular event (e.g., a big storm locally), and reference to the students' work when a related event happens beyond the locality (e.g., a hurricane in the southeast, drought in the Midwest, floods on West Coast) will reinforce the real-world connections.

NONTRADITIONAL EDUCATIONAL OPPORTUNITIES

In addition to the three strategies for making relevant connections, other educational settings can be used to facilitate the teaching of science: at play, on excursions, and while engaging with environmental issues. The play situation can be found on the school grounds, but here we focus on students' natural settings outside school, such as the yard around the home, a local park or playground, and the neighborhood in general—places where students play ball, ride bikes, skate, and so on.

Another type of nontraditional setting for studying science is places where students might go on field trips, either with their class or with a group of friends or relatives, such as museums, zoos, planetariums, aquariums, nature centers, hiking trails, local, state, or national parks and wildlife refuges, and beaches. Many other possibilities for science excursions exist, such as amusement parks, farms, airports, train stations, manufacturing plants, fire stations, water purification facilities, professional sports arenas, and marinas.

A third opportunity for nontraditional experiences with science is through environmental issues. This option helps students see not only the relevance of science to their local world but also the connections to the larger society. The scope of these issues can be as narrowly focused as concerns related to the local community, such as waste disposal, noise pollution, and traffic congestion, or as broad as national and global issues, such as global climate change, fossil fuel depletion, or biodiversity loss.

At Play

Naturally, students enjoy playing with their toys, games, and sporting equipment. Not so obvious are the possibilities for learning. However, there are many opportunities for the study and application of science in playful settings. Whether students are playing ball, skating, skateboarding, swimming, surfing, skiing, or even building forts, science applications exist. We will present examples to illustrate relevant science in playful settings related to each of the three strategies discussed in this section.

Real-World Demonstration

Suppose a class has been studying simple machines. From the adult perspective, the connection between simple machines and their use in everyday life is obvious. To help students recognize the significance of simple machines, a teacher could ask students to do a relevant documentation activity such as recording examples of simple machines in their own homes. However, simple machines rarely exist in isolation. Most often they are combined with other simple machines. It is this situation that will make identifying them difficult for students. A *real-world demonstration* can be used to increase student awareness of the frequency of simple machines and demystify the process of identification. For example, students are familiar with the bicycle, yet few have probably ever taken one apart or even examined the components to see how they interact and make the bicycle work. A real-world demonstration can prepare students to do relevant documentation identifying other simple machines around the home. Figure 7.6 is an example of a data sheet a student may have completed during the demonstration.

Relevant Documentation at Play

In the bicycle demonstration, students identify simple machines within other machines. It is appropriate now to ask them to conduct a relevant

Figure 7.6   Example of Data Collection Sheet for the Bicycle Activity

Bicycle Data Sheet

Name: *Lindsey*

Subsystems	Parts	Simple Machines
Forward motion	Back wheel	Wheel and axle
	Pedals	Lever, inclined plane
	Gears	Wheel and axle
	Chain	
	Derailleur	Lever
	Cable	
	Frame	
Steering	Handlebar	Lever
	Front wheel	Wheel and axle
Braking	Hand grips	Lever
	Cables	
	Brake pads	Lever
Comfort and safety	Seat	
	Grips	
	Fenders	
	Lights	
	Basket	

What simple machines did you find?

5 levers, 3 wheel and axles, and 1 inclined plane

Copyright © 2007 by Corwin Press. All rights reserved. Reprinted from *Teaching Constructivist Science, K–8: Nurturing Natural Investigators in the Standards-Based Classroom* by Michael L. Bentley, Edward S. Ebert II, and Christine Ebert. Thousand Oaks, CA: Corwin Press, www.corwinpress.com. Reproduction authorized only for the local school site or nonprofit organization that has purchased this book.

documentation activity identifying simple machines that are not associated with bicycles. These searches for simple machines may occur in students' back yards, parks, or other places in the neighborhood.

Other content within the science curriculum can be connected to play through documentation. Students could be asked to document examples of toys or sporting activities that involve such topics as friction (e.g., roller skating, sledding, air hockey, skateboarding), air or its movement (e.g., whistling, blowing bubbles, kites, balls), or transfer of energy (e.g., Slinky, trampoline, balls, bicycling). The first time an investigation of this sort is assigned, students' lists may not be very lengthy because they may not be used to thinking about connections between school studies and play. With a little practice and some encouragement, however, students begin to recognize relationships and even enjoy making the relevant connections.

Individual Investigations at Play

Students can be challenged to conduct individual investigations related to their play. The partially completed investigation form in Figure 7.7 is an

Figure 7.7 Example of Individual Investigation Related to Play

Gliders

Name: *Toby* **Date**: *October 15*

Type of Investigation: *Experiment*

Desired Outcome: *Information about the flight of paper gliders*

Procedures: *I thought about the various things that might affect the flight of my paper glider and decided to try changing the weight: how much and where it was located. First I launched the glider with no paper clips (weights) and measured how far it flew. Next I added 1, then 2, then 3 paper clips and measured how far it flew each time. Finally I added only 1 paper clip, first under the nose of the glider, and measured how far it flew. Then I moved the paper clip under the front part of the wings, and finally just behind the wings. Each time I flew the glider, I measured how far it flew.*

Distance of Flight

    1 paper clip _____   *2 paper clips* _____   *3 paper clips* _____
    front _____   *under wings* _____   *behind wings* _____

Results: *I found out that . . .*

Copyright © 2007 by Corwin Press. All rights reserved. Reprinted from *Teaching Constructivist Science, K–8: Nurturing Natural Investigators in the Standards-Based Classroom* by Michael L. Bentley, Edward S. Ebert II, and Christine Ebert. Thousand Oaks, CA: Corwin Press, www.corwinpress.com. Reproduction authorized only for the local school site or nonprofit organization that has purchased this book.

example of an experiment conducted by a student interested in paper gliders. Although experimenting may not be a frequently used form of investigation because it requires special considerations for controlling variables, investigations such as prediction testing, trial and error, and product testing may be more applicable for students in this type of setting.

Students may want to study and seek improvement of their own sport skills, such as batting in softball, passing a football or lacrosse ball, or shooting baskets (Activity 7.1). These movements can all be documented. For example, a student could vary his or her stance, hand position, or amount of follow-through and observe the effects on the direction of the thrown or hit ball. Other students may be interested in studying the effects of the length of and type of tails on kites or type of detergent used in making bubbles. These studies may not be very precise scientifically, but they allow students to study things of personal interest in a systematic way.

Activity 7.1 Relevant Connections at Play

Now it is your turn to create a relevant learning opportunity. Select one of the following play activities. Explain how students could conduct a scientific investigation of the activity. Identify your choice of strategy as a real-world demonstration, relevant documentation, or individual investigation.

Opportunities for Relevant Connections Related to Play

Archery	Badminton	Softball	Basketball
Tennis	Football	Soccer	Flying kites
Horseshoes	Ice skating	Roller skating	Skateboarding
Golf	Throwing a Frisbee	Throwing a boomerang	

Science Excursions

Science excursions are field trips that take the students outside the regular classroom. The specific intent is educational. Real-world connections, planned in advance of the excursion, help to keep a scientific focus without diminishing the novelty of the experience. Here we discuss ways of debriefing the experience back in the classroom.

Real-World Demonstrations for a Science Excursion

Real-world workplaces often offer many opportunities for science connections, but such sites may provide only a limited amount of space for visitors. In these situations, it may be better to have a guest speaker visit your classroom before an on-site visit. An example is a field trip to a local law enforcement agency crime laboratory. If you were to ask a crime scene investigator (CSI) to visit the classroom first, he or she would be able to explain the various types of laboratory techniques used during criminal investigations, providing the students with an advance organizer or set for their field trip. The CSI might even demonstrate specific techniques used to collect or examine evidence. In addition to answering students' questions, the CSI could also make suggestions for specific observations for a visit to the lab itself. An observation sheet such as the one in Figure 7.8 would also facilitate student observation.

Relevant Documentation While on a Science Excursion

A trip to an amusement park or a local fair can provide opportunities for making relevant connections. Students may not suspect that there are many science links to the feelings they experience on amusement park rides, yet a study of force and motion becomes really meaningful when experienced first-hand and while having fun. The incomplete form in Figure 7.9 illustrates the type of information students can collect on such an excursion. The information can be discussed back in the classroom.

Individual Investigations While on a Science Excursion

Good planning for science excursions is very important but often doesn't get much beyond doing the logistics, recruiting volunteers to chaperone, and packing the first aid kit. Thorough planning can ensure academic quality by challenging each student to conduct an individual investigation. Before the trip

Figure 7.8 Sample Observation Sheet for a Science Excursion to a Forensic
Laboratory

Criminal Investigations

Test Conducted	Equipment and Materials Used	Evidence Collected
Fingerprints		
Lifting prints	_____	_____
Matching prints	_____	_____
Blood tests		
Types	_____	_____
Substance analysis	_____	_____
Fiber identification	_____	_____
Other	_____	_____

Copyright © 2007 by Corwin Press. All rights reserved. Reprinted from *Teaching Constructivist Science,
K–8: Nurturing Natural Investigators in the Standards-Based Classroom* by Michael L. Bentley, Edward S.
Ebert II, and Christine Ebert. Thousand Oaks, CA: Corwin Press, www.corwinpress.com. Reproduction
authorized only for the local school site or nonprofit organization that has purchased this book.

Figure 7.9 Example of a Data Collection Sheet for an Amusement Park Science
Excursion

Amusement Park

Amusement Ride	Direction of Force	Gravitational Force	Resultant Force
Tilt-a-whirl	Counterclockwise	Downward	Strong
Roller coaster	Circles within circle	Outward	_____
Ferris wheel	Counterclockwise	Pressed down	_____

Copyright © 2007 by Corwin Press. All rights reserved. Reprinted from *Teaching Constructivist Science,
K–8: Nurturing Natural Investigators in the Standards-Based Classroom* by Michael L. Bentley, Edward S.
Ebert II, and Christine Ebert. Thousand Oaks, CA: Corwin Press, www.corwinpress.com. Reproduction
authorized only for the local school site or nonprofit organization that has purchased this book.

you might ask each student to identify a topic of interest related to the site and
formulate a question. Providing a simple data sheet such as the one in Figure
7.10 will help guide student observations. In the example, the field trip is to a
zoo. Appropriate student questions might include, "How do young monkeys
behave differently from the adults?" or "What conditions are necessary for an
amphibian habitat?" or "How is the platypus environment controlled?" When
the class returns to school, the information gathered can be recalled and
shared, enhancing the impact of the excursion. The last entry on the data sheet
can guide individual research as a follow-up activity so that relevant connections are made before and after the field trip.

Figure 7.10 Data Sheet

Visit to the Zoo

My question is _____

I observed _____

I asked _____

I found out that _____

I want to find out more about _____

Copyright © 2007 by Corwin Press. All rights reserved. Reprinted from *Teaching Constructivist Science, K–8: Nurturing Natural Investigators in the Standards-Based Classroom* by Michael L. Bentley, Edward S. Ebert II, and Christine Ebert. Thousand Oaks, CA: Corwin Press, www.corwinpress.com. Reproduction authorized only for the local school site or nonprofit organization that has purchased this book.

Facing Environmental Issues

Environmental issues are generally thought to be big problems that are properly the concern of the adults of the world, the people who caused the problems, or the people who have the power to make decisions about dealing with the problems. However, facing environmental issues is something that students as well as adults can do. Facing issues is a way of becoming aware of the environment and the impact people have on it. It also involves finding ways in which people can do something, no matter what their age.

If you design science opportunities related to environmental issues at the right level, your students will not become frightened or overwhelmed. The nuclear reactor waste disposal problem or worldwide disasters such as global climate change might be issues too big to tackle at a young age. But there are many other issues of local concern and smaller problems that are good experiences for the novice. These experiences help students see themselves as good problem solvers and as important people in the community. Examples of appropriate local issues, depending on where you live, might be rezoning of farmland for development, the location of proposed recreational facilities, strip mining or mountaintop removal, chip mills, industrial pollution of a river, or the disposition of local brownfields. One issue this year in our locality was what to do about a pair of beavers who had colonized the stream and pond in a suburban subdivision (the poor beavers were euthanized after much protest).

Real-World Demonstrations of Environmental Issues

In every community that has to deal with a local issue, opportunities exist for people to attend forums or meetings to inform the local citizenry. Rarely do students get to attend these meetings, and they naturally have little inclination to do so. However, interest can be fostered through real-world demonstrations or "science talks" in the classroom. If taking students to such a meeting isn't an option, you can create a forum in your classroom. Invite people who represent opposing sides of an issue to share their views with your class. Prepare the students in advance by going over available information from the local newspaper or government Web site. Ask student teams to create a graphic organizer to compare and contrast, to visualize, and to construct the different positions on the issue. Then help students prepare a few questions to interview the experts or representatives. After the presentations, your students may want to extend the lesson by forming teams of partisans to debate possible solutions. Alternatively, you could use the Four Corner strategy and ask your students to take one of four positions on the issue: strongly agree, agree, disagree, or strongly disagree.

Relevant Documentation Related to Environmental Issues

Environmental issues of one kind or another affect citizens in most communities. Such issues are relevant to students and their families who live in those communities. Students can survey people in their neighborhood to learn about local issues and the degree of concern of the locals. One problem that affects many neighborhoods is littering. Students can easily make relevant documentation of the type, amount, and location of litter where they live. Rather than collect the litter, which may be hazardous if done unsupervised, students can list what they find using a form like the one in Figure 7.11. Having completed the documentation and discussed their findings with the class, students can make more informed decisions about their own behaviors. They also may infer the source of the litter and communicate with the owner or manager of the responsible commercial establishment to suggest a way to ameliorate the problem. For example, your students may recognize that there is a need for more trash receptacles or for putting receptacles in another place. The location of these containers could be determined on the basis of the information already

Figure 7.11 Environmental Issues Documentation Form

Litter List for _____

Type of Litter	Amount	Location
_____	_____	_____
_____	_____	_____
_____	_____	_____

What amount of litter did you find between your home and school?

Which objects in the litter could be reused?

Which things could be recycled?

Copyright © 2007 by Corwin Press. All rights reserved. Reprinted from *Teaching Constructivist Science, K–8: Nurturing Natural Investigators in the Standards-Based Classroom* by Michael L. Bentley, Edward S. Ebert II, and Christine Ebert. Thousand Oaks, CA: Corwin Press, www.corwinpress.com. Reproduction authorized only for the local school site or nonprofit organization that has purchased this book.

collected or provide an impetus for further investigation. Particular strategies for preventing litter might also be generated.

Individual Investigations With Environmental Issues

"Dragon Fly Pond" is an interesting activity from Project WILD (see http://www.projectwild.org/) that allows students to assume the roles of people working in agriculture, business and manufacturing, local government, and local utilities. All of these people have an interest in Dragon Fly Pond, a local source of water. They all use the water and create waste, which affects the water quality. The object of the simulation activity is for students to assume the roles of the town council members, who must consider the whole community in prioritizing access to the water and solve the pollution problem.

Simulation activities such as this can provide opportunities for students to assume different perspectives and lobby for those interests. Various other questions can be added to the scenario, such as the following:

- If you were to build a new house, where would you locate it? Why?
- If the population continues to increase at the current rate, more subdivisions and schools will have to be built. Where would you locate them?

Such questions highlight how environmental issues pervade modern life and the importance of community input into decision making. Your lesson activities might lead students to recognize other issues in their community. They might want to ask government officials or reporters from the media to meet with the class about local environmental concerns. Such activities contribute to cognitive and affective development and citizenship formation.

Summary

Making real-world connections between school science and science in students' lives is not difficult. Your lessons will take on new life with these connections to the outside world. Make use of the considerable community resources at your disposal. The local newspaper can be a wonderful resource. Students can track the newspaper to see how often stories about a particular issue are reported (relevant documentation). From there, plans for excursions or individual investigations will naturally emerge.

CONCLUSION

Many possibilities exist for making classroom instruction relevant to the lives of students. The teacher is responsible for structuring those opportunities to provide appropriate guidance and scaffolding so that the task is within the abilities of the student while not dictating details to such a degree that the activity becomes just another burdensome assignment. As a guide, we have identified three strategies to making relevant connections that integrate well with the inquiry approach: real-world demonstrations, relevant documentation, and individual investigations. Each strategy reflects different levels of student involvement and can be regarded as complementary in lesson design; the use of one may set the stage for the others. In this chapter we described how each of the strategies can be applied in three nontraditional educational settings, making connections at play, on science excursions, and when facing environmental issues. If you incorporate activities that relate classroom experiences to experiences outside the school, you can expect more interest and involvement from your students.

PART III

Planning, Management, Assessment, and Resources

The three chapters of this section represent what goes into your science program beyond the pedagogy and the standards. We think of this as classroom pragmatics. That is, these are the practical and necessary activities teachers perform in addition to the presentation of a lesson. In addition, we offer you a practical and, we hope, valuable compendium of resources to support teaching.

Effective science education, perhaps more than any other discipline, requires the appropriate use of many different resources. Chapter 8, "Nuts and Bolts: Organizing and Managing the Classroom for Inquiry," is concerned with identifying and organizing those resources. Among other topics, the chapter discusses learning centers, subject integration, and arranging experiences outside of the classroom.

Chapter 9, "Assessment and Evaluation," addresses the important questions of accountability. Although the standardized, selected-response test continues its tenacious hold on school districts as a tool for policy decisions, there are alternative forms of assessment that allow the teacher to determine what the students understand, how they have changed their thinking, and how they have grown in a cognitive sense over the course of the instruction. The emphasis of this chapter is on demonstrating understanding rather than relying on one's best guess.

And finally, Chapter 10, "A Compendium of Resources," provides you with a wealth of information to help make yours the most fascinating and engaging science classroom in the school. You will find information about safety in the elementary classroom, sample interview questions, planning science field trips, useful recipes and formulas, animal care in the classroom, and additional resources for teaching science.

8

Nuts and Bolts

*Organizing and Managing
the Classroom for Inquiry*

Multiple Contexts Require Multiple Approaches

Spaces That Foster Interaction and Learning

Alternative Patterns for Teaching Science

Science Culture of the Classroom

Planning in Support of Inquiry

Your Academic Roadmap

This chapter should help you to understand the following ideas:

- Science education occurs in contexts that can be expected to vary from region to region.
- An activity-rich classroom science program is facilitated by effective classroom design.
- Science can be the school subject that integrates many other subject areas.

"The point is not to cover the subject but to help uncover part of it."

—Victor Weisskopf

MULTIPLE CONTEXTS
REQUIRE MULTIPLE APPROACHES

In previous chapters we considered the content of the classroom science program. We considered a number of strategies for fostering students' thinking and helping them construct scientific knowledge and knowledge of the nature of science and science-technology-society interactions. This chapter is about planning and managing science instruction in the K–8 classroom. This chapter focuses on the nuts and bolts of the science program, the processes that occur inside and outside the classroom that most directly enable students' learning.

Classroom management is a concern of many teachers, particularly for beginning teachers. Simultaneously coping with a classroom of diverse youngsters and trying to enact a meaningful curriculum can be daunting. There is great diversity in K–8 education in the United States, with a million and a half elementary teachers, 600,000 middle school teachers, and more than 36 million students in some 110,000 public schools (U.S. Census Bureau, 2005; Bureau of Labor Statistics, 2005).

The first point to remember is that there is no one right way to go about your planning and management activities. Your million and a half colleagues go about these activities in many, many different ways, some more effective, some less so.

A second point to remember is that the science content of the curriculum can and should reflect the uniqueness of the school's locale and the multiple cultures of its students. That is, the context in which science education occurs can be expected to vary from region to region. Fourth graders in Illinois might be studying the prairie, whereas students in Florida would be studying the Everglades. Detroit sixth graders might study force and motion in the context of automobile transportation, whereas Seattle students might study the same topic through airplanes or boats. How the content is taught should reflect the unique environment and community.

If you now teach in a school close to where you grew up, then you may be familiar with these contextual matters already. However, if you are teaching in a locale that is new to you, do not dismiss the importance of finding out more about the values and expectations of the community in which your students live. The more you know, the more likely it is that you will be able to help your students make relevant connections between science and their worlds, as we discussed in Chapter 7.

Teachers will tell you that their classes are different each year. Most teachers recognize that the effectiveness of instructional activities depends on the particular students in their classes. Much also depends on the circumstances of the moment. Thus, even though you have planned your lessons in advance, a lot of interactive planning may occur right on the spot in response to students' interests or needs. Teachers need to be flexible in order to take advantage of teachable moments.

All in all, classroom life is affected by myriad variables, so the educational enterprise has to be among the most complex systems in society. Clearly, then, no one formula for planning and managing science in the classroom possibly could apply in all or even most situations. There is no way you can predict every kind of student or every teaching situation with which you might have to cope. Yet despite the constraints and challenges, teachers and students in different kinds of schools manage year after year to create communities where science learning flourishes. Here is one piece of advice based on our own classroom experiences: Be patient with the complexity and keep yourself open to learning on the job.

Nevertheless, through thoughtful planning, many of the tasks and problems of managing the science program can be anticipated ahead of time. Your colleagues usually will be helpful in sharing their own solutions to management problems.

In the typical self-contained elementary classroom your first tasks each year include setting the daily and weekly schedule and organizing the classroom space. Depending on the type of school furniture, you may have some options in how to arrange the desks and how to store and make materials and equipment accessible. Take a moment to consider the following questions:

- How would you prefer to arrange the classroom furniture be arranged (e.g., your desk, the students' tables and chairs)?
- In terms of storage and work areas, what would be ideal for your classroom?

SPACES THAT FOSTER INTERACTION AND LEARNING

Even when they are empty, classrooms can be all kinds of spaces. Some are organized in multiclass open space; others are located in transportable modules. Some have sinks and water. Some have nooks and crannies and even separate breakout rooms or preparation and storage. In some classrooms students keep their books and belongings in their desks, whereas in others they use lockers or cubbies located in the classroom or hallway. From your own observations, what kind of classroom spaces do you think facilitate good, investigative, problem-oriented science teaching? Which do not?

Small things can make a big difference. Classroom furniture is an example. Slant-topped desks and desks or tables bolted to the floor are an obstacle for many hands-on activities. Movable furniture and flat-topped desks offer more flexibility.

Some teachers prefer student desks to be separate from others and typically arrange them in rows facing the chalkboard. This setup emphasizes individual work. An alternative is to group four desks together or to use tables instead of desks as workspaces. Desks in clusters facilitate students' conversations, cooperative learning, and the teacher's movement around the classroom. Also consider the location of your own desk in the classroom. What's the message to students when your desk is in the back or the front of the classroom?

Learning Centers

Centers are special classroom workplaces. A classroom might have one or more subject-related centers, or a single center might be used for different subjects at different times. A science center is appropriately supplied with materials and directions to allow independent or small-group investigations and study. Students and teachers alike share responsibility for recording progress in center work.

A fourth-grade teacher has a science and math center consisting of a table and several shelves for storage. On one shelf is a terrarium housing a pair of anoles. Another shelf contains math manipulatives: Cuisenaire rods, pattern blocks, attribute blocks, unifix cubes, number bars, chip trading materials, geoboards, and color cubes. Another shelf has materials used in both math and science, such as blank paper and graph paper, calculators, rulers, measuring cups, plastic beakers, a trundle wheel, meter sticks, spring scales, and an equal-arm platform balance. Science supplies in the center include microscopes, containers, eyedroppers, magnifiers, magnets, a collection of seashells and various other specimens, and reference books and data sheets for recording observations.

A science center also can be created to complement a particular instructional unit. For example, for a unit on "mini-beasts" a center could feature Peterson's *A Field Guide to Insects* (Borror & White, 1998) and magnifiers set up for students to examine specimens. The center might also include periodicals with features on insects (such as *National Geographic Kids*), posters, and games such as Predator-Prey. Activity 8.1 will provide you with practice in conceptualizing how to set up a science learning center. Keep in mind the goal of a differentiated classroom and be sure to provide reading materials at different levels.

Activity 8.1   **Conceptualizing a Science Center**

Select one of the following situations and develop a plan for your classroom.

- Design a science center to accompany a first-grade unit about animals and their characteristics.
- Design a science center for a fourth-grade unit on weather.
- Choose a science topic based on your own interests, and design a science center for a group of students at a level you would like to teach.
- What would you do to guide students in their work in the science center?

Creating an Inviting Environment

All in all, providing opportunities for students to learn science involves creating an environment with a variety of materials and supplies and with spaces that can be used for different purposes. Nicholson's (1972) classic *The Theory of Loose Parts* states that in any environment both the degree of inventiveness and creativity and the possibility of discovery are directly proportional to the number and kind of variables in that environment. Some classroom environments do not work simply because they do not have enough "loose parts" to generate learning. "Loose parts," properly provided, will make your classroom an interesting and stimulating place for everyone, a space that is both aesthetically pleasing and well organized. Also, have your students help you display their work around the room, such as lab reports, sketches, and concept maps. This shows that you value their work and encourages them to take ownership and contribute to a positive classroom environment.

A simple way to enhance the classroom environment is to add plants. The same plants can be a source of investigations. Dependable choices include geraniums, begonias, coleus, impatiens, spider plants, *Tradescantia,* ivy, snake plants, nephthytis, pothos, Chinese evergreens, and philodendrons. Hardy plants that can tolerate water are best for the primary classrooms because young students like to care for them often. If the room has good sun, you might try miniature roses, sensitive plants (e.g., *Mimosa pudica*), and dwarf and scented geraniums. African violets also make good classroom plants, and forcing daffodil or tulip bulbs is a great activity.

An aquarium can house aquatic plants and fish, or it can be used as a terrarium for many kinds of organisms. If your budget is tight, a terrarium can be made in a large jar, such as a super-size pickle jar, or even in a 2-liter clear plastic bottle. There are many other interesting investigations involving plants. Using hydroponics is an example. Table 8.1 describes the basic process for making a woodland habitat terrarium, which could be modified for simulated desert or marshland ecosystems.

Managing Learning Centers

Students can use the science center if they are working on an individual or group project, but that is not the only way to use centers. In some instances you may want all students to gain particular experiences in small groups. This can be accomplished by creating a number of centers and having groups rotate through them during the same class time or on successive days. Table 8.2 describes a hassle-free procedure for moving groups of students from center to center (Novelli, 1995).

Workshop or lab time in the Table 8.2 schedule might look something like the following. At Time 4 the Kangas are at the computer center working together on a laptop, entering data they collected about light-dark preferences of isopods. The Cubbies are recording observations of ants in an ant farm in the science center in their science journals. The Ravens are writing, creating a skit based on a book they read together, a biography of the life of Rachel Carson, and the Bears are working with a plastic model illustrating insect anatomy.

Table 8.1   How to Make a Classroom Terrarium

1. Put several centimeters of small, washed gravel on the bottom of the container. Intersperse several pieces of activated charcoal to absorb impurities (available in the plant section of home and garden stores). Top this with 5–10 centimeters of commercial potting soil mixed with peat or mulch. Sprinkle the surface with water to moisten but not saturate (too much water will encourage the growth of mold and mildew).

2. Collect small woodland plants to place in the terrarium. These might include mosses, small ferns, lichens, wintergreen, and partridgeberry. They can be placed around rocks or decorative pieces of wood.

3. When the plants have established themselves, small animals can be introduced to the terrarium. Students can be encouraged to bring organisms to add to the ecosystem, such as isopods (sow bugs or pill bugs, often called "roly-polies") and earthworms. One small animal, such as a salamander or frog, is suitable for your simulated woodland habitat. For food, frogs and salamanders will need small live worms or insects such as crickets from a pet shop.

4. Loosely cover the terrarium to maintain the internal humidity while permitting air circulation. Avoid direct sunlight because it might cause too much heat to build up inside.

Table 8.2   A Simple Procedure for Moving Groups Through Classroom Activity Centers

1. Divide the class into groups. Ask each group to choose a name or color.

2. Create a master schedule such as the one below, with center names or numbers going across and days or times going down. Write group names on small cards (or use color-coded cards if you're using colors to differentiate groups). Assign one group to each center (going across) on Day 1 or Time 1 by tacking cards into place on a schedule board.

3. Explain the rotation schedule and have students take a practice run. Soon, with a quick glance, they will know exactly where they are supposed to be and what center they have next.

	Center 1	Center 2	Center 3	Center 4	Center 5
Time 1	Cats	Bears	Kangas	Cubbies	Ravens
Time 2	Ravens	Cats	Bears	Kangas	Cubbies
Time 3	Cubbies	Ravens	Cats	Bears	Kangas
Time 4	Kangas	Cubbies	Ravens	Cats	Bears
Time 5	Bears	Kangas	Cubbies	Ravens	Cats

Meanwhile, the Cats are examining and drawing insects in amber they are viewing under a microscope.

Science Needs Space

You have probably noticed that teaching science requires stuff. It is never too early to begin collecting science center materials. In Chapter 10 you will find a useful list of materials frequently used for science activities. Some stuff will need to be stored much of the time. You may be fortunate to have an adequate storage area, but in many classrooms space for storing materials and equipment is at a premium. Teachers often use cardboard file boxes or plastic containers and bins of different sizes to store science materials. Organizing your materials is a key to making hands-on science manageable.

In addition to storage space, there is a need for space in the classroom for students to temporarily house science projects and investigations in progress. Space also may be is needed for one or more computers and their peripherals (e.g., printer, scanner, external hard drive). See Activity 8.2.

Activity 8.2 Your Ideal Classroom

Assume you have a typical rectangular self-contained classroom containing a teacher desk and 25 student desks. You are free to add any other items that are reasonably available.

Arrange the furniture as you prefer. Be sure that your plan includes

- Centers
- Storage areas
- Individual and group work areas

  1. What are some advantages and limitations of each aspect of your design?
  2. What might be the advantages and disadvantages of placing the desks in rows or in clusters?
  3. What is an advantage to where you placed your desk in your plan? And a disadvantage?

Summary

For science to be active it is not necessary that students scurry around or call out data across the room (they could do so, but not necessarily). Moving through a learning center provides a certain degree of dynamism simply by its nature. The differentiated classroom provides many opportunities for students to work independently and in small groups. Learning centers are one mechanism for facilitating both situations.

Two points are significant: One is that the success of the classroom science program can be facilitated by classroom design, and the second is that science requires stuff and space, for its doing and for its preparation and for storage. Thus, the teacher contributes much behind the scenes to maintain a high-quality classroom science program by handling logistics and organizing materials for use and for storage. One plus to all this is that being prepared will give you more confidence as you enact your classroom curriculum.

There are many ways to organize. For example, you might color-code your storage bins and label them clearly. You might want to use shelves so that you can access each bin without removing the ones above. Whatever system you choose, don't be afraid to modify it so that it works for your particular situation and style.

ALTERNATIVE PATTERNS FOR TEACHING SCIENCE

The self-contained classroom under the supervision of a single teacher is the most typical staffing pattern for schools in the United States, at least for K–5. Nevertheless, many teachers team teach or work in the classroom with a variety of specialists and paraprofessionals. Teaming can increase relevance and demonstrate the real connectedness of the curriculum. For example, the music teacher can contribute to your lessons on sound, as could the physical education teacher on forces and motion. Paraprofessionals, teachers' aides, could facilitate students' work in learning centers while you are occupied with other students in groups.

Prime Time for Science

A big advantage of self-contained classrooms is that teachers usually have some latitude in deciding details of the daily and weekly schedule and how the room is to be organized. Just as no one pattern of furniture arrangement is the best for all purposes, there are advantages and disadvantages to different staffing patterns and schedules. The choices you make as a teacher may facilitate science learning.

In terms of scheduling, the professional wisdom is that "students become more engaged in their own learning when the daily routine is predictable and consistent" (Fisher, 1992, p. 57). Opening and closing routings and transitions throughout the day are especially important. For example, one teacher begins his third-grade students' day with sharing time and typically ends in the afternoon with a journaling activity. The routine that opens the day can serve as the set or advanced organizer for the day's learning tasks.

Here is an example of a daily schedule a teacher created for her first-grade class:

8:40 A.M.	Settling-in time
9:00	Group meeting: community circle
9:30	Science or workshop
11:00	Snack and recess
11:20	Math
12:10 P.M.	Specialist (e.g., art, music, physical education)
12:45	Lunch
1:30	Social studies or workshop
2:10	Shared reading

2:30	Independent and collaborative reading
2:55	Group meeting, community circle
3:10	Dismissal

You can see from this schedule that this teacher considers science important. Science is taught early in the school day—prime time—and a generous amount of time is allotted for the lesson. You can also see that the teacher places value on both individual and group work. We can infer that this primary teacher does some subject integration in her classroom curriculum, but not a great deal, and that she probably uses methods such as projects and group work.

In self-contained classrooms, teachers may be able to schedule science in the morning, although they may have to work around the schedules of others, including specialist teachers (e.g., music, art, physical education, English language learner program, gifted program). This constraint aside, the teacher's personal priorities often are revealed in his or her scheduling. Unfortunately, elementary teachers typically schedule science late in the afternoon rather than in the morning. In the afternoon students experience their postprandial dip, a low-energy and low-attention period that is part of everyone's diurnal metabolic cycle. Some countries even shut down commerce for afternoon siestas. The early afternoon is not a time your class is likely to be the most creative or excited about tackling a tough problem or issue.

Another consequence of the typical afternoon scheduling for science is that science time is more likely to be cut short for assemblies, parent-teacher conferences, and half-days. Science classes scheduled at the end of the day may even be bumped or abbreviated as preceding lessons run over. These factors help explain why the time spent on science instruction in U.S. schools averages only about 20 minutes a day.

We readily admit our bias in considering science as an important subject, and we believe science deserves prominent placement in the daily schedule. To us, science and social studies are the curriculum's core subjects, around and through which most other skills and content can and should be taught. Science and social studies are content-rich subjects, whereas reading, language arts, and mathematics are skill-rich subjects. Many skills can be taught in the context of problems and issues, and these are abundant in science and social studies. Therefore, we favor a subject-integrated curriculum.

Despite our bias, we concede that teachers may be compelled by school or district policies to divide teaching time in a particular way, and we realize that not everyone agrees that science and social studies are the "real subjects" in the curriculum. We recommend at the very least that instead of spreading the time for science equally throughout the week, you bunch it together to provide longer, investigation-oriented science periods. To pursue an investigation in depth, students usually need an hour or more. Students need time to develop and implement their investigations and to discuss and deliberate. A longer period allows students more opportunity to break with everyday experience and make the transition to an appropriate frame of mind for scientific thinking. Changing too frequently from subject to subject in a day's schedule can fragment students' thought processes, preventing them from having a coherent instructional experience.

An example of creating longer periods for science would be to designate Mondays, Wednesdays, and Thursdays as science days with hour and a half periods (math might be blocked for this period on Tuesdays and Fridays). In our experience, most students are flexible enough to handle some daily variation. The professional wisdom is to aim for a predictable schedule for students but not necessarily with the same routine every day.

Schedules also must be organized within larger frames than the day. There is the weekly schedule and the grading period, which could be 6 weeks, a quarter (9 weeks), or a semester. An example of framing science instruction in a weekly schedule is illustrated by the teacher who on Monday introduces the assignments that she expects to be completed by Friday. Her assignments might include science observations, a commentary on a science book from the library, or a drawing or model of something related to the lesson being studied.

Then there is the case of schools that have bells. Middle schools especially may be departmentalized, and teachers in these schools specialize in one or more subjects. Students move at the bell from place to place, changing classes. There are many variations in middle school staffing and scheduling, however. For example, in one school a core team of teachers is responsible for the main subjects, which are block scheduled. Within that large block of time, the teaching team and the students can allot the time as they choose. One advantage of this approach is that it allows science to be taught in an integrated fashion with other subjects.

Value of Planning for Subject Integration

Teachers often feel overwhelmed by the amount of content they are expected to teach. Nothing ever seems to be subtracted from the curriculum, but new topics and programs often are added (e.g., drug and alcohol abuse education, sex education, and domestic abuse and violence education). The only approach to this situation, at least in terms of preserving your sanity, is to teach the subjects in an integrated fashion. In terms of scheduling, this means creating blocks of time for teaching. Some topics in science lend themselves naturally to integration with mathematics, whereas other topics are more naturally integrated with social studies. Language arts, or English, nearly always can be integrated with science. The sense of what fits best is something that develops with experience.

Summary

Teachers will tell you that they teach math or reading first in the morning because that is when their students are fresh. If they are honest they may also admit that science is squeezed in when and where it can be. However, if you take our advice about integrating what you do in science with the other subject areas, science can be the vehicle that launches everything else. What's more, your classroom curriculum will demonstrate a definite sense of connectedness between the subjects.

SCIENCE CULTURE OF THE CLASSROOM

So far in this chapter, we have considered some practical matters, such as scheduling, arranging the classroom, and working with colleagues. Now we want to stress again that learning is a *social* process. Knowledge itself is a social construct that is influenced by the cultures of the classroom, family, and community. And don't think that a student reading a book in a corner is constructing knowledge in isolation. Rather, she is engaged in a social process; she is interacting with the authors and illustrators of the book, assimilating and accommodating as she ponders the ideas she encounters, the familiar and the new. The learning happens in the *interactions* (e.g., student to student, student to adult, student to author), and therefore it is the quality of these interactions that you will want to consider as you develop your teaching. You will want to plan activities that optimize the interactions. Students will demonstrate their knowledge, skills, attitudes, and appreciations in what they write or say as they consider the merits of different ways of solving a problem, for example.

Vygotsky (1978) pointed out that cognitive functions in general are internalizations of social actions. If you provide students access to appropriately nourishing experiences, such as opportunities to carry out investigations or to read a good science book, learning will come about naturally. The experience of the activity itself (reading the book) does *not* produce the knowledge. Vygotsky and others argue that knowledge does not derive directly from experience per se, from the sensory data alone, but rather from the student *making sense* of the experience, actively constructing knowledge through the interaction, by inquiring in the context of a particular cultural setting (reading the book). Thus we are back to Dewey's claim that we *learn by thinking.*

Because learning is a natural consequence of positive social interactions focused on challenging problems and issues, you can do much to enhance students' opportunities for science learning by attending to the cultural setting of your classroom. Your task is to facilitate students' engagement with each other and with the subject matter. As Chaillé and Britain (1991) point out, "Good environments for young students permit, encourage, and even necessitate interaction with others, from simple communicative interaction to the complex negotiation of conflicts. But social interaction is important not only because it is a part of life, but also because it actively contributes to students' theory building" (p. 9). Unfortunately, the social interaction between students often is neglected in the classroom while attention is focused on the teacher-class interaction.

Student-to-student social interaction happens naturally in cooperative group work. We recommend that your repertoire of science teaching strategies include a variety of cooperative learning strategies. Table 8.3 provides some tips on how to get the most out of this important teaching method.

PLANNING IN SUPPORT OF INQUIRY

Teachers have different personalities and different learning styles and consequently plan in different ways, and that planning can occur at any time. As we have said, there is no one right way to plan your lessons. Albert Einstein once

Table 8.3 Suggestions for Effective Use of Cooperative Groups

- Arrange student desks to allow discussion between students; think circular instead of straight lines.

- Early in the school year provide some explicit instruction in communication, conflict management, and leadership before assigning group work. Have students practice listening, taking turns, disagreeing politely, managing time, asking for help, being supportive, sharing feelings, keeping everyone involved, paraphrasing, expressing appreciation, making everyone feel important, and making eye contact.

- Design tasks to encourage all students in the group to contribute, with everyone having a stake in the learning of others in the group. This might be achieved by assigning a group grade or by assigning roles and dividing labor.

- Avoid providing opportunities for some students to hitchhike on the work of others in the group. This may be achieved by individual accountability, such as by questioning students at random or by having students share in the reporting back to the whole class.

- Use pairs whenever possible; avoid trios and groups larger than four. Group members can self-select, or you can use structured procedures for forming groups, such as by counting off, drawing a playing card, or pairing up within categories. ("Walk around and pair up with *red* as the category; those wearing red pair, and those not wearing red pair.")

- Use paired reading for science texts: Have partners take turns reading aloud to each other, and when they have finished reading, have each pair talk about the reading, write in their journals, or prepare to report to another group. Pairs can rotate for another task ("Okay, identify a person in your pair as 'A' and the other as 'B'; the A's remain seated, and the B's move to a new 'A' to be your partner. B's will share . . .").

- Option display: A group works on a problem or issue, aiming to display several options for solving the problem or addressing the issue, the likely consequences of each option, and the group's overall recommendation.

- Best choice debate: Pairs prepare either a pro or con position on an issue; a "pro pair" and a "con pair" then meet to explain their position to each other and seek an agreement on an overall recommendation (similar to Johnson & Johnson's [1987] constructive controversy method).

- Project work usually aims to produce a product. Teams can be organized around an action project whose focus is taking action rather than studying; projects may be based on student interests; guidelines should include clear timelines and progress reports (tasks might involve interviewing, comparing opinions, making models, designing an ideal something, finding contrasting views, producing a graphic, or creating a dramatic skit for another class).

- Allow students to celebrate a group success and to consider how their work could have been improved. Students should ask questions such as "What contribution did each of us make?" and "How could our work together have been better?"

Source: Jensen, Moore, and Hatch (2002).

remarked that he could relate all of his greatest insights to the "3 B's": the bed, the bathroom, and the bus. Veteran teachers will tell you that they are often most creative when they are occupied with something else, such as driving home from school, working in the garden, or washing dishes—almost anyplace other than school. These teachers will also tell you that they write down their plans in some fashion, perhaps as an outline, a semantic web or concept map, or a written narrative. Some schools require teachers to write plans that are kept on file. You will have to find which method best fits your own style and your school's requirements. One helpful device is to use a list of *guiding or driving questions.* Questions to guide your planning are offered in Table 8.4.

Table 8.4   Example of Guiding Questions to Facilitate Planning Science Units and Lessons

Think about the following:

1. What is the topic? (theme? issue? problem?) What is (are) its source(s)?

2. Why is this topic (theme, issue, problem) important? Why should students learn this? What influence, if any, will it have on their lives?

3. What do the students already know? How do their explanations or beliefs differ from those of the scientific community?

4. What knowledge will students construct?
   o "Big understandings"
   o Concepts
   o Facts

5. What processes and skills will students develop?
   o Knowledge acquisition skills
   o Thinking processes
   o Social skills

6. What habits of mind will students develop?
   o Attitudes and dispositions
   o Values

7. What other parts of the curriculum can be naturally integrated with this content?

8. What resources are available?

9. How will students be engaged and stimulated to investigate the topics?

10. What can be done so that students share their knowledge with peers?

11. How can students be motivated to apply and extend what they know?

12. How will I assess what they learned?

13. How will I evaluate my teaching?

Source: Powell, Needham, and Bentley (1994).

Figure 8.1   One Teacher's Initial Concept Map for Planning a Unit on Forces

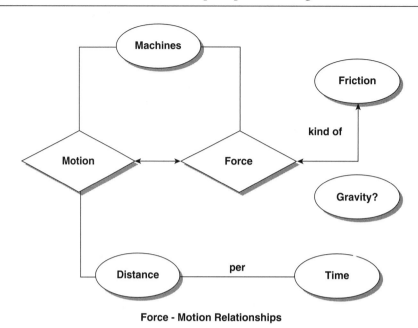

Force - Motion Relationships

When you are teaching your students, you will have to draw on your own background knowledge of the content. One thing we recommend you do in instructional planning is to read up on the science topics you plan to teach (an encyclopedia is one good starting place, and several can be found on the Internet; see http://www.britannica.com and http://encarta.msn.com/). One of the most creative thought processes you will ever experience is modifying the content in your mind for use in instruction, or creating your own "pedagogical content knowledge" (Shulman, 2003, p. 119). This transformation, or "translation," as physicist Richard Feynman called it, changes the content to make it more concrete and understandable to your students.

After reading up on the content, some teachers like to outline or web the information to highlight the main concepts. One teacher's initial concept map for planning a physical science unit on forces is illustrated in Figure 8.1. As you can see, this teacher was not sure about using gravity as an example of a kind of force.

Planning for Challenging Science Projects

Science is the perfect subject for long-term, challenging projects, something that your students might take on over the course of several weeks. Such projects provide opportunities for integrating the curriculum and doing investigations.

An example of a project in a unit on forces is for students to build a catenary arch. This is an arch that distributes the forces over it smoothly throughout the curve of the arch. Once the keystone, or top piece of the arch, is put in place between the two ascending sides, the arch supports itself. First, have students draw the arch on paper. Patterns made from the drawings are used to cut pieces from corrugated cardboard boxes. The pieces are glued together to form blocks, and the blocks are stacked to form arches, without glue or fasteners. You can view an example of an arch project at http://www.coker.edu.

Another example of an integrative project is to have students build a greenhouse. The basic ingredients include PVC pipe, PVC fittings, and plastic sheeting. After the construction is completed students can plan investigations related to plant growth and life cycles by planting seeds and recording plant growth measurements. To see student-built greenhouses, visit http://www.coker.edu/educationdept/ebert.htm

Planning for Excursions and Using Community Resources

Every community has resources you can tap to enrich your science program. One of the most underused resources for science is the great outdoors. Even the school's playground is underused, but so are the neighborhood, local parks and public spaces, footpaths and biking trails, and resources you might never have thought about, such as the farm owned by one of your students' grandparents. Your local community represents an even broader category of resources, which includes these as well as people and institutions.

Field trips often are among students' most memorable school experiences. They require advance planning and attention to detail, but a good field trip can enrich classroom life for days and weeks, before and after the trip. Field trips should be planned that fit naturally into the curriculum. For example, a visit to an aquarium or a saltwater marsh would be appropriate when you are teaching a unit about marine life or the oceans.

If you are new to a locale, you can find out about its resources by visiting the public library, the Chamber of Commerce, the local newspaper, a science museum or nature center, or the science department at a community college. Knowledgeable parents are another source of information about community resources and field sites.

In planning excursions you must be aware of school and district policies and regulations regarding field trips. There might be constraints on the number of field trips per class per year or a limit on the amount students' caregivers can be asked to pay for transportation, admissions, or other costs. Typically a field trip request form must be submitted to your school administration for advance approval. Such forms ask you to indicate the date of the proposed trip, the site address, and the name of an on-site contact. You may be required to provide a rationale that specifies your objectives and states how the field trip activities fit into the curriculum.

We recommend that you involve your students in planning trip logistics and deciding which activities will take place. If your students are invested in the process, they will learn more, and you will have fewer management problems. Most students recognize that excursions are special learning opportunities and are eager to cooperate. The countdown days before the trip can be used as a series of deadlines for getting tasks finished and getting everyone prepared for the special event.

You will probably want to solicit parents to participate as chaperones. Often room mothers or fathers can provide the extra support you need. You will have to send a notice about the trip home with students a week or more in advance, and most schools require a permission form signed by parents or guardians.

Field trip success is enhanced if you create an investigative atmosphere—one of excitement and expectancy of different possibilities and discoveries. It is hard to fail if students go off on the field trip with inquiring frames of mind, confident in their roles as observers, problem solvers, and data recorders. On the other hand, failure is almost certain if students head off on a field trip not knowing what they are responsible for doing.

The problems and questions that provide the focus for a field trip are established during pretrip activities. Some teachers have students keep science logs or journals, and these are often very useful on field trips for sketching and recording observations. Depending on the field trip, other tools and materials also might be useful. Here is a list of things frequently used to support students' observing and learning on science excursions:

- A first aid kit (including, depending on season, insect repellent)
- Binoculars
- Magnifiers, such as hand lenses and jeweler's loupes
- Field microscopes
- Plastic bags
- Containers (bug boxes, small cages, or collection jars)
- Tweezers, scissors, probes (or dissecting kits)
- Nets (aquatic or insect)
- Field guides (e.g., to insects, wildflowers, trees, birds, rocks and minerals)
- Maps (e.g., roadmaps, topographic maps, geological maps)
- Compasses
- Camera and film or digital cameras
- Tape recorders and blank tapes
- Field logs or journals
- Paper, pencils, colored pencils, or markers

Making a field collection is an educational and rewarding activity for students on field trips. Before collecting organisms, however, check with your county extension agent or a park agent regarding regulations that prohibit collecting particular plants or animals. Never collect rare, threatened, or endangered species, but insects usually are okay to collect.

If you are going to be on private property, always get a landowner's written permission to visit or collect. Be sure students pick up after themselves: "Leave nothing but footprints." Encourage students to show respect for wildlife, for example, by putting logs and rocks that they have moved back into their original positions and by releasing organisms after examining them back into the natural habitat.

Your school grounds and neighborhood are valuable as an outdoor resource. One elementary school in Winnetka, Illinois, is located next to a forest preserve. A fifth-grade teacher in the school used the site for students to study native flora. She invited a local forester to help. This led to the beginning of a project for the class. The students learned to identify and remove alien plant species that had invaded the native prairie. The teacher and forester trained parent volunteers to take groups of students out on study and work expeditions periodically throughout the year. Each group was responsible for caring for an area in the preserve. The students' enthusiasm in tackling the project to restore the native flora led to a lot of worthwhile physical exercise and science learning as well.

Few schools are fortunate enough to be located adjacent to an area managed for nature, such as a forest preserve. However, many other valuable activities and investigations can be done outdoors. Gardening is one of them. A school garden can offer many opportunities for science lessons, connecting with topics such as reproduction, growth, plants, the structure of flowers, seeds, leaves, stems, and roots, photosynthesis, capillarity, nitrogen fixation, the water cycle and other biogeochemical cycles, food chains, trophic levels, and parasitism. There are many kinds of gardens, such as butterfly, rock, herb, vegetable, flower, and desert. An example of a project is an heirloom seed garden (note that seed catalogs often have interesting historical and scientific information). Information and assistance are available in every part of the United States from land grant university extension agents. Local garden clubs may also be willing to contribute.

A garden must be maintained, and so you can work with students to create a calendar of reminders about watering and weeding the garden. One way is to schedule pairs of students to handle tasks on a rotating basis. The calendar could also record students' predictions about germination time. You will find useful resources on school gardening from the National Gardening Association (www.garden.org) and from Kidsgardening.com (www.kids gardening.com).

A variation on the garden idea is a nature trail. In this case, what grows around your school is left undisturbed except for a path through the area. Once a pathway is cleared, the plants that are indigenous to the area can be identified and labeled. In addition to seeing what is there, students can observe changes over time. Over the course of several years, these changes could be dramatic. A marker indicating the height of a sapling when initially measured would be interesting years later to another class.

Your Community's Human Resources

Teachers often overlook the human resources their community offers. Students in your classroom may have relatives who work in science fields or who have to use science in their work. Some connections might even surprise you. For instance, examples of simple machines are to be found in the toolbox of a carpenter or plumber. There are always community members who are willing and interested in helping students learn and many willing to help with student investigations. Your local science museum, zoo, aquarium, arboretum, botanical garden, nature center, planetarium, children's museum, and parks department can be among your greatest allies in teaching science. They are not just places where exhibits are stored; each is a treasure trove of ideas for investigations. Also, they have people with special expertise and hands-on resources for investigations.

Science Homework

In the past, science homework often was dry and boring: "Read the chapter, answer questions 1–6 at the end of the chapter" or "Look up the vocabulary words in the glossary and write the definitions." This kind of homework rarely challenges students and rarely results in meaningful learning. On the other hand, linking classroom instruction with the home can be motivating. There are many simple science activities that students and their parents or guardians can conduct at home. Instructions can be provided on a take-home handout, or you can let the investigative teams come up with their own procedures. These kinds of activities strengthen the connections between student, school, and home and give a student's caregivers opportunities to help and show interest in their child's work.

One elementary teacher sends the students in her third-grade class home on Friday with a science activity packed in a plastic bag. Included in the bag are the science materials, instructions for carrying out one or more investigations, a data sheet or worksheet, and a "Science Wizard Form" for the parent to verify that the student completed the activity at home. On Monday, the teacher re-creates the activity that the student and parent have done at home. This teacher says that she receives immediate responses from most students because they have done the activity. Students are encouraged to discuss questions that came up at home. Examples of some take-home activities include exploring magnets, investigating the properties of seltzer tablets, building an aluminum foil barge and then estimating the number of pennies that can be placed in it before it sinks, seed sorting and graphing, estimation activities, graphing and sorting gummy bears, and finding the center of gravity of a ball of clay.

Animals in the Classroom

Living things are what the life sciences are all about. When it comes to studying the life sciences there is no substitute for *living things.* Students can learn much from observing and documenting the characteristics and behaviors of organisms in the classroom. Plants are easier to care for than animals. Proper care for an animal includes providing an appropriate artificial habitat that is cleaned regularly. Your classroom animals should be able to get adequate exercise and should have hiding spaces to prevent undue stress. Also, food and clean water must be provided in suitable containers, and they need proper ventilation, light, and heat (especially important for reptiles).

Many different organisms can be kept in the classroom. Mammals that are usually selected include varieties of rodents (guinea pigs, mice, rats, hamsters, and gerbils). These animals are clean and easy to care for. Rabbits need special attention because they typically are stressed in a busy and crowded environment such as a classroom. Be aware that some students may be allergic to fur; find out before bringing animals into the classroom.

Among our favorite animals are anoles (lizards), red-eared slider turtles, and "fancy" rats. Most students are open-minded about the latter and immediately become rat fans. However, adults tend to be squeamish (perhaps it's the naked tail). We also like fish and invertebrates such as isopods ("roly-polies"), mealworms, and earthworms.

In captivity, reptiles (except snapping turtles) should have access to an appropriate supplemental heat source for their metabolic needs. Most reptiles need a hot spot where they can raise their body temperature whenever they want (at least during the day) to about 38°C or even higher depending on species, which allows the animal to digest food and fight off disease. The reptile should be able to move away from the heat source to cool off.

Students usually are highly motivated to care for classroom animals and often are willing to care for them at home over school holidays. Chapter 10 contains information on the feeding needs of several kinds of animals. School and public libraries have books on animals and their care, and there is a lot of information on the World Wide Web.

Some people argue that animals do not belong in the school. In his book *Animal Liberation,* Australian professor Peter Singer coined the term *speciesism,* which he compared to racism and defined as "a prejudice or attitude of bias toward the interest of members of one's own species and against those of members of other species" (1975, p. 7). Some animal rights advocates say the educational benefits of using animals in the classroom are overstated and the suffering of the animals involved is underestimated. What do you think about this issue?

Planning for a Safe Environment

Both inside and outside the classroom, safety must be the first consideration for planning for science. In fact, you and the students in your class should talk about safety right at the start of the school year. Safety has been described as simply using common sense in planning ahead. Of course, nothing you do can guarantee that an accident will never happen in your classroom. We consider ourselves aware of safety issues, but we have had to manage emergencies in both classroom and field situations.

The first thing to do is to look ahead and be prepared. In your school, know the location of fire extinguishers and how to use them. Keep your classroom doors free of obstructions, and never store flammable material near doors. Know school procedures for handling student injuries. Unless circumstances offer no alternative, never treat injuries yourself. Excluding life-saving measures, teachers should only stop bleeding and apply water (as to burns or acid spills).

Engage your students in discussing safety early in the year. They should be able to contribute suggestions in determining appropriate safety rules, and involving them fosters their investment in maintaining a safe environment. Post the resulting standards for safe behavior prominently in the classroom. Chapter 10 has a list of general safety guidelines.

Plan for safety, but don't let worrying about accidents inhibit your use of hands-on activities. After all, students could injure themselves by misusing many things, even scissors and pencils. Before beginning activities involving potential risks, remind students of safety concerns. These include activities involving a lighted flame (e.g., burning candles or alcohol lamps) and the use of chemicals or sharp instruments. Require safety glasses in investigations where a splash or projectile might harm the eyes (and be aware that particular types of goggles are designed for different hazards). Remember that contact lenses can be dangerous if a chemical splashes into the eyes because capillary action carries the irritant to the eye's surface. If the chemical is an alkali, eye damage can occur within seconds.

Although you will never be able to create an absolutely injury-proof environment, you always can and should be conscientious about safety. Your liability as a teacher falls under *tort law*, which governs negligence or breach of contract or trust that results in injury to another person or damage to property. A student generally acquires the status of an *invitee*, which means that no contractual basis exists for assumed risk on his or her part. The law assumes students do not know the potential dangers or appreciate the risks involved. The teacher's responsibility is related to the legal concept of *negligence*, which is about neglecting instruction, supervision, or proper maintenance of equipment and supplies. If no precedent or statute is involved, then the actions or inactions of the teacher are measured against what a hypothetical reasonably prudent individual would have done under the same circumstances. *The reasonable person is one who anticipates what might happen.* For older students, a good strategy is to work with the class to develop safety contracts that everyone in class will sign. These should be kept on file. A sample student safety contract can be found in Chapter 10. However, keep in mind that such a document does not absolve you of responsibility.

Summary

Try to break free of the idea that all science must occur on the top of a student's desk. Look outside the classroom window and consider how you can make what's out there a part of your science program. And ask *who* might be out there who can help with those lessons. Always make safety a part of your plan rather than a reason not to plan. Although it is simply not possible to plan for every contingency that might arise when students are involved, take time to consider the *likely* contingencies and what you can do to respond if necessary.

CONCLUSION

Planning and management, nuts and bolts, have been our focus in this chapter. We've looked at how teachers can work with students to plan and manage an inquiry-oriented classroom, a place where students' interests and ideas are respected and are the starting point of program planning. We have addressed practical matters, such as organizing the classroom space, scheduling, ensuring safety, conducting excursions, and selecting tools and resources to support science learning. How you set up the room reflects what you think is important about the learning that is to go on there. Providing prime time for science is important, too; students need time to investigate and to reflect, through discussions, drawing and writing, and other process activities.

We have also mentioned the importance of working with students to establish reliable classroom routines. But lesson plans are meant to guide, not bind. Excitement about learning grows when routines give way to exploration and adventure, as in taking studies into the field and community. Yet science investigations in and out of the classroom should be planned carefully to take into account risks and hazards. The bottom line is that safe conditions for learning require a proactive teacher.

9

Assessment and Evaluation

Distinguishing Between Assessment and Evaluation

Indirect Versus Direct Assessment

Alternative Forms of Assessment

Authentic Assessment Using Portfolios

Scoring Guides

Your Academic Roadmap

This chapter should help you to understand the following ideas:

- Assessment serves many purposes, from diagnostic to lesson design to evaluation.
- The application of acquired skills is performance-based assessment.
- There are alternative forms of assessment that are dynamic and encourage thinking on higher levels of Bloom's taxonomy of educational objectives.
- The outstanding advantage of portfolios as authentic assessment is that they provide evidence of individual gains in cognitive growth.
- Effective alternative assessment techniques appropriately reflect the content required by the curriculum, though in a manner most suitable for a student constructing new knowledge.

What happens to the stars during the day?

> *"They go to the Sun. After the stars go into the Sun, the Sun gets brighter and brighter. The stars make the Sun light up."*

—Sha'Lee, 6 years old

DISTINGUISHING BETWEEN ASSESSMENT AND EVALUATION

If we want to know how well students are doing in their science class, we must examine more than just one science learning domain (See Chapter 4 for the six domains of science education). We must assess not just students' acquisition of knowledge but also their development of skills of investigation and their affective development, the domain of feeling and valuing. Unfortunately, too many educators equate assessment with testing, and traditional means of testing have focused almost exclusively on the knowledge domain, which is the lowest level of Bloom's taxonomy—what the students can recall. The higher levels of understanding, the process skills, and the affective domain often have been overlooked. With the *National Science Education Standards* (National Research Council, 1996) the emphasis in the teaching of science has shifted to the active process of investigation, and therefore the process skills and inquiry must become integrated into assessment as well as instruction.

Assessment is the examination of student performance in order to appraise progress in meeting curriculum goals and objectives. Assessment involves the collection of materials to indicate learning. Assessment information is used to drive instruction. Evaluation, on the other hand, is the making of formal statements of judgment about the quality or value of the materials examined. Evaluation tends to be more summative and is the step *after* assessment.

In assessing you look at what changes have occurred as a result of your instruction. You want to know what your students know now, what skills they have acquired or further developed, and how their attitudes have changed. What you find out helps you to decide what further instruction will be appropriate. When the information collected through assessment is used to assign a grade or to revise the curriculum, it becomes *evaluation.* The two terms often are used interchangeably, but there is a distinction. Our focus in this chapter is primarily on assessment in two areas: designing effective instruction and measuring student performance.

INDIRECT VERSUS DIRECT ASSESSMENT

Traditional tests measure learning indirectly. That is, a question prompts a response that will indicate whether something is known. There was a time when this may have been appropriate, for instance, when information was not as readily available as it is in our day. However, given our access to resources today, such as the World Wide Web, an emphasis on recall in assessing science learning is no longer warranted. Instead, we need to find out what meanings students have constructed as a result of instruction and whether they can apply what they have learned.

Instead of tests, student products and performances that provide direct measures of cognitive changes are more consistent with current best practices for instruction, such as teaching science through inquiry. Performance-based assessment and, in particular, *performance tests,* which are conducted as hands-on science activities, represent direct measures of learning, in contrast to multiple-choice tests, for example. The latter elicit student responses that only indirectly demonstrate that learning has occurred. A demonstration of understanding includes both what students know and their ability to apply their knowledge. Thus, performance-based assessment is an advance over traditional paper-and-pencil testing. It reflects the ancient Chinese proverb:

I hear, and I forget.

I see, and I remember.

I do, and I understand.

Art, music, and physical education are components of the K–8 curriculum that are typically conducted outside students' regular classrooms. Other teachers are likely to be responsible for planning instruction in those subjects and assessing your students in them. Teachers in these areas have used performance-based assessment for many years. It is obvious that in physical education the best way to determine how well a student is doing is to observe the student's performance: If you want to know how well a student can swim, watch her swim. A paper-and-pencil test would not be of much use to determine the student's mastery of swimming.

Performance-based assessments such as this are equally useful in science education. Such assessments can determine how well your students have met your science lesson objectives. It is our responsibility as teachers to put students in situations where they supply *and* apply information. Performance-based assessment requires that students be actively involved in solving a problem or interpreting a situation rather than merely recalling information or eliminating distractors, as in a multiple-choice quiz. There are many techniques and alternative forms of assessment that you can use. Common to all forms are the characteristics listed in Table 9.1.

Table 9.1   Characteristics of Performance-Based Assessment

Assessment tasks require active student involvement.
Answers are created by students rather than identified from a list of choices.
Responses are produced by students rather than recalled from a text.

Source: Baron (1991).

ALTERNATIVE FORMS OF ASSESSMENT

Many alternative forms of assessment, in contrast to traditional assessment techniques, require students to construct responses to open-ended tasks rather than to select responses from a set of options. Some alternative forms, such as interviews and checklists, require teachers to observe or interact with students as their data are collected. Teachers may provide guidelines or initiate activities, but students generate the products to be used for assessment.

Interviews

Chapter 3 examined interviewing as a means of eliciting what students know about a topic before instruction. Because interviewing allows one-on-one conversation and follow-up probing, a student's personal explanations for natural phenomena can be accessed, and misconceptions can be identified. If several students are sampled, group patterns can be identified. In this case the assessment is *diagnostic* and is used directly for instructional planning.

Interviews can also be used as a means of assessment *after* instruction. By interviewing a sample of students after a unit has been taught, you can determine any changes that occurred in multiple domains. Areas of persistent misunderstanding can also be noted. Although interviewing can be time-consuming, much is to be gained in using interviewing as a means of assessment. You can use probing questions in order to identify subtleties in student understanding that would otherwise go unnoticed.

Checklists

Checklists are useful in observing students as they conduct individual and group work. For example, you might want to see whether students are following your directions correctly, making appropriate measurements, properly testing predictions, or classifying objects. Checklists allow you to record observable behaviors or demonstrations of skills that are key to learning in science. If checklists, such as the one in Figure 9.1, are designed in advance, you can simply indicate the desired behavior as "present" or "absent," "demonstrated" or "not demonstrated," or "observed" or "not observed." This minimizes the need to write a long description about individual behavior yet provides useful data for instructional decision making.

The main function of a checklist is to provide an organized way to document student progress in a minimum amount of time. There is a downside to simple checklists, however. Although using a checklist is an efficient way for you to document student performance during classroom activities, unless you include a column for your comments, a checklist does not tell you anything about the quality of the work demonstrated. Comments are optional but worthwhile because they provide detail.

Open-ended (divergent) questions usually do not have one correct answer but are designed to allow a variety of acceptable responses. They encourage thinking on multiple levels simultaneously and allow you to value all the ideas expressed by your students. Used formally or informally, open-ended questions

Figure 9.1 Sample Checklist Assessment

Checklist for Basic Process Skills

Name: _____   Date: _____

	Yes	No	Comments
Made prediction:	_____	_____	_____
Shared prediction:	_____	_____	_____
Tested prediction:	_____	_____	_____
Listed observations:	_____	_____	_____
Constructed inference:	_____	_____	_____
Open-ended questioning:	_____	_____	_____

Copyright © 2007 by Corwin Press. All rights reserved. Reprinted from *Teaching Constructivist Science, K–8: Nurturing Natural Investigators in the Standards-Based Classroom* by Michael L. Bentley, Edward S. Ebert II, and Christine Ebert. Thousand Oaks, CA: Corwin Press, www.corwinpress.com. Reproduction authorized only for the local school site or nonprofit organization that has purchased this book.

challenge students to supply *and* apply information. Contrasted with convergent questions, the divergent nature of open-ended questions allows different kinds of responses that may draw on personal experiences and new information acquired through instruction.

The way you word your questions is important. For instance, if you were to ask "What color is this object?" the answers offered would tend to be identical. However, by rewording the question to make it a divergent question, "How would you describe this object?," you would probably get varied responses and generate more student thinking. The responses might give the color but also shape and size, and nonvisual senses might be used with descriptions of texture, smell, or a sound produced by the object. The convergent question limits the potential responses, whereas the open-ended, divergent question encourages diversity and elaboration.

A different type of limitation occurs in this next example. Consider the different responses that would be evoked by these two questions about an investigation involving mealworms.

How many different behaviors did you notice?

What different behaviors did you notice?

Do you think that this teacher really wanted to know only the number of mealworm behaviors, or do you think that her intent was to have students generate a list of several ways in which the mealworms behaved in the presence of various stimuli? In oral questioning it is difficult to save student answers to use as evidence of understanding. A notebook with a page for each student is one way to keep a record of such anecdotal information. On the other hand, if the question is asked for a written response, student answers can be retained as evidence of their performance.

Science Journals

Journals can serve many purposes that may vary according to the subject, but journal entries can provide evidence of student progress in multiple domains. Students might use science journals to collect data during investigations, for example. That work can be used to assess skill development. If you consider it important for students to connect what they do in class to their lives outside school, you can ask them to make entries that do so. For example, your students might complete the following: "What we did in class today is similar to . . ." You can also ask them to make summative entries such as "Today, I learned . . ." and "My question now is . . ."

Your assessment of your students' journals depends on your objectives. If the intent is to chronicle activities such as observing bird behavior at a bird feeder, then the *regularity* of entries becomes important. If your purpose for the journal is to collect and record data from an experiment, then *accuracy* and *organization* become important. If you want your students to reflect on what they learned, then providing *feedback* and encouragement to elaborate or consider alternatives is most appropriate. In any case, it is important for you to decide ahead of time what your objectives are and to communicate that purpose to the students. Journal entries are also an excellent source of assessment data about students' attitudes and values.

Inquiry Reports

Inquiry reports are created by students in order to document the procedures and results of their investigations. An inquiry project may begin with a question from the teacher or, ideally, from the student. The student identifies a topic of personal interest, usually related to something being studied in the classroom. For example, the class may be studying oceans and ocean life. Some of your students may be content with what they have already learned, and others may be stimulated by the topic and want to know more. One student might be particularly interested in sharks, and another might want to know more about how hurricanes are formed, and still another might be interested in beaches and beach erosion. You invite each student to formulate a question that will serve as a focus of his or her inquiry. Each student or team of students might collect information in a variety of ways, ranging from Internet searches to visits to a local beach or aquarium to corresponding with an oceanographer (many institutional Web sites provide a "Contact us" link).

Once the information has been collected, each student can be called on to share what was learned with the class. This could be done either informally in a "science talk" or formally, as in a poster or PowerPoint presentation. Thus, the actual reporting can take many forms. It might be a combination of oral and written material and include inscriptions such as drawings and charts and artifacts such as photographs, concept maps, and charts.

Although inquiry reports provide evidence of student performance, they present special challenges for evaluation. One student's inquiry project may arise from an intense desire to learn more about a topic or the need to resolve personal uncertainty. Another inquiry project may result from a more superficial interest. A wide range of time and effort might have gone into each of those projects. Previous student experience with such assignments is also going to affect the quality of the product. Because one objective for this type of experience is that students learn to value and use a variety of sources of information to answer their questions, the criteria for evaluation may include gradually increasing the number of sources or types of sources accessed in subsequent inquiry projects.

When it comes to assessing the *amount* of information learned from an individual inquiry, perhaps the student is the best one to make that determination. General guidelines such as those in Figure 9.2 may be used to help students evaluate their own progress. Notice that the guidelines focus on reflection rather than on self-evaluation. This process is more apt to provide useful assessment data than if the student thought that a grade was on the line.

Inquiry projects are found in many commercial K–8 curricula that have an integrated or interdisciplinary focus. And although they may not be confined to science per se, they do exemplify an appropriate kind of science learning.

Figure 9.2   Reflection Form for Inquiry Reports

What I Learned During My Inquiry Project

Name: _____   Date: _____

Circle the number that best reflects how you feel about each statement.

A little bit   *A lot*
    1   2   3   4   5

1. I know more about this topic now than I did before I started my project.
    1   2   3   4   5

2. I used a variety of sources to find information.
    1   2   3   4   5

3. I am able to explain what I have learned to somebody else.
    1   2   3   4   5

4. Answering my inquiry question has increased my interest in the topic.
    1   2   3   4   5

Complete each of the following statements:

5. The most important or interesting thing I learned during the inquiry was _____.

6. If somebody else were to study this topic, my advice would be _____.

Copyright © 2007 by Corwin Press. All rights reserved. Reprinted from *Teaching Constructivist Science, K–8: Nurturing Natural Investigators in the Standards-Based Classroom* by Michael L. Bentley, Edward S. Ebert II, and Christine Ebert. Thousand Oaks, CA: Corwin Press, www.corwinpress.com. Reproduction authorized only for the local school site or nonprofit organization that has purchased this book.

Investigation Reports

Investigation reports are similar to inquiry reports in being open-ended. As before, the student conducts an investigation and then makes a report. But in this case, the form of investigation is in one of the formats we discussed in Chapter 5: trial and error, documenting, prediction testing, product testing, generating models, experimenting, reflecting, and inventing. Although the student's investigation is largely self-directed, the investigative technique has a particular structure to be followed.

Reporting on their investigation helps students organize their results, analyze what happened, apply their knowledge of the science, and share what they learned. As students construct their own understanding, you will note subtle differences in their observations and conclusions. Open-ended reports, as opposed to more traditional laboratory worksheets, allow these differences to be expressed. If students have only textbook-based lab worksheets to complete, that diversity in learning might go unnoticed.

This is not to say that there are no guidelines for the student report; guidelines vary according to the form of investigation being conducted. Teacher and students discuss and even negotiate expectations and the criteria to be used to evaluate the report. Common to all of the reports would be the following elements:

- A statement of the problem or question that focused the investigation.
- A description of all the steps involved in the investigation.
- A summary of the data or information collected (if applicable).
- A presentation of the solution to the problem or answer to the question.

The quality of the student's presentation and the level of detail in the report depend on his or her developmental level, ability, and experience, among other factors. In the differentiated classroom, as discussed in Chapter 6, you need to set standards by which to evaluate student performance based on individual learner characteristics. It is possible to have high standards for student achievement and at the same time maintain some flexibility in applying those standards case by case. Each student is going to personalize his or her investigation in terms of questions, observations, inferences, and insights. The activity leads the student to develop the skills and confidence to solve real problems. Therefore, your evaluation of the investigation report should emphasize the process over the product.

Inventions and Models

Investigations can also focus on the development of inventions and models. However, reports are not necessary for assessment to occur because the resulting model or invention provides the teacher with a concrete example of the student's work. When students generate their own models they include previously existing components and indicate how those parts are related. Inventions are unique in that the product is something that did not previously exist. The students combine the parts or ideas into newly created systems. Either type of investigation leads to the generation of a novel and personally satisfying product. So how do you assess something that has never existed before?

Whether assessing inventions or models, it is once again important to focus on the *process* rather than the product. These forms of investigation are opportunities for students to apply information in creative ways. Students with weak verbal skills typically do not perform well on written tests, yet they often excel when provided opportunities to demonstrate their understanding in this very concrete manner.

The purpose of the activity must be reflected in assessment criteria. If the invention is a Rube Goldberg contraption, then by definition it must be humorous and complex. If the purpose is to identify a personal problem and subsequently invent a practical solution to the problem, then the criteria should judge the effectiveness and practicality of the solution.

Modeling activities typically are done at first as a means of considering possibilities before exploring an existing model or the one used by the scientific community. If done the other way around, the student is under pressure to come up with a model that is better than what scientists already use. And when it is time to assess your students' work it would be inappropriate to judge their models against the scientifically accepted one. Instead, you should value ideas that express reasonable and possible solutions. The principal ingredients to look for are the recognition of the various components involved and some understanding of how the parts work together. Perhaps a modification of the reflection form in Figure 9.2 would also be appropriate.

Performance Tests

The techniques discussed thus far fall into the category of projects rather than testing techniques. However, there is a place in your science program for testing, although multiple-choice testing is not the option we prefer. In science, *performance tests* are used to assess students' abilities to supply and apply newly acquired knowledge and skills under the same time and access constraints normally associated with traditional testing. The difference is that performance tests are not limited to pencil-and-paper activities. The activities require that students interact with manipulatives just as they do during instruction. This type of testing allows students to demonstrate their skills rather than just write about them.

For example, if the class has been learning how to classify leaves, a performance test would be for them to actually classify a sample of leaves that you provide. The leaves may or may not be the same as those used during instruction. The challenge for the student is to be able to classify similar objects in a slightly different situation. Students would be provided with the leaves and then asked to classify them using a multistage classification scheme. In addition, they may be required to translate the scheme that they developed into a dichotomous key.

AUTHENTIC ASSESSMENT USING PORTFOLIOS

Authentic assessment is a recent approach to assessment that involves requiring students to demonstrate the behavior the lesson is intended to produce. A variety of alternative assessment strategies can be used in authentic assessment, including performance assessments, as just discussed, portfolio assessments, and even tests in the form of open-ended exams. The idea is that multiple sources of information about each student will lend more validity to your ultimate evaluation. In Table 9.2 various assessment methods are distributed into categories of tests, tasks, and observations. Tests are divided into selected response and open-ended or constructed response categories, and tasks are divided into products and performances. Portfolios are listed under "tasks" and are the most comprehensive form of authentic assessment in that they combine several forms of alternative assessments and provide multiple and diverse examples of student-generated products.

Table 9.2   Categories of Assessment Methods

Tests		Tasks		Systematic Observation
Answers Selected	Answers Constructed	Artifact or Inscription	Performance	
Multiple choice	Fill-in blank	Individual or team project	Oral presentation	Oral responses
True–false	Short answer	Report of an investigation	Report of an investigation	Interview data
Matching	Open-ended response	Science portfolio	Demonstration	Record of behaviors
	Graphic organizer or concept map	Science journal or log	Debate or structured controversy	Check list
	Diagram or figural representation	Web page or PowerPoint	Multimedia presentation	Running record or anecdotal record
	Essay	Physical or drawn model	Musical or dance performance	
	Drawing with labels	Graphic organizer or concept map	Skit or dramatic performance	
	"Show your work" or explanation	Exhibit, poster, or display	Contest	
		Essay or research paper		
		Story		
		Videotape		
		Poem		

Source: Adapted from Doll (1996, pp. 258–259).

Table 9.3   Assumptions About Portfolios as Used in Assessment

Portfolios are systematic, purposeful, and meaningful collections of student work in one or more subjects.

Students of any age can learn not only to select pieces to be placed into their portfolios but also to establish criteria for selection.

Portfolios should be ongoing so that they show student effort, progress, and achievement over a period of time.

In all cases, portfolios should reflect the actual day-to-day learning activities of students.

Portfolios may contain several compartments or subfolders and may include input by teachers, parent, administrators, and peers.

Selected works in portfolios may be in a variety of media and may be multidimensional.

Source: De Fina (1992, pp. 13–16).

The Nature of Portfolios

Portfolios are representative collections of student work samples over a given period of time (Hope, 2005). Typically students select the samples of their own work to be included, and the process allows reflection and self-evaluation. Whereas tests provide a snapshot of student achievement at a particular moment, portfolios allow a longer-term view of student achievement. They focus on personal growth by displaying performance on a variety of tasks over time, whether a 6- or 9-week grading period, a semester, or multiple years of schooling. In addition, portfolios can include samples across various subject areas. Portfolios not only reflect student skills and knowledge, but they also tell teachers something about how students organize and communicate information.

Portfolios go beyond assessment for its own sake, beyond sampling student work, to providing evidence of *individual gains* in cognitive growth. They show how much improvement a student has made. Samples of work from September can be compared with similar work in January and again in May. Progress will be apparent and available for consideration by the student, the teacher, and the parents or other interested parties.

Portfolios are defined in various ways, including definitions based on the *intent* of portfolios, which reflects the individual application of the process. However, the assumptions about portfolios listed in Table 9.3 may help you understand portfolio assessment.

In some cases, teachers may select entries that go into the student portfolios. More often, teachers give students guidance about the selection of materials that go into their portfolios, and the student selects the entries. The purpose of the portfolio will influence the actual items selected for inclusion.

Although portfolios often are used to examine student achievement in an interdisciplinary fashion, they can also be subject specific. A list of various

Table 9.4   Types of Evidence Appropriate for Science Portfolios

Investigation reports
Inventions and models
Observational checklists completed by students or teachers
Inquiry records
Reports of group work
Logs or journals
Graded tests
Individual questions and wonderings
Reflections and self-evaluations (on the portfolio as a whole, on each section, or on particular projects or work samples)

types of science-related documentation that could serve as evidence for learning are provided in Table 9.4.

An effective science portfolio design should reflect the conceptualization of science as having multiple domains (see Chapter 4, Figure 4.1). The *process* dimension of science has been described in terms of the science process skills (e.g., observing, predicting, classifying) and various forms of scientific investigation (e.g., documenting, inventing, experimenting). The *knowledge* dimension of science is described as the information gained through listening, reading, and investigation and research. It can take the form of answers to questions or new questions that continue the search. The domain of feeling and valuing, or *attitude* dimension, is the driving force of learning. The student's curiosity and inquisitiveness generate investigations and subsequently the construction of new knowledge. Elements of this category could be demonstrated in the *reflection and evaluation* component of the portfolio. The portfolio should include an appropriate balance of the various domain elements, and that balance should reflect the instructional setting.

For instance, if you are teaching first or second grade, where more emphasis and instructional time (perhaps half) are placed on activities that foster the science process skills and investigations, then the portfolio entries ought to also reflect that. Perhaps 50% of the work samples will demonstrate skills, 20% will demonstrate content learning, and the remaining 30% will demonstrate a positive attitude toward science. On the other hand, if you are teaching fifth or sixth graders, then a higher percentage of items selected for the portfolio might demonstrate cognitive development.

Students will need to be informed early on about the criteria you will use to evaluate their portfolios. A rubric might be developed for this purpose, and you should go over it with students so that they are clear about your expectations. Depending on the grade level, typical evaluation criteria might include evidence of appropriate mastery of several forms of investigation conducted in the time period (e.g., prediction testing, documenting, and experimenting), construction of two or more different types of graphs of data collected, drawings or graphics showing competence in multistage classification, an inquiry project report, journal entries demonstrating personal wonderings or questions that are to be pursued in the future, and the student's evaluation of the materials in the portfolio and a statement concluding what it represents in terms of change, growth, or achievement. The first three criteria concentrate on the process, one examines newly acquired information, and two reflect the attitudes the teacher wants to foster. Thus, the portfolio is a vehicle for collecting materials and products that represent student performance, skills, and attitudes.

Some student work will be in written in the form of reports, journal entries, personal wonderings, and test results. The collection may include photographs and inscriptions related to the students' projects, as in the case of inventions and models. The collection also might include objects such as audiotapes or videotapes, in which case the portfolio takes on multimedia dimensions. It will be important to decide how student projects can best be represented in the portfolio, by photographs, drawings, or even pages indicating where the project is stored and can be accessed. Regardless, the portfolio should not be limited to a folder, and older students may even want to create an electronic portfolio.

The nature of portfolios is to provide an ongoing record of progress. In order to demonstrate individual student gains, samples of work must be placed in the portfolios at regular intervals throughout the instructional period. Perhaps our most valuable recommendations are these: Communicate the purpose of the portfolios and the evaluation criteria to your students, and allow them an active role in deciding what examples of their work should be placed in the portfolio.

Activity 9.1 Designing a Portfolio

Consider how you would design a portfolio to represent your own work in a recent course you have taken. Think about the activities, projects, and tests you completed and decide what you would include in your own portfolio. Write out your plan as if it were to be distributed to new students just beginning the course. Be sure that your design indicates the following:

A balance of the science domains

Specific items that will be included

A description of how reflection and self-evaluation will be a part of the portfolio

An indication of how much emphasis the portfolio should receive if it is to count for a portion of your grade in the course

Alternatively, consider the design of a portfolio to represent your achievements and abilities for the purpose of seeking a teaching position.

SCORING GUIDES

Alternative assessments and portfolios become more meaningful when criteria for evaluation are established and communicated to students. In Kuhs's (1997) discussion of portfolio evaluation and grading, she stresses the importance of guides or rubrics in this way: "Evaluation that involves more than a 'right answer' approach requires guidelines to govern scoring. If the criteria, or focus, of the evaluation are not specifically defined and made known to students, the teachers' subjectivity may be questioned" (p. 58).

Scoring guides provide a means for teachers to know what they expect and for students to know what is expected of them. For each learner outcome, the guide describes anticipated levels or standards of accomplishment. Once the guide is generated, the teacher can compare each student's work sample with the guide and determine a rating or score. The scoring guide in Table 9.5 is a modification of Price and Hein's (1994) General Scoring Rubric. It provides descriptions in terms so general that they would apply to almost any project. From this example, you could develop specific guides for your own classroom situation. Although this example has five categories, you may want to give more weight to one category than to another. You can establish point values that are appropriate based on your own instructional goals. Again, be sure to communicate this to your students before an assignment is due.

A more specific example may help demonstrate the versatility of scoring guides. The students in Ms. Davis's class conducted product tests, examining several dishwashing liquids to determine which makes the largest and the longest-lasting soap bubbles. When each student team designed a test and determined an outcome, the class results were tabulated on the board. A logical extension of the activity would be to graph the data. In the past, Ms. Davis's students have worked on graphing skills. Because graphing is an appropriate way to analyze the data collected in product testing, she decided to ask each team to construct a graph that represented the results of the activity. So far, so good.

Table 9.5   Adapted General Scoring Rubric

Poor:	The product was not completed or shows no evidence that the student comprehends the activity.
Inadequate:	The product does not satisfy many of the criteria, contains errors, or does not accomplish the given task.
Fair:	The product does not contain major errors or omit crucial information and does meet some of the criteria.
Good:	The product substantially or completely meets the criteria.
Outstanding:	All criteria are met, and the product exceeds expectations or includes additional, outstanding features.

Source: After Price and Hein (1994).

Figure 9.3 Ms. Davis's Scoring Guide for Graphing

Criteria	Yes	No
Accurate display of data using a graph	_____	_____
Both axes of graph labeled appropriately	_____	_____
Key to graph is accurate	_____	_____
Title of graph is relevant	_____	_____
Data are displayed at equal intervals on both axes	_____	_____

Points _____ (score equals the total number of checks under "Yes")

Copyright © 2007 by Corwin Press. All rights reserved. Reprinted from *Teaching Constructivist Science, K–8: Nurturing Natural Investigators in the Standards-Based Classroom* by Michael L. Bentley, Edward S. Ebert II, and Christine Ebert. Thousand Oaks, CA: Corwin Press, www.corwinpress.com. Reproduction authorized only for the local school site or nonprofit organization that has purchased this book.

As the teacher, Ms. Davis must then evaluate her students' work. She needs to provide feedback to her students on whether their work met the lesson objectives and her expectations. She also knows that there is not just one way of graphing the information. The assessment must allow some flexibility while also meeting certain standards. So how can Ms. Davis decide how well each student has done on the graphing?

First, appropriate criteria for judging the quality and accuracy of the work must be identified. Once criteria are listed, statements that describe the levels of quality can be written. The scoring guide that Ms. Davis thought would be appropriate for evaluating the graphing activity is provided in Figure 9.3.

A scoring guide has its greatest value when it is understood by the teacher and the students before the activity begins. The teacher can better define his or her own instructional plans by first establishing what will be considered important in terms of assessment. The students will be able to perform with more focus if they know what is expected of them. It is often beneficial in this regard to involve the students in the design of the scoring guide. Certainly this is not appropriate under all circumstances, but even young students can indicate what they think are important outcomes when given particular tasks to accomplish. You can then negotiate with the students regarding additional criteria you consider to be important. Notice that this does not necessarily lead to a lowering of standards but in fact can result in *raising* standards. Consider the last time you were given input into establishing expectations on an assignment. Did you or any of your classmates first look to find the easiest way out? What do you suppose would be the result if all students went through school having input in setting realistic and challenging standards for their work?

CONCLUSION

In many ways teaching is both an art and a science. What makes it so is the creativity needed to align *curriculum* (expectations for student learning), *instruction* (experiences to facilitate acquisition of new skills and information), and *assessment* (the means for ascertaining student progress). The educational theory, instructional strategies, and assessment techniques we've described specifically seek to accomplish such an alignment. Our vision is to make K–8 science education an interactive and positive learning experience for all students, an experience that capitalizes on students' natural curiosity and the cognitive process of constructing knowledge.

Assessment is something that many educators are reluctant to address because for them it is hard to make value judgments about someone's work and to assign a grade to it. And that is true. It is often difficult to declare one set of values to be the correct one. However, without assessment there would be no way of describing your students' developmental progress in the various domains. With assessment, teachers can describe students' level of understanding at the beginning of the school year and again at the end of the year. Assessment allows you to collect evidence and describe individual growth and improvement for each student.

The several alternative forms of assessment discussed in this chapter are consistent with the types of activities known to be most effective in instructional settings. That is, assessment can be embedded in instruction. No longer do we have to think of instruction as a time of activity and purposeful problem solving and consider testing a totally different type of activity. Whereas instruction allows discovery, exploration, and clarification, performance-based assessment allows application of newly acquired skills and information. Effective assessment techniques are those that reflect the goals and objectives the curriculum.

10

A Compendium
of Resources

Safety in the Elementary Classroom

Concept Interviews: Sample Interview Questions

Planning Science Field Trips

Useful Recipes and Formulas

Animal Care in the Classroom

Resources for Teaching Science

Your Academic Roadmap

This chapter is a compendium of resources for the teaching of science.

The roads that lead to knowledge are as wondrous as that knowledge itself.

—Johannes Kepler, 1604

SAFETY IN THE ELEMENTARY CLASSROOM

First Aid

Excluding life-saving measures, teachers may only stop bleeding and apply water (as to burns, acid spills).

Safety Goggles

In general, whenever any chemicals are used in any science activities, or where objects or liquids might fly into the air, children should wear safety goggles. Purchase safety glasses according to purpose: Some types of goggles protect against chemical splashes, other types against object impacts. Be aware of students who wear contact lenses because these can be dangerous if a chemical is splashed into the eyes.

General Safety Practices for Teachers Related to Science

• Know state and local safety regulations and school policies and procedures for dealing with accidents.

• Check your classroom regularly to be sure that safety is being maintained. Equipment and materials should be stored properly. Hazardous materials should never be left in the classroom.

• Before handling equipment and materials, be familiar with possible hazards.

• Be particularly cautious when using fire.

• Be familiar with school fire regulations, evacuation procedures, and the location and use of fire extinguishers.

• Point out potential hazards and precautions to be taken at the start of a science activity.

• Limit the number of students working in a group so that the activity can be carried out without creating confusion or an accident.

• Allow sufficient time for students to perform activities. Have equipment and materials properly cleaned and stored after use.

• Remind students never to taste or touch substances in the science classroom without first obtaining the teacher's permission.

• Tell students to report accidents or injuries to you immediately, no matter how minor.

- Tell students not to touch their face, mouth, eyes, or other parts of the body while working with plants, animals, or chemical substances until they have washed their hands.

- Whenever possible and appropriate, substitute plastic for glassware in activities.

- Hard glass test tubes should not be heated from the bottom; instruct students to tip them slightly but not toward themselves or anyone else.

- Have a whisk broom and dustpan available for cleaning up.

- Caution students not to drink from containers used for science activities.

- Thermometers used in the K–8 classroom should be filled with alcohol, not mercury.

- Doors must not be blocked, and flammable materials should never be stored near doors.

Suggestions for Working With Chemicals

- Do not allow students to mix chemicals "just to see what happens."

- Tell students never to taste chemicals and to wash their hands after use.

- Don't allow students to mix acids and water.

- Combustible materials should be kept in a locked metal cabinet.

- Lock away chemicals in a cool, dry place but not in a refrigerator.

- Store only small amounts of chemicals in the classroom. Unused chemicals that could become unstable should be discarded properly. Consult with your school administrator.

Suggestions for Working With Electricity

- Provide safety instruction related to the use of electricity.

- Caution students not to play with the electric current of their home circuits.

- Keep extension cords in good condition. Connecting cords should be short and plugged in at the closest outlet. Grasp the plug, not the cord, when disconnecting.

- Do not use extension cords for electrical tools such as heating elements for terraria and aquaria, hot plates, or small motors; use only three-prong (grounded) plugs.

- Explain to students that tap water conducts electricity. Children should dry their hands before touching electrical cords, switches, or appliances.

Copyright © 2007 by Corwin Press. All rights reserved. Reprinted from *Teaching Constructivist Science, K–8: Nurturing Natural Investigators in the Standards-Based Classroom* by Michael L. Bentley, Edward S. Ebert II, and Christine Ebert. Thousand Oaks, CA: Corwin Press, www.corwinpress.com. Reproduction authorized only for the local school site or nonprofit organization that has purchased this book.

Upper elementary and middle school students should be asked to sign a safety contract at the beginning of the school year.

Student Safety Contract

I agree to:

_____ Obey my teacher's written and verbal instructions in the classroom, lab, and in the field.

_____ Keep my eyes, face, hands, and body safe while participating in activities.

_____ Keep my work area clean and tidy.

_____ Know where to find and how to use the first aid kit and fire extinguisher.

_____ Report all injuries, no matter how minor, to my teacher.

_____ Know what to do in an emergency.

_____ Always be responsible while participating in activities in the classroom, lab, and in the field.

I, _____, have read and agree to abide by these safety guidelines.

Date: _____

Student Signature _____

To the Parent/Guardian

Your child will be participating in science investigations in the classroom and in the field during this course. In order to assure his/her personal safety and the safety of others, it is important the above rules are followed. Failure to do so may result in restricting the offending student from completing the activity.

We have read, understand, and agree to follow the safety rules and procedures as written in this document.

Date _____ Parent/Guardian _____

[__] *Please check here if student wears contact lenses.*

CONCEPT INTERVIEWS: SAMPLE INTERVIEW QUESTIONS

Day and Night

1. Where does the light of day come from?

2. Where does the darkness of night come from?

3. Why does a day end?

4. What makes day change to night?

5. What happens to the Sun during the day?

6. What happens to the stars during the day?

7. What happens to the Moon during the day?

8. Have you ever seen the Moon at night? If yes, what did it look like? If no, why not?

9. Have you ever seen the Moon during the day? If no, why not? If yes, what did it look like?

10. Is the Moon always the same shape? If yes, why? If no, why does the Moon's shape change?

11. If you were on the Moon and looked up at the sky *during the day,* what would the sky look like?

12. If you were on the Moon and looked up at the sky *during the night,* what would the sky look like?

Sound

For this interview you will need two glass soft drink bottles partially filled with water. One bottle must have noticeably more water than the other bottle.

1. What is sound?

2. Where does sound come from?

3. How does sound travel?

4. Does sound travel through air? How? or Why not?

5. Does sound travel through water? How? or Why not?

6. Does sound travel through solid wood? How? or Why not?

7. How is it that you can hear sounds from one room while you are in another room?

8. (Point to the bottle with the small amount of water.) If you were to blow air across the top of this bottle, would it make a higher or lower sound than the other bottle? Why?

9. (Point to the bottle with the large amount of water.) If you were to blow air across the top of this bottle, would it make a higher or lower sound than the other bottle? Why?

10. (Point to the bottle with the larger amount of water.) If you were to tap this bottle with an object, would it make a sound? Why? or Why not?

11. (Point to the bottle with the larger amount of water.) If you were to tap this bottle with an object, would it make a higher or lower sound than the other bottle? Why?

12. Why can't you hear the broadcast from a radio station unless you have a radio turned on?

Light and Shadows

For this interview you will need a rod-shaped object, such as a wooden dowel or unused piece of chalk.

1. What can you tell me about shadows?

2. Where does a shadow come from?

3. Can you make a shadow disappear? How? or Why not?

4. Can you make a shadow appear where you want it? How? or Why not?

5. Can you make your own shadow smaller? How? or Why not?

6. Can you make your own shadow larger? How? or Why not?

7. (Show the student the rod.) What would the shadow of this object look like? Might the shadow be another shape? What would that shape be?

8. Can you make the shadow of this object smaller? How? or Why not?

9. Can you make the shadow of this object larger? How? or Why not?

10. What is the largest shadow you have ever seen?

Light

1. Does a candle make light? How? or Why not?

2. How far from the candle does the light go?

3. How is it that you are able to see the light of the candle?

4. How is it that you can see the candle?

Repeat questions in the same sequence, substituting *Sun, Moon,* and *flashlight* for the word *candle.*

Seasons

These questions are for the temperate zone and may need to be changed depending on your locale. If you have rainy and dry seasons, then the questions should reflect that situation.

1. What can you tell me about the seasons? Can you name them?

2. Why are there different seasons? Is there a particular order for the seasons? What is the order? or Why not?

3. How can you tell when it is winter? Are there any other signs that it is winter?

4. How can you tell when it is spring? Are there any other signs that it is spring?

5. How can you tell when it is summer? Are there any other signs that it is summer?

6. How can you tell when it is autumn? Are there any other signs that it is autumn?

7. What causes the seasons to change?

Electricity

1. What is electricity?

2. Where does electricity come from?

3. How does electricity make a light bulb light?

4. What happens inside the bulb?

5. What happens inside the wires?

6. How does a battery make electricity?

7. What is the difference between *static electricity* and *current electricity*?

8. What is the difference between *parallel* and *series* circuits?

9. Can you *make* electricity? How? or Why not?

Magnetism

1. What is a magnet?

2. Where do magnets come from?

3. Can you make a magnet?

4. Is a penny (dime, nickel, aluminum foil, paper clip, pencil) attracted to a magnet? Why or Why not?

5. Will a magnet attract an object if the object is in water?

6. Will a magnet attract an object if the object is in a cardboard box?

7. What is the difference between a temporary magnet and a permanent magnet?

8. Can you make a magnet with electricity? How? or Why not?

9. Can you make electricity with a magnet? How? or Why not?

10. Why is a magnet marked with an *N* and an *S*?

11. If like poles repel each other, why does the north magnetic pole of a compass point to the North Pole of the Earth?

PLANNING SCIENCE FIELD TRIPS

Field Trip Safety

When an excursion is well organized, a few precautions can promote safety for all participants.

• Never be complacent when children are in your care, and always be alert for the unexpected.

• One or more additional responsible adults, known and approved by the school administration, should accompany the teacher on the trip.

- Parent or guardian permissions should be solicited and received before a student is allowed to go on a field trip.

- Send home with each participant a list identifying appropriate clothing to be worn and the equipment and supplies students should bring to school to take on the trip.

- To prevent ticks and other insect bites, plant poisoning, or scratches, participants should wear clothing that covers legs and arms.

- Carry a first aid kit on the trip. Maintain the kit so that that it contains the essential first aid items.

- No trip should be taken to any body of water unless an adult in the group is familiar with rules of water safety as described in first aid handbooks or the *American Red Cross Senior Lifesaving Manual*.

- If the trip is near or in the water of a stream, river, lake, or ocean, participants should be taught to recognize any dangerous aquatic or marine plants and animals common to the area.

- If wading in the water is part of the field experience, footwear should be worn, and the buddy system should be used. Personal flotation devices (PFDs) should be available for wading when appropriate.

- Trips to industrial or construction sites and laboratories must be well supervised. An official plant representative should be present.

- When in the field, children should be taught never to pick any unknown wildflowers, seeds, berries, or cultivated plants and never to eat any fungi (mushrooms).

Toxic Plants

The following is only a partial list of toxic plants. Become aware of poisonous (toxic) plants in your field trip locality.

Plants Poisonous to the Touch

Poison ivy (often found on school grounds), poison oak, poison sumac

Plants Poisonous When Eaten

Many fungi (mushrooms)

Aconite

Belladonna

Wake robin

Henbane

Hemlock

Pokeweed (berries)

Tansy

Foxglove

Indian tobacco

Jimsonweed

Plants With Toxic Saps

Oleander

Poinsettia

Trumpet vine

Note: Many common houseplants also are toxic (Hardin & Arena, 1977).

USEFUL RECIPES AND FORMULAS

Measures are given here in customary units for teacher convenience. However, when working with students you may want to convert the measures into metric units. Several Internet sites perform such conversions automatically (see www.convertit.com or www.convert-me.com).

Sterilizer for Safety Goggles

Pour one-half cup chlorine bleach in a pail (5 gallons) of water. Dip the goggles and dry.

Everyday Cleaning Solution

Mix 2 oz. trisodium phosphate and 1 oz. sodium oleate in 1 pint distilled water. Soak apparatus in a warm solution 10–15 minutes, then brush with stiff brush. The chemicals are available from paint supply stores.

Goop

Keep goop in a well sealed jar or can. Goop can be refreshed by adding water (caution: will stain wood and fabrics).
Recipe (makes about 1 1/2 cups):

1/2 tsp. borax detergent (soap and detergent section in supermarkets)

1/4 cup water

1/4 cup cornstarch

1/2 cup white craft glue

2 tsp. food coloring (optional)

Dissolve the borax in the water. Put the cornstarch in another bowl, add the glue, and stir until mixed. Add the borax liquid, stirring constantly for about 2 minutes, even after the goop forms. Knead until no longer sticky.

Play Dough

Store play dough for up to 6 months in sealed plastic bags or lidded plastic containers in the refrigerator (return to room temperature before use). Food coloring can be mixed in as play dough is made. The work surface can be protected with wax paper.

Recipe (makes 2 cups):

1 1/2 cups water

2 tsp. food coloring

2 tbsp. cooking oil

2 cups flour

1/2 cup salt

4 tbsp. cream of tartar

Combine water, coloring, and oil in a bowl. Put flour, salt, and cream of tartar in a saucepan. Pour the liquid mix into the saucepan, stirring and heating (medium heat) until a ball of dough forms (about 5 minutes). Cool for several minutes, and knead until uniform.

Bubble Mix

Store in half-liter plastic soda bottles. Children can create bubble makers from a variety of materials, including a pair of glasses without lenses, a length of wire or clothes hanger curved into a wand, or the tops cut off of a plastic soda bottle.

Recipe (makes 2 cups):

1 cup dishwashing detergent

1/2 cup or less glycerine (available at pharmacies)

1/2 cup water

Combine all ingredients and mix. Pour into containers that have a large opening for dipping wands. Mix can also be poured on flat Formica tabletops in thin puddles, then bubbles can be blown into the puddle with soda straws. When these bubbles pop they leave a footprint that can be measured with a ruler or measuring tape. An investigation might be to compare various recipes or different detergents for the largest bubble. A math link would be to measure radius, diameter, and circumference. If you can't obtain glycerine, clear corn syrup can be added to a water-detergent mix to make better bubbles. For a small quantity, mix 1/2 cup water with 3 tbsp. of liquid detergent and 1 1/2 tbsp. of corn syrup, or try experimenting with proportions for the best mix.

Fingerpaint

Recipe makes 3/4 cup of each color.

1 envelope unflavored gelatin

2 1/2 cups cold water

1 cup cornstarch

1/2 cup soap flakes

2 drops each of four colors of icing color paste (available at craft or baking supply stores)

Put half a cup of the water into a bowl and sprinkle in the gelatin until dissolved. In a saucepan over medium heat, mix the cornstarch, the soap flakes, and the rest of the water. Stir in the gelatin mixture and continue to stir until the mixture thickens. Prepare four containers for the different colors. Strain the warm mix equally into the containers. Let cool for about an hour, then fold in icing color paste for each container. Store in the refrigerator. The materials are safe for students to use but should not be eaten.

Beet Juice Indicator

Beet juice is an indicator that changes color as the pH of a solution changes. Beet juice is red in acidic solutions and blue in basic solutions.

Wash and slice a fresh beet. Place several slices of beet into a pan containing 1 cup of water.

Heat until boiling and continue heating for about 5 minutes.

Remove the beet slices and allow the red liquid to cool. Store in dropper bottles.

Iodine Indicator

Iodine indicator is a test for the presence of starch. It turns blue-black when starch is present.

Dissolve 10 g of potassium iodide in 100 ml of water.

Add 5 g of iodine crystals and mix. Store the solution in brown dropper bottles.

Tincture of iodine obtained from a drugstore may also be used as an indicator.

Note: Iodine stains hands and clothes and is toxic. Have students wear goggles and follow safety precautions when using iodine indicator.

Red Cabbage Juice Indicator

Red cabbage juice is an indicator that changes to red in acidic solutions and green or blue in basic solutions.

Tear about five leaves of red cabbage into small pieces and place them in a saucepan.

Add 1 liter (or 1 quart) of water, bring to a boil, and simmer until the water turns a deep purple.

Pour the liquid through a strainer or cheesecloth into a bottle. Keep refrigerated.

ANIMAL CARE IN THE CLASSROOM

Personnel at the local humane society or zoo are good sources of information about providing healthy habitats for animals in the classroom. Mammals may bite, scratch, and kick to protect themselves and their young. Dogs, cats, rabbits, guinea pigs, and similar pets should be handled with care and should not be disturbed when eating. The following are some points to consider when planning rules to adopt for your classroom.

• Do not allow students to bring wild animals, either alive or deceased, into the classroom. Snapping turtles, snakes, insects, or arachnids (spiders, ticks, mites) should be restricted or handled only by competent adults.

• Provide appropriate habitats for animals. Keep animal quarters clean and free from contamination. Be sure the enclosure can be closed securely. Plan ahead for animal care on weekends and holidays.

• Obtain your classroom animals from a reputable supplier. Choose fish from tanks in which all the fish appear healthy.

• When observing unfamiliar animals, don't permit children to touch or pick them up.

• Children should be told never to tease animals or to put fingers or objects through wire mesh cages. Children with animal bites or scratches should be taken to the school nurse.

• Pick up rats, rabbits, hamsters, and mice by the scruff of the neck, placing a hand under the body to give support. Because the mother will be protective if young animals are being handled, move the mother to another cage.

• Use gloves for handling animals, and have children wash their hands before and after they handle animals.

For additional information, see the Humane Society of the United States Web site (www.hsus.org).

RESOURCES FOR TEACHING SCIENCE

Materials and Supplies Commonly Used in Teaching Science

Glue	Extension cords	Rubber bands
Aquarium	Pipe cleaners	Thermometers (metric)
Rulers (metric)	Funnels (small and large)	Egg cartons
Bags (paper, plastic)	Sandpaper	Hotplate
Iron filings	Pulleys	Food coloring
Balances	Buttons	Shoeboxes
Lenses	Balloons	Aluminum foil
Magnets	Balls	Magnifiers or hand lenses
Scissors	Barometer and wind vane	Seeds (such as radish)
Medicine droppers	Sponges	Clothespins
Meter sticks	Steel wool	Coat hangers
Metric weights	String, twine, and rope	Compasses
Microscopes	Styrofoam cups	Construction paper
Mirrors	Modeling clay	Copper wire
Masking tape	Paper cups	Cotton balls
Cellophane tape	Dowel rods	Craft sticks
Paper towels	Rocks	Mineral specimens
Containers	Baby food jars	Pill bottles
Film canisters	Batteries	Toothpicks
Tweezers	Plastic spoons and knives	Waxed paper
Plastic wrap	Flashlight	Vinegar
Sand	Paraffin wax	Tongs
Baking soda	Small bulbs, flashlight size	Sugar
Salt	Matches or lighter (keep secure)	Measuring cups (metric and customary)

Multipurpose small animal cage	Mechanical toys (e.g., tops, toy cars)	Straws and plastic tubing
Saw, hammer, screwdriver, pliers	Candles (birthday candles and table size)	

Internet Search Engines

Commercial Web sites change frequently. Use your favorite Internet browser search engine to find the Web sites for the magazines and journals below and for the science equipment and material suppliers.

Google: www.google.com

Yahoo: www.yahoo.com

Ask.com: www.ask.com/

SavvySearch, which allows you to conduct keyword Net searches using 19 search engines simultaneously (via Colorado State University): guaraldi.cs .colostate.edu:2000/

Argus Clearinghouse, a metadirectory that lists only guides and directories, not content sites themselves: www.clearinghouse.net/

Periodicals

Journals and Magazines for Developing Content

American Scientist, Science, Nature, Scientific American, The Ecologist, The Sciences (New York Academy of Science), *New Scientist, American Scientist, Technology Review, Issues in Science and Technology, New England Journal of Medicine, Discover Magazine, Science News, Popular Science, National Geographic, Natural History, Smithsonian Magazine, Science Daily, Geotimes*

Magazines That Address Issues in Science, Technology, and Society

Audubon, E: The Environmental Magazine, Environment Magazine, Greenpeace Magazine, National Wildlife, Sierra Magazine, On Earth Magazine, World Watch Magazine, Science in Society, Mother Earth News, Grist Magazine, Our Planet Magazine (U.N.E.P.), *Orion Magazine, EarthLight Magazine, Skeptical Inquirer*

Professional Journals Relevant to Science Education

Australian Science Teachers Journal, Electronic Journal of Science Education, Journal of Research in Science Teaching, Journal of Science Teacher Education, Journal of Science Education and Technology, Journal of Elementary Science Education, School Science and Mathematics, Science Education, Science Education International (Journal of the International Council of Associations for Science Education), Science Education Review, Journal of Chemical Education

Periodicals for Teaching Ideas

Science Activities, Science and Children (elementary journal of the National Science Teachers Association), *Science Scope* (middle grades), *AIMS Magazine, Teaching PreK–8, Scholastic*

Periodicals With Science Content for Children

Dig (archeology, ages 5–9), *Chickadee* (ages 5–9), *Kids Discover* (ages 6 and up), *Muse* (from Smithsonian, ages 9–14), *National Geographic Kids* (ages 8–14), *Odyssey: Adventures in Science* (ages 10–16), *Owl Magazine* (ages 8 and up), *Ranger Rick* and *Your Big Backyard* (from National Wildlife Federation, ages 7 and up for *Ranger Rick* and 3–7 for *Backyard*), *Yes Mag* (ages 8–14), *Cousteau Kids* (from Cousteau Society, formerly *Dolphin Log*, ages 7–13), *Science Weekly* (K–6 editions), *Zoobooks* (ages 5–12)

Suppliers of Equipment, Textbooks, Materials, and Media for Teaching Science

Biological Sciences Curriculum Study (BSCS)

Broderbund Software

Cambridge Development Laboratory, Inc.

Carolina Biological

Central Scientific Co.

Charles Scribner's

Charles E. Merrill Books

Churchill Media

Delta Education (materials kits and general elementary and middle school science equipment)

D.C. Heath and Co.

Edmund Scientific

Encyclopedia Britannica Educational Corporation

Fisher Scientific

Frey Scientific

HarperCollins Publishers

Holt, Rinehart and Winston

Hubbard Scientific

Insights Visual Productions, Inc.

Instructional Video

Lawrence Hall of Science Discovery Corner

Macmillan/McGraw-Hill

Microsoft Corporation

Nasco

National Geographic Society

Optical Data Corporation

Phoenix/BFA Films and Video, Inc.

Raintree Publishers, Inc.

Sargent-Welch

Scholastic

Science Kit & Boreal Laboratories

Science News Books

Scott, Foresman and Co.

Silver Burdett and Ginn

Society for Visual Education

Sunburst Communications, Inc.

Tom Snyder Productions

Troll Associates

Vernier Software (for probeware, electronic measuring instruments that transfer data directly into computer data processing software)

Videodiscovery, Inc.

Wards

Internet Homepages of Professional Associations Related to Science Education

American Association of Physics Teachers (AAPT): www.aapt.org/

American Chemical Society (ACS): www.acs.org

American Federation of Teachers (AFT): www.aft.org

Council for Elementary Science International (CESI): www.cesiscience.org/

National Association of Biology Teachers (NABT): www.nabt.org/

National Association of Geoscience Teachers (NAGT): www.nagt.org

National Association for Multicultural Education (NAME): www.nameorg.org

National Association for Research in Science Teaching (NARST): www.educ.sfu.ca/narstsite/

National Education Association (NEA): www.nea.org/

National Marine Educators Association (NMEA): www.marine-ed.org/

National Middle Level Science Teachers' Association (NMLSTA): www.nsta.org/nmlsta/

National Science Teachers Association (NSTA): www.nsta.org

North American Association for Environmental Education (NAAEE): www.naaee.org/

School Science and Mathematics Association (SSMA): www.ssma.org/

Research and Resource Web Sites

Online Encyclopedias

Microsoft Encarta: http://encarta.msn.com
IBM World Book: www.worldbook.com
Grolier Multimedia Encyclopedia: www.grolier.com
Britannica Online: www.eb.com
Compton's Interactive Encyclopedia: www.comptons.com

Internet Resources for Science Educators

Although these links were good at time of publication, Web sites change frequently. If you find that a link fails, use your favorite Internet browser search engine to find the organization's Web sites.

Education Resource Information Center (ERIC): www.aspensys.com/eric

Library of Congress: http://rs6.loc.gov/ammem/ndlpedu/primary.html

On-line Educator: www.ole.net/ole/

Middle School Resource Guide: www.nap.edu/readingroom/

U.S. Food and Drug Administration (FDA) Kids homepage: www.fda.gov/oc/opacom/kids/

EE-Link (National Consortium for Environmental Education and Training): www.nceet.snre.umich.edu/

Chem4Kids: www.chem4kids.com

Eureka Alert gateway to science, medicine, and technology news: www.eurekalert.org/

United Nations Food and Agriculture Organization (FAO): www.fao.org/

Astronomical Society of the Pacific: www.aspsky.org

U.S. Census Bureau (check out the "popclock"): www.census.gov/

Massachusetts Institute of Technology database of information on American inventions and discoveries: http://web.mit.edu/invent/

Rainforest Action Network: www.igc.apc.org/ran/

PBS Online (Web of Life, NOVA, Scientific American Frontiers, Nature, Bill Nye, Newton's Apple, National Geographic, the Magic School Bus): www.pbs.org/

National Aeronautics and Space Administration (NASA): www.hq.nasa.gov/education

NASA's K–12 Internet Initiative: http://quest.arc.nasa.gov/

NASA Spacelink (current and historical information related to aeronautics and space research): http://spacelink.nasa.gov

National Wildlife Federation: www.nwf.org/

U.S. Fish and Wildlife Service: www.fws.gov/

U.S. National Oceanic and Atmospheric Administration (NOAA) Office of Oceanic and Atmospheric Research (OAR): www.oar.noaa.gov/education/

Project WILD: http://eelink.umich.edu/wild/wildhome.html

National Geographic (lots of pictures and articles): www.nationalgeographic.com

USA Today: www.usatoday.com/classlin/clfront.htm

The Why Files (NSF site explaining science behind current events in the news): http://whyfiles.news.wisc.edu/index.html

Annenberg Guide to Math and Science Reform: www.learner.org/k12/ The_Guide/

Concord Consortium (educational technology): www.concord.org/

Earth Island Institute: www.earthisland.org

A Professional Development Bibliography

Abd-El-Khalick, F., & Akerson, V. L. (2004). Learning as conceptual change: Factors mediating the development of preservice elementary teachers' views of nature of science. *Science Education, 88*(5), 785–810.

Abd-El-Khalick, F., Boujaoude, S., Duschl, R., Lederman, N. G., Mamlok-Naaman, R., & Hofstein, A. (2004). Inquiry in science education: International perspectives. *Science Education, 88*(3), 397–419.

Allchin, D. (2003). Scientific myth-conceptions. *Science Education, 87*(3), 329–351.

Allchin, D. (2004). Should the sociology of science be rated X? *Science Education, 88*(6), 934–946.

Allen, S. (2004). Designs for learning: Studying science museum exhibits that do more than entertain. *Science Education, 88* (Suppl.), S17–S33.

Anderson, D., Lucas, K. B., & Ginns, I. S. (2003). Theoretical perspectives on learning in an informal setting. *Journal of Research in Science Teaching, 40*(2), 177–199.

Andrée, M. (2005). Ways of using "everyday life" in the science classroom. In K. Boersma, M. Goedhart, O. De Jong, & H. Eijkelhof (Eds.), *Research and the quality of science education* (pp. 107–116). Dordrecht, the Netherlands: Springer.

Appleton, K. (2002). Science activities that work: Perceptions of primary school teachers. *Research in Science Education, 32*(3), 393–410.

Ash, D. (2003). Dialogic inquiry in life science conversations of family groups in a museum. *Journal of Research in Science Teaching, 40*(2), 138–162.

Aubusson, P. (2002). An ecology of science education. *International Journal of Science Education, 24*(1), 27–46.

Bakas, C., & Mikropoulos, T. A. (2003). Design of virtual environments for the comprehension of planetary phenomena based on students' ideas. *International Journal of Science Education, 25*(8), 949–967.

Barab, S. A., & Luehmann, A. L. (2003). Building sustainable science curriculum: Acknowledging and accommodating local adaptation. *Science Education, 87*(4), 454–467.

Barnett, J., & Hodson, D. (2001). Pedagogical context knowledge: Toward a fuller understanding of what good science teachers know. *Science Education, 85*(4), 426–453.

Barnett, M., & Morran, J. (2002). Addressing children's alternative frameworks of the moon's phases and eclipses. *International Journal of Science Education, 24*(8), 859–879.

Bartholomew, H., & Osborne, J. (2004). Teaching students. "Ideas-about-science": Five dimensions of effective practice. *Science Education, 88*(5), 655–682.

Barton, A. C., Koch, P. D., Contento, I. R., & Hagiwara, S. (2005). From global sustainability to inclusive education: Understanding urban children's ideas about the food system. *International Journal of Science Education, 27*(10), 1163–1186.

Bazin, M., Tamez, M., & the Exploratorium Teacher Institute. (2003). *Math and science across cultures: Activities and investigations from the Exploratorium.* San Francisco: The Exploratorium.

Bell, R. L., & Lederman, N. G. (2003). Understandings of the nature of science and decision making on science and technology based issues. *Science Education, 87*(3), 352–377.

Ben-Zavi Assaraf, O. & Orion, N. (2005). Development of system thinking skills in the context of earth system education. *Journal of Research in Science Teaching, 42*(5), 518–560.

Berg, C. A. R., Bergendahl, V. C. B., & Lundberg, B. K. S. (2003). Benefiting from an open-ended experiment? A comparison of attitudes to, and outcomes of, an expository versus an open-inquiry version of the same experiment. *International Journal of Science Education, 25*(3), 351–372.

Beykont, Z. (Ed.). (2002). *The power of culture: Teaching across language differences.* Cambridge, MA: Harvard Education Publishing Group.

Biddle, B. (Ed.). (2001). *Social class, poverty, and education: Policy and practice.* New York: Routledge Falmer.

Biological Science Curriculum Study. (2006). *Why does inquiry matter? Because that's what science is all about!* Dubuque, IA: Kendall/Hunt.

Boujaoude, S., Sowwan, S., & Abd-El-Khalick, F. (2005). The effect of using drama in science teaching on students' conceptions of the nature of science. In K. Boersma, M. Goedhart, O. De Jong, & H. Eijkelhof (Eds.), *Research and the quality of science education* (pp. 259–267). Dordrecht, the Netherlands: Springer.

Bourne, B. (2000). *Taking inquiry outdoors: Reading, writing, and science beyond the classroom walls.* York, ME: Stenhouse.

Bowers, C. (2003). *Mindful conservatism: Rethinking the ideological and educational basis of an ecologically sustainable future.* Lanham, MD: Rowman & Littlefield.

Brickhouse, N. W. (2001). Embodying science: A feminist perspective on learning. *Journal of Research in Science Teaching, 38*(3), 282–295.

Brown, B. A., Reveles, J. M., & Kelly, G. J. (2005). Scientific literacy and discursive identity: A theoretical framework for understanding science learning. *Science Education, 89*(5), 779–802.

Bryan, L. A., & Atwater, M. M. (2002). Teacher beliefs and cultural models: A challenge for science teacher preparation programs. *Science Education, 86*(6), 821–839.

Calabrese-Barton, A., Ermer, J., Burkett, T., & Osborne, M. (2003). *Teaching science for social justice.* New York: Teachers College Press.

Campbell, B., & Fulton, L. (2003). *Science notebooks: Writing about inquiry.* Portsmouth, NH: Heinemann.

Caravita, S. (2001). A re-framed conceptual change theory? *Learning and Instruction, 11*(4–5), 421–429.

Carter, L. (2005). Globalisation and science education: Rethinking science education reforms. *Journal of Research in Science Teaching, 42*(5), 561–580.

Chin, C., Brown, D. E., & Bruce, B. C. (2002). Student-generated questions: A meaningful aspect of learning in science. *International Journal of Science Education, 24*(5), 521–549.

Chin, C., & Chia, L.-G. (2004). Problem-based learning: Using students' questions to drive knowledge construction. *Science Education, 88*(5), 707–727.

Chinn, C., & Malhotra, B. A. (2001). Epistemologically authentic inquiry in schools: A theoretical framework for evaluating inquiry tasks. *Science Education, 86*(2), 175–218.

Chiu, M.-H., & Lin, J.-W. (2005). Promoting fourth graders' conceptual change of their understanding of electric current via multiple analogies. *Journal of Research in Science Teaching, 42*(4), 429–464.

Cobern, W. W., & Loving, C. C. (2001). Defining "science" in a multicultural world: Implications for science education. *Science Education, 85*(1), 50–67.

Cobern, W. W., & Loving, C. C. (2002). Investigation of preservice elementary teachers' thinking about science. *Journal of Research in Science Teaching, 39*(10), 1016–1031.

Committee on Development of an Addendum to the National Science Education Standards on Scientific Inquiry, Center for Science, Mathematics, and Engineering Education, National Research Council. (2000). *Inquiry and the national science education standards.* Washington, DC: National Academy Press.

Committee on Science Learning, Kindergarten Through 8th Grade, Division of Behavioral and Social Sciences and Education of the National Academies. (2007). *Taking science to school: Learning and teaching science in grades K–8.* Washington, DC: National Academy Press.

Cox-Petersen, A. M., Marsh, D. D., Kisiel, J., & Melber, L. M. (2003). Investigation of guided school tours, student learning, and science reform recommendations at a museum of natural history. *Journal of Research in Science Teaching, 40*(2), 200–218.

Craven, J. A. III, Hand, B., & Prain, V. (2002). Assessing explicit and tacit conceptions of the nature of science among preservice elementary teachers. *International Journal of Science Education, 24*(8), 785–802.

Dagher, Z. R., & Boujaoude, S. (2005). Students' perceptions of the nature of evolutionary theory. *Science Education, 89*(3), 378–391.

Davis, E. A. (2003). Untangling dimensions of middle school students' beliefs about scientific knowledge and science learning. *International Journal of Science Education, 25*(4), 439–468.

Davis, K. S. (2003). "Change is hard": What science teachers are telling us about reform and teacher learning of innovative practices. *Science Education, 87*(1), 3–30.

Dawes, L. (2004). Talk and learning in classroom science. *International Journal of Science Education, 26*(6), 677–696.

DeBoer, G. E. (2000). Scientific literacy: Another look at its historical and contemporary meanings and its relationship to science education reform. *Journal of Research in Science Teaching, 37*(6), 582–601.

Dedes, C. (2005). The mechanism of vision: Conceptual similarities between historical models and children's representations. *Science & Education, 14*(7–8), 699–712.

Dhingra, K. (2003). Thinking about television science: How students understand the nature of science from different program genres. *Journal of Research in Science Teaching, 40*(2), 234–256.

Diakidoy, I.-A., & Kendeou, P. (2001). Facilitating conceptual change in astronomy: A comparison of the effectiveness of two instructional approaches. *Learning and Instruction, 11*(1), 1–20.

Dickens, S. (2005). How students use empirical evidence to draw conclusions. In H. E. Fischer (Ed.), *Developing standards in research on science education* (pp. 87–92). London, UK: Taylor & Francis.

Dierking, L. D., Ellenbogen, K. M., & Falk, J. (2004). In principle, in practice: Perspectives on a decade of museum learning research (1994–2004). *Science Education, 88* (Suppl. 1), S1–S3.

Dodick, J., & Orion, N. (2003). Cognitive factors affecting student understanding of geologic time. *Journal of Research in Science Teaching, 40*(4), 415–442.

Donnelly, J. F. (2004). Humanizing science education. *Science Education, 88*(5), 762–784.

Donovan, C., & Smolkin, L. (2002). Considering genre, content, and visual features in the selection of trade books for science instruction. *The Reading Teacher, 55*, 502–520.

Douglas, R., Klentschy, M. P., & Worth, K. (Eds.). (2006). *Linking science and literacy in the K–8 classroom.* Arlington, VA: NSTA Press.

Dove, J. (2002). Does the man in the moon ever sleep? An analysis of student answers about simple astronomical events: A case study. *International Journal of Science Education, 24*(8), 823–834.

Duit, R., & Treagust, D. F. (2003). Conceptual change: A powerful framework for improving science teaching and learning. *International Journal of Science Education, 25*(6), 671–688.

Ebbers, M. (2002). Science text sets: Using various genres to promote literacy and inquiry. *Language Arts, 80*, 40–50.

Eick, C. J., & Reed, C. J. (2002). What makes an inquiry-oriented science teacher? The influence of learning histories on student teacher role identity and practice. *Science Education, 86*(3), 401–416.

Eisenkraft, A. (2003). Expanding the 5E model. *The Science Teacher, 70*(6), 56–59.

Elby, A., & Hammer, D. (2001). On the substance of a sophisticated epistemology. *Science Education, 85*(5), 554–567.

Ellenbogen, K. M., Luke, J. J., & Dierking, L. D. (2004). Family learning research in museums: An emerging disciplinary matrix? *Science Education, 88*(Suppl.), S48–S58.

Enger, S., & Yager, R. (2001). *Attitudes toward science inventory.* Thousand Oaks, CA: Corwin Press.

Eryilmaz, A. (2002). Effects of conceptual assignments and conceptual change discussions on students' misconceptions and achievement regarding force and motion. *Journal of Research in Science Teaching, 39*(10), 1001–1015.

Fathman, A. K., & Crowther, D. T. (2005). *Science for English language learners: K–12 classroom strategies.* Arlington, VA: NSTA Press.

Fischler, H. (2005). Interviews in science education research. In H. E. Fischer (Ed.), *Developing standards in research on science education* (pp. 29–38). London, UK: Taylor & Francis.

Falk, J. (2004). The director's cut: Toward an improved understanding of learning from museums. *Science Education, 88*(Suppl.), S83–S96.

Falk, J. H., & Adelman, L. M. (2003). Investigating the impact of prior knowledge and interest on aquarium visitor learning. *Journal of Research in Science Teaching, 40*(2), 163–176.

Falk, J., & Storksdieck, M. (2005). Using the contextual model of learning to understand visitor learning from a science center exhibition. *Science Education, 89*(5), 744–778.

Flinders, D. J., & Thornton, S. J. (Eds.). (2004). *The curriculum studies reader.* New York: Routledge.

Ford, D. J. (2005). The challenges of observing geologically: Third graders' descriptions of rock and mineral properties. *Science Education, 89*(2), 276–295.

Freeman, L. A., & Jessup, L. M. (2004). The power and benefits of concept mapping: measuring use, usefulness, ease of use, and satisfaction. *International Journal of Science Education, 26*(2), 151–169.

Galili, I., Weizman, A., & Cohen, A. (2004). The sky as a topic in science education. *Science Education, 88*(4), 574–593.

Garcia, J., Spalding, E., & Powell, R. R. (2001). *Contexts of teaching: Methods for middle and high school instruction.* Upper Saddle River, NJ: Merrill Prentice Hall.

Gilbert, J., & Calvert, S. (2003). Challenging accepted wisdom: Looking at the gender and science education question through a different lens. *International Journal of Science Education, 25*(7), 861–878.

Gill, G., & Levidow, L. (Eds.). (1987). *Anti-racist science teaching.* London, UK: Free Assn. Books.

Gil-Pérez, D. (2003). Constructivism in science education: The need for a clear line of demarcation. In D. Psillos, P. Kariotoglou, V. Tselfes, E. Hatzikraniotis, G. Fassoulopoulos, & M. Kallery (Eds.), *Science education research in the knowledge-based society* (pp. 9–17). Dordrecht, the Netherlands: Kluwer.

Girod, M., Rau, C., & Schepige, A. (2003). Appreciating the beauty of science ideas: Teaching for aesthetic understanding. *Science Education, 87*(4), 574–587.

Glassman, M. (2001). Dewey and Vygotsky: Society, experience, and inquiry in educational practice. *Educational Researcher, 30*(4), 3–14.

Glasson, G. E., & Bentley, M. L. (2000). Epistemological undercurrents in scientists' reporting of research to teachers. *Science Education, 84*(4), 469–485.

Grandy, R. E. (2003). What are models and why do we need them? *Science & Education, 12*(8), 773–777.

Grotzer, T. A. (2003). Learning to understand the forms of causality implicit in scientifically accepted explanations. *Studies in Science Education, 39,* 1–74.

Gutierrez, R. (2001). Mental models and the fine structure of conceptual change. In R. Pinto & S. Surinach (Eds.), *Physics teacher education beyond 2000* (pp. 35–44). Paris: Elsevier.

Hammer, D., & Schifter, D. (2001). Practices of inquiry in teaching and research. *Cognition and Instruction, 19*(4), 441–478.

Hammerman. E. (2006). *Essentials of inquiry-based science, K–8.* Thousand Oaks, CA: Corwin Press.

Hammond, L., & Brandt, C. (2004). Science and cultural process: Defining an anthropological approach to science education. *Studies in Science Education, 40,* 1–47.

Hansen, L. (2006). Strategies for ELL success. *Science & Children, 43*(4), 22–25.

Harding, P., & Hare, W. (2000). Portraying science accurately in classroom: Emphasizing open-mindedness rather than relativism. *Journal of Research in Science Teaching, 37*(3), 225–236.

Hart, C., Mulhall, P., Berry, A., Loughran, J., & Gunstone, R. (2000). What is the purpose of this experiment? Or can students learn something from doing experiments? *Journal of Research in Science Teaching, 37*(7), 655–675.

Hartman, H. J., & Glasgow, N. A. (2002). *Tips for the science teacher: Research-based strategies to help students learn.* Thousand Oaks, CA: Corwin Press.

Hayes, M. T., & Deyhle, D. (2001). Constructing difference: A comparative study of elementary science curriculum differentiation. *Science Education, 85*(3), 239–262.

Hickey, D. T., & Zuiker, J. (2003). A new perspective for evaluating innovative science programs. *Science Education, 87*(4), 539–563.

Hiler, W., & Paul, R. (2005). *Active and cooperative learning.* Dillon Beach, CA: Foundation for Critical Thinking. Available: www.criticalthinking.org

Hoffman, J. L., Wu, H.-K., Krajcik, J. S., & Soloway, E. (2003). The nature of middle school learners' science content understandings with the use of on-line resources. *Journal of Research in Science Teaching, 40*(3), 323–346.

Irvine, J. J. (2003). *Educating teachers for diversity: Seeing with a cultural eye.* New York: Teachers College Press.

Izquierdo-Aymerich, M., & Aduriz-Bravo, A. (2003). Epistemological foundations of school science. *Science & Education, 12*(1), 27–43.

Jarman, R. (2005). Science learning through scouting: An understudied context for informal science education. *International Journal of Science Education, 27*(4), 427–450.

Johnson, P. (2002). Children's understanding of substances, part 2: Explaining chemical change. *International Journal of Science Education, 24*(10), 1037–1054.

Johnson, P. (2005). The development of children's concept of a substance: A longitudinal study of interaction between curriculum and learning. *Research in Science Education, 35,* 41–61.

Kaartinen, S., & Kumpulainen, K. (2002). Collaborative inquiry and the construction of explanations in the learning of science. *Learning and Instruction, 12*(2), 189–212.

Kailin. J. (2002). *Antiracist education: From theory to practice.* Lanham, MD: Rowman & Littlefield.

Kallery, M. (2001). Early-years educators' attitudes to science and pseudo-science: The case of astronomy and astrology. *European Journal of Teacher Education, 24*(3), 329–342.

Kang, S., Scharmann, L. C., & Noh, T. (2004). Reexamining the role of cognitive conflict in science concept learning. *Research in Science Education, 34*(1), 71–96.

Kattmann, U. (2001). Aquatics, flyers, creepers and terrestrials: Students' conceptions of animal classification. *Journal of Biological Education, 35*(3), 141–148.

Keeley, P. (2005). *Science curriculum topic study.* Arlington, VA, and Thousand Oaks, CA: NSTA Press and Corwin Press.

Keeley, P., Eberle, F., & Farrin, L. (2005). *Uncovering student ideas in science, Vol. 1: 25 assessment probes.* Arlington, VA: NSTA Press.

Khishfe, R., & Abd-El-Khalick. (2002). Influence of explicit and reflective versus implicit inquiry-oriented instruction on sixth graders' views of nature of science. *Journal of Research in Science Teaching, 39*(7), 551–578.

Kipnis, N. (2005). Scientific analogies and their use in teaching science. *Science & Education, 14*(3–5), 199–233.

Kliebard, H. (2002). *Changing course: American curriculum reform in the 20th century.* New York: Teachers College Press.

Kolstoe, S. D. (2001). Scientific literacy for citizenship: Tools for dealing with the science dimension of controversial socioscientific issues. *Science Education, 85*(3), 291–310.

Kozoll, R. H., & Osborne, M. D. (2004). Finding meaning in science: Lifeworld, identity, and self. *Science Education, 88*(2), 157–181.

Krnel, D., & Glazar, S. S. (2003). The development of the concept of "matter": A cross-age study of how children classify materials. *Science Education, 87*(5), 621–639.

Kubli, F. (2005). Science teaching as a dialogue: Bakhtin, Vygotsky and some applications in the classroom. *Science & Education, 14*(6), 501–534.

Kurth, L. A., Kidd, R., Gardner, R., & Smith, E. L. (2002). Student use of narrative and paradigmatic forms of talk in elementary science conversations. *Journal of Research in Science Teaching, 39*(9), 793–818.

Laugksch, R. C. (2000). Scientific literacy: A conceptual overview. *Science Education, 84*(1), 71–94.

Lawson, A. E. (2003). The nature and development of hypothetico-predictive argumentation with implications for science teaching. *International Journal of Science Education, 25*(11), 1387–1408.

Leach, J. S. P. (2003). Individual and sociocultural views of learning in science education. *Science & Education, 12*(1), 91–113.

Lee, H. S., & Butler Songer, N. (2003). Making authentic science accessible to students. *International Journal of Science Education, 25*(8), 923–948.

Lethelae, P.-L. (2001). Role-playing, conceptual change, and the learning process: A case study of 7th grade pupils. In H. Behrendt, H. Dahncke, R. Duit, W. Graeber, M. Komorek, & A. Kross (Eds.), *Research in science education: Past, present, and future* (pp. 211–216). Dordrecht, the Netherlands: Kluwer.

Limon, M. (2001). On the cognitive conflict as an instructional strategy for conceptual change: A critical appraisal. *Learning and Instruction, 11*(4–5), 357–380.

Lin, C.-Y., & Hu, R. (2003). Students' understanding of energy flow and matter cycling in the context of the food chain, photosynthesis, and respiration. *International Journal of Science Education, 25*(12), 1529–1544.

Lindemann-Matthies, P. (2005). "Loveable" mammals and "lifeless" plants: How children's interest in common local organisms can be enhanced through observation of nature. *International Journal of Science Education, 27*(6), 655–677.

Liu, X. (2004). Using concept mapping for assessing and promoting relational conceptual change in science. *Science Education, 88*(3), 373–396.

Liu, X. (2006). Student competence in understanding the matter concept and its implications for science curriculum standards. *School Science and Mathematics, 106*(5), 220–227.

Lloyd, D., & Wallace, J. (2004). Imaging the future of science education: The case for making futures studies explicit in student learning. *Studies in Science Education, 40*, 139–178.

Long, K., & Kamii, C. (2001). The measurement of time: Children's construction of transitivity, unit iteration, and conservation of speed. *School Science and Mathematics, 101*(3), 125–135.

Louv, R. (2005). *Last child in the woods: Saving our children from nature-deficit disorder.* Chapel Hill, NC: Algonquin Books of Chapel Hill.

Martinez, M. E. (2006). What is metacognition? *Phi Delta Kappan, 87*(9), 696–699.

Martinez-Delgado, A. (2002). Radical constructivism: Between realism and solipsism. *Science Education, 86*(6), 840–855.

Mason, L. (2001). Introducing talk and writing for conceptual change: A classroom study. *Learning and Instruction, 11*(4–5), 305–329.

Mason, L. (2002). Developing epistemological thinking to foster conceptual change in different domains. In M. Limon & L. Mason (Eds.), *Reconsidering conceptual change. Issues in theory and practice* (pp. 301–335). Dordrecht, the Netherlands: Kluwer.

McNair, S. (2005). *Start young! Early childhood science activities.* Arlington, VA: NSTA Press.

Menthe, J. (2005). Acquisition and encouragement of decision making processes in science classes. In H. E. Fischer (Ed.), *Developing standards in research on science education* (pp. 155–163). London: Taylor & Francis.

Mikkilae-Erdmann, M. (2002). Science learning through text: The effect of text design and text comprehension skills on conceptual change. In M. Limon & L. Mason (Eds.), *Reconsidering conceptual change: Issues in theory and practice* (pp. 337–356). Dordrecht, the Netherlands: Kluwer.

Morge, L. (2005). Teacher–pupil interaction: A study of hidden beliefs in conclusion phases. *International Journal of Science Education, 27*(8), 935–956.

Moss, D. M. (2003). A window on science: Exploring the JASON project and student conceptions of science. *Journal of Science Education and Technology, 12*(1), 21–30.

Moss, D. M., Abrams, E. D., & Robb, J. (2001). Examining student conceptions of the nature of science. *International Journal of Science Education, 23*(8), 771–790.

Murphy, P. (2005). Young people's perspectives on genetics, identity and society using film and discussion. In H. E. Fischer (Ed.), *Developing standards in research on science education* (pp. 165–170). London: Taylor & Francis.

Nakhleh, M. B., Samarapungavan, A., & Saglam, Y. (2005). Middle school students' beliefs about matter. *Journal of Research in Science Teaching, 42*(5), 581–612.

Nemirovsky, R., Rosebery, A. S., Soomon, J., & Warren, B. (Eds.). (2005). *Everyday matters in science and mathematics: Studies of complex classroom events.* Mahwah, NJ: Lawrence Erlbaum.

Niaz, M. (2001). Understanding nature of science as progressive transitions in heuristic principles. *Science Education, 85*(6), 684–690.

Niaz, M., Aguilera, D., Maza, A., & Liendo, G. (2001). Arguments, contradictions, resistances, and conceptual change in students' understanding of atomic structure. *Science Education, 86*(4), 505–525.

Norris, S. P., Guilbert, S. M., Smith, M. L., Hakimelahi, S., & Phillips, L. M. (2005). A theoretical framework for narrative explanation in science. *Science Education, 89*(4), 535–563.

Norris, S. P., & Phillips, L. M. (2003). How literacy in its fundamental sense is central to scientific literacy. *Science Education, 87*(2), 224–240.

Novak, J. D. (2005). Results and implications of a 12-year longitudinal study of science concept learning. *Research in Science Education, 35*, 23–40.

Nunley, K. F. (2003). Layered curriculum brings teachers to tiers. *Education Digest, 69*(1), 31–36.

Nunley, K. F. (2004). *Layered Curriculum™: The practical solution for teachers with more than one student in their classroom* (2nd ed.). Amherst, NH: Brains.org.

Odegaard, M. (2003). Dramatic science. A critical review of drama in science education. *Studies in Science Education, 39*, 75–102.

Ogborn, J. (2005). 40 years of curriculum development. In K. Boersma, M. Goedhart, O. De Jong, & H. Eijkelhof (Eds.), *Research and the quality of science education* (pp. 57–65). Dordrecht, the Netherlands: Springer.

Oppenheimer, T. (2003). *The flickering mind: Saving education from the false promise of technology.* New York: Random House.

Osborne, J. C. S., Ratcliffe, M., Millar, R., & Duschl, R. (2003). What "ideas-about-science" should be taught in school science? A Delphi study of the expert community. *Journal of Research in Science Teaching, 40*(7), 692–720.

Österlind, K. (2005). Concept formation in environmental education: 14-year-olds' work on the intensified greenhouse effect and the depletion of the ozone layer. *International Journal of Science Education, 27*(8), 891–908.

Paavola, S., & Hakkarainen, K. (2005). The knowledge creation metaphor: An emergent epistemological approach to learning. *Science & Education, 14*(6), 535–557.

Palmer, D. (2001). Students' alternative conceptions and scientifically acceptable conceptions about gravity. *International Journal of Science Education, 23*(7), 691–706.

Pedretti, E. (2001). T. Kuhn meets *T. rex:* Critical conversations and new directions in science centres and science museums. *Studies in Science Education, 37*, 1–42.

Pedretti, E. G. (2004). Perspectives on learning through research on critical issues-based science center exhibitions. *Science Education, 88*(Suppl.), S34–S47.

Pellegrino, J., Chudowsky, N., & Glaser, R. (Eds.). (2001). *Knowing what students know: The science and design of educational assessment.* Washington, DC: Center for Education, National Research Council.

Pena, B. M., & Quiles, M. J. P. (2001). The importance of images in astronomy education. *International Journal of Science Education, 23*(11), 1125–1135.

Penick, J. E., & Harris, R. L. (2005). *Teaching with purpose: Closing the research–practice gap.* Arlington, VA: NSTA Press.

Perla, R. J., & Carifio, J. (2005). The nature of scientific revolutions from the vantage point of chaos theory. *Science & Education, 14*(3–5), 263–290.

Plucker, J. A. (2001). What's in a name? Young adolescents' implicit conceptions of invention. *Science Education, 86*(2), 149–160.

Polman, J. L. (2000). *Designing project-based science: Connecting learning through guided inquiry.* New York: Teachers College Press.

Rahm, J. (2004). Multiple modes of meaning-making in a science center. *Science Education, 88*(2), 223–247.

Reiner, M., & Eilam, B. (2001). Conceptual classroom environment: A system view of learning. *International Journal of Science Education, 23*(6), 551–568.

Reiss, M. J., & Tunnicliffe, S. D. (2001). Students' understandings of human organs and organ systems. *Research in Science Education, 31*(3), 383–399.

Rennie, L. J., & Johnston, D. J. (2004). The nature of learning and its implications for research on learning from museums. *Science Education, 88*(Suppl.), S4–S16.

Rennie, L. J., & Williams, G. F. (2002). Science centers and scientific literacy: Promoting a relationship with science. *Science Education, 86*(5), 706–726.

Rescher, R. (2000). *Inquiry dynamics.* New Brunswick, NJ: Transaction.

Rhoton, J., & Shane, P. (Eds.). (2005). *Teaching science in the 21st century.* Arlington, VA: NSTA Press.

Rice, D., Dudley, A., & Williams, C. (2001). How do you choose science trade books? *Science and Children, 38*, 18–22.

Rivard, L. P. (2004). Are language-based activities in science effective for all students, including low achievers? *Science Education, 88*(3), 420–442.

Rodriguez, A. (1997). The dangerous discourse of invisibility: A critique of the National Research Council's National Science Standards. *Journal of Research in Science Teaching, 34*(1), 19–37.

Romberg, T. A., Carpenter, T. P., & Dremock, F. (Eds.). (2005). *Understanding mathematics and science matters.* Mahwah, NJ: Lawrence Erlbaum.

Roth, W.-M. (2001). Gestures: Their role in teaching and learning. *Review of Educational Research, 71*(3), 365–392.

Roth, W.-M., & Tobin, K. (2002). *At the elbow of another: Learning to teach by coteaching.* New York: Peter Lang.

Rowell, P. M., & Ebbers, M. (2004). Shaping school science: Competing discourses in an inquiry-based elementary program. *International Journal of Science Education, 26*(8), 915–934.

Rowlands, M. (2001). The development of children's biological understanding. *Journal of Biological Education, 35*(2), 66–68.

Rudolph, J. L. (2003). Portraying epistemology: School science in historical context. *Science Education, 87*(1), 64–79.

Rudolph, J. L. (2005). Inquiry, instrumentalism, and the public understanding of science. *Science Education, 89*(5), 803–821.

Russel, T., & McGuigan, L. (2003). Promoting understanding through representational redescription: An exploration referring to young pupils' ideas about gravity. In D. Psillos, P. Kariotoglou, V. Tselfes, E. Hatzikraniotis, G. Fassoulopoulos, & M. Kallery (Eds.), *Science education research in the knowledge-based society* (pp. 277–284). Dordrecht, the Netherlands: Kluwer.

Ryder, J., Hind, A., & Leach, J. (2005). Teaching about the epistemology of science in school science classrooms: Case studies of teachers' experiences. In K. Boersma, M. Goedhart, O. De Jong, & H. Eijkelhof (Eds.), *Research and the quality of science education* (pp. 283–293). Dordrecht, the Netherlands: Springer.

Sadler, T. D. (2004). Informal reasoning regarding socioscientific issues: A critical review of research. *Journal of Research in Science Teaching, 41*(5), 513–536.

Sadler, T. D., Chambers, F. W., & Zeidler, D. L. (2004). Student conceptualizations of the nature of science in response to a socioscientific issue. *International Journal of Science Education, 26*(4), 387–409.

Sadler, T. D., & Zeidler, D. L. (2004). The morality of socioscientific issues: Construal and resolution of genetic engineering dilemmas. *Science Education, 88*(1), 4–27.

Sandoval, W. A. (2005). Understanding students' practical epistemologies and their influence on learning through inquiry. *Science Education, 89*(4), 634–656.

Sandoval, W. A., & Reiser, B. J. (2004). Explanation-driven inquiry: Integrating conceptual and epistemic scaffolds for scientific inquiry. *Science Education, 88*(3), 345–372.

Saul, W., & Dieckman, D. (2005). Choosing and using information trade books. *Reading Research Quarterly, 40,* 502–513.

Schmidt, H.-J., & Volke, D. (2003). Shift of meaning and students' alternative concepts. *International Journal of Science Education, 25*(11), 1409–1424.

Schreiner, C., Henriksen, E. K., & Hansen, P. J. K. (2005). Climate education: Empowering today's youth to meet tomorrow's challenges. *Studies in Science Education, 41,* 3–50.

Schwartz, R. S., Lederman, N. G., & Crawford, B. A. (2004). Developing views of nature of science in an authentic context: An explicit approach to bridging the gap between nature of science and scientific inquiry. *Science Education, 88*(4), 610–645.

Scott, W., & Gough, S. (2003). *Key issues in sustainable development and learning: A critical review.* London, UK: RoutledgeFalmer.

Scott, W., & Gough, S. (2003). *Sustainable development and learning: Framing the issues.* London, UK: RoutledgeFalmer.

Shayer, M. (2003). Not just Piaget, not just Vygotsky, and certainly not Vygotsky as alternative to Piaget. *Learning and Instruction, 13*(5), 465–485.

She, H.-C. (2004). Fostering radical conceptual change through dual-situated learning model. *Journal of Research in Science Teaching, 41*(2), 142–164.

Shepardson, D. P. (2002). Bugs, butterflies, and spiders: Children's understanding about insects. *International Journal of Science Education, 24*(6), 627–644.

Shepardson, D. P., & Britsch, S. J. (2001). The role of children's journals in elementary school science activities. *Journal of Research in Science Teaching, 38*(1), 43–69.

Siegel, H. (2002). Multiculturalism, universalism, and science education: In search of common ground. *Science Education, 86*(6), 803–820.

Simmons, P., McMahon, M., Sommers, R., DeBaets, D., & Crawley, F. (Eds.). (2006). *Assessment in science: Practical experiences and education research.* Arlington, VA: NSTA Press.

Simpson, G. B. (2004). Critical constructivism, neo-relativism, and the place of values in science education, *Science Education Review, 3*(1), 23–28.

Snively, G., & Corsiglia, J. (2001). Discovering indigenous science: Implications for science education. *Science Education, 85*(1), 6–34.

Solomon, J. (2001). Science stories and science texts: What can they do for our students? *Studies in Science Education, 37,* 85–106.

Solomon, J. (2003). Risk: Why don't they listen to us? *Studies in Science Education, 39,* 125–142.

Southerland, S., Kittleson, J., Settlage, J., & Lanier, K. (2005). Individual and group meaning-making in an urban third grade classroom: Red fog, cold cans, and seeping vapor. *Journal of Research in Science Teaching, 42*(9), 1032–1061.

Spiliotopoulou, V., & Alevizos, P. (2001). Entities of the world and causality in children's thinking. In H. Behrendt, H. Dahncke, R. Duit, W. Graeber, M. Komorek, & A. Kross (Eds.), *Research in science education: Past, present, and future* (pp. 113–118). Dordrecht, the Netherlands: Kluwer.

Stanley, W. B., & Brickhouse, N. W. (2001). Teaching sciences: The multicultural question revisited. *Science Education, 85*(1), 35–49.

Stavridou, H., & Marinopoulos, D. (2001). Water and air pollution: Primary students' conceptions about "itineraries" and interactions of substances. *Chemistry Education: Research and Practice in Education, 2*(1), 31–41.

Sungur, S., Tekkaya, C., & Geban, O. (2001). The contribution of conceptual change texts accompanied by concept mapping to students' understanding of the human circulatory system. *School Science and Mathematics, 101*(2), 91–101.

Sutherland, D., & Dennick, R. (2002). Exploring culture, language and the perception of the nature of science. *International Journal of Science Education, 24*(1), 1–26.

Taber, K. S. (2001). Shifting sands: A case study of conceptual development as competition between alternative conceptions. *International Journal of Science Education, 23*(7), 731–754.

Taylor, I., Barker, M., & Jones, A. (2003). Promoting mental model building in astronomy education. *International Journal of Science Education, 25*(10), 1205–1225.

Tolley, K. (2003). *The science education of American girls: A historical perspective.* London, UK: RoutledgeFalmer.

Tomkins, S. P., & Tunnicliffe, S. D. (2001). Looking for ideas: Observation, interpretation and hypothesis-making by 12-year-old pupils undertaking science investigations. *International Journal of Science Education, 23*(8), 791–814.

Tomlinson, C. (2004). The Mobius effect: Addressing learner variance in schools. *Journal of Learning Disabilities, 37*(6), 516–524.

Tomlinson, C. (2005). Differentiating instruction for academic diversity. In J. M. Cooper (Ed.), *Classroom teaching skills* (8th ed., pp. 151–184). Boston: Houghton-Mifflin.

Tomlinson, C. (2005). Grading and differentiation: Paradox or good practice. *Theory Into Practice, 44*(3), 262–269.

Tomlinson, C., Kaplan, S., Purcell, J., Leppien, J., Burns, D., & Strickland, C. (2005). *The parallel curriculum model in the classroom, Book 2: Units for applications across the content areas, K–12.* Thousand Oaks, CA: Corwin Press.

Tomlinson, C., & McTighe, J. (2006). *Integrating differentiated instruction and understanding by design: Connecting content and kids.* Alexandria, VA: Association for Supervision and Curriculum Development.

Treagust, D. F., Jacobowitz, R., Gallagher, J. L., & Parker, J. (2001). Using assessment as a guide in teaching for understanding: A case study of a middle school science class learning about sound. *Science Education, 85*(2), 137–157.

Trumper, R. (2001). A cross-age study of junior high school students' conceptions of basic astronomy concepts. *International Journal of Science Education, 23*(11), 1111–1123.

Tsai, C.-C. (2003). Using a conflict map as an instructional tool to change student alternative conceptions in simple series electric-circuits. *International Journal of Science Education, 25*(3), 307–327.

Tsai, C.-C., & Chang, C.-Y. (2005). Lasting effects of instruction guided by the conflict map: Experimental study of learning about the cause of the seasons. *Journal of Research in Science Teaching, 42*(10), 1089–1111.

Tsai, C.-C., & Liu, S.-Y. (2005). Developing a multidimensional instrument for assessing students' epistemological views toward science. *International Journal of Science Education, 27*(13), 1621–1638.

Tuan, H.-L., Chin, C.-C., & Shieh, S.-H. (2005). The development of a questionnaire to measure students' motivation towards science learning. *International Journal of Science Education, 27*(6), 639–654.

Tytler, R., & Peterson, S. (2001). Deconstructing learning in science: Young children's response to a classroom sequence on evaporation. *Research in Science Education, 30*(4), 339–356.

Tytler, R., & Peterson, S. (2003). Tracing young children's scientific reasoning. *Research in Science Education, 33*(4), 433–465.

Tytler, R. P., & Peterson, S. (2004). From "try it and see" to strategic exploration: Characterizing young children's scientific reasoning. *Journal of Research in Science Teaching, 41*(1), 94–118.

Tytler, R., & Peterson, S. (2005). A longitudinal study of children's developing knowledge and reasoning in science. *Research in Science Education, 35,* 63–98.

Unsworth, L. (2001). Evaluating the language of different types of explanations in junior high school science texts. *International Journal of Science Education, 23*(6), 585–610.

van Horn, R. (2006). Technology: Generation "M" and 3G. *Phi Delta Kappan, 87*(10), 727, 792.

van Rens, L., & Dekkers, P. (2001). Learning about investigations: The teachers' role. In H. Behrendt, H. Dahncke, R. Duit, W. Graeber, M. Komorek, & A. Kross (Eds.), *Research in science education: Past, present, and future* (pp. 325–330). Dordrecht, the Netherlands: Kluwer.

Venville, G., Adey, P., Larkin, S., & Robertson, A. (2003). Fostering thinking through science in the early years of schooling. *International Journal of Science Education, 25*(11), 1313–1331.

Venville, G., Gribble, S. J., & Donovan, J. (2005). An exploration of young children's understandings of genetics concepts from ontological and epistemological perspectives. *Science Education, 89*(4), 614–633.

Vosniadou, S. (2001). Conceptual change research and the teaching of science. In H. Behrendt, H. Dahncke, R. Duit, W. Graeber, M. Komorek, & A. Kross (Eds.), *Research in science education: Past, present, and future* (pp. 177–188). Dordrecht, the Netherlands: Kluwer.

Vosniadou, S., Dimitrakopoulou, A., & Papademetriou, E. (2001). Designing learning environments to promote conceptual change in science. *Learning and Instruction, 11*(4–5), 381–419.

Vosniadou, S., Skopeliti, I., & Ikospentaki, K. (2005). Reconsidering the role of artifacts in reasoning: Children's understanding of the globe as a model of the earth. *Learning and Instruction, 15,* 333–351.

Ward, R. E., & Wandersee, J. H. (2002). Struggling to understand abstract science topics: A roundhouse diagram-based study. *International Journal of Science Education, 24*(6), 575–592.

Ward, R. E., & Wandersee, J. H. (2002). Students' perceptions of roundhouse diagramming: A middle-school viewpoint. *International Journal of Science Education, 24*(2), 205–225.

Warren, B., Ballenger, C., Ogonowski, M., Rosebery, A. S., & Hudicourt-Barnes, J. (2001). Rethinking diversity in learning science: The logic of everyday sense-making. *Journal of Research in Science Teaching, 38*(5), 529–552.

Watson, J. R., & Swain, J. R. L. (2004). Students' discussions in practical scientific inquiries. *International Journal of Science Education, 26*(1), 25–45.

Westra, R. (2005). Systems thinking in ecology education: Modeling ecosystems. In H. E. Fischer (Ed.), *Developing standards in research on science education* (pp. 235–240). London, UK: Taylor & Francis.

Wetzel, D. R. (2005). *How to weave the Web into K–8 science.* Arlington, VA: NSTA Press.

Wickman, P.-O., & Oestman, L. (2002). Learning as discourse change: A sociocultural mechanism. *Science Education, 86*(5), 601–623.

Williams, R. L. II, Chen, M.-Y., & Seato, J. M. (2003). Haptics-augmented simple-machine educational tools. *Journal of Science Education and Technology, 12*(1), 1–12.

Windschitl, M. (2001). The diffusion and appropriation of ideas in the science classroom: Developing a taxonomy of events occurring between groups of learners. *Journal of Research in Science Teaching, 38*(1), 17–42.

Windschitl, M. (2001). Using simulations in middle school: Does assertiveness of dyad partners influence conceptual change? *International Journal of Science Education, 23*(1), 17–32.

Wiser, M., & Amin, T. (2001). "Is heat hot?" Inducing conceptual change by integrating everyday and scientific perspectives on thermal phenomena. *Learning and Instruction, 11*(4–5), 331–355.

Wittmann, M. C., Steinberg, R. N., & Redish, E. F. (2003). Understanding and affecting student reasoning about sound waves. *International Journal of Science Education, 25*(8), 991–1013.

Wong, D., & Pugh, K. (2001). Learning science: A Deweyan perspective. *Journal of Research in Science Teaching, 38*(3), 317–336.

Wu, Y.-T., & Tsai, C.-C. (2005). Development of elementary school students' cognitive structures and information processing strategies under long-term constructivist-oriented science instruction. *Science Education, 89*(5), 822–846.

Yager, R. E. (2005). *Exemplary science in grades 5–8: Standards-based success stories.* Arlington, VA: NSTA Press.

Yager, S. O., & Yager, R. E. (2006). The advantages of an STS approach over a typical textbook dominated approach to middle school science. *School Science and Mathematics, 106*(5), 248–260.

Yair, Y., Schur, Y., & Mintz, R. (2003). A "thinking journey" to the planets using scientific visualization technologies: Implications to astronomy education. *Journal of Science Education and Technology, 12*(1), 43–49.

Yanowitz, K. L. (2001). Using analogies to improve elementary school students' inferential reasoning about scientific concepts. *School Science and Mathematics, 101*(3), 133–142.

Yip, D. Y. (2003). Developing a better understanding of the relationship between transpiration and water uptake in plants. *Journal of Science Education and Technology, 12*(1), 13–19.

Zee, E., Iwasyk, M., Kurose, A., Simpson, D., & Wild, J. (2001). Student and teacher questioning during conversations about science. *Journal of Research in Science Education, 38*(2), 159–190.

Zeidler, D. L., Sadler, T. D., Simmons, M. L., & Howes, E. V. (2005). Beyond STS: A research-based framework for socioscientific issues education. *Science Education, 89*(3), 357–377.

Zeidler, D. L., Walker, K. A., Ackett, W. A., & Simmons, M. L. (2002). Tangled up in views: Beliefs in the nature of science and responses to socioscientific dilemmas. *Science Education, 86*(3), 343–367.

Zembylas, M. (2005). Three perspectives on linking the cognitive and the emotional in science learning: Conceptual change, socio-constructivism and poststructuralism. *Studies in Science Education, 41*, 91–116.

Zembylas, M., & Isenbarger, L. (2002). Teaching science to students with learning disabilities: Subverting the myths of labeling through teachers' caring and enthusiasm. *Research in Science Education, 32*(1), 55–79.

References

American Association for the Advancement of Science. (1989). *Science for all Americans (Project 2061)*. Washington, DC: Author.

American Association for the Advancement of Science. (1990). *The liberal art of science: Agenda for action*. Washington, DC: Author.

American Association for the Advancement of Science. (1993). *Benchmarks for science literacy: Project 2061*. New York: Oxford University Press.

Atkin, J. M., & Black, P. (2003). *Inside science education reform: A history of curricular and policy change*. New York: Teachers College Press.

Atkins, J. M., & Karplus, R. (1962, September). Discovery or invention? *The Science Teacher, 29*, 45–51.

Baron, J. (1991). Performance assessment: Blurring the edges of assessment, curriculum, and instruction. In G. Kulm & S. Malcom (Eds.), *Science assessment in the service of reform*. Waldorf, MD: American Association for the Advancement of Science.

Bohm, D., & Peat, F. D. (1987). *Science, order, and creativity*. New York: Bantam.

Borror, D. J., & White, R. E. (1998). *A field guide to insects*. The Peterson Field Guide Series. Boston: Houghton Mifflin.

Brooks, J. G. (1990, February). Teachers and students: Constructivists forging new connections. *Educational Leadership*, pp. 68–71.

Brown, L. R., Flavin, C., & Postel, S. (1990). Picturing a sustainable society. In L. Starke (Ed.), *State of the world, 1990: A Worldwatch Institute report on progress toward a sustainable society* (pp. 173–190). New York: W.W. Norton.

Bruner, J. S. (1960). *The process of education*. New York: Vintage.

Bureau of Labor Statistics, U.S. Department of Labor. (2005). *Occupational outlook handbook, 2004–05 ed. Teachers: Preschool, kindergarten, elementary, middle, and secondary*. Retrieved August 17, 2005, from http://www.bls.gov/oco/ocos069.pdf

Bybee, R. (1977). The new transformation of science education. *Science Education, 61*(1), 85–97.

Caine, R. N., & Caine, G. (1991). *Making connections: Teaching and the human brain*. Alexandria, VA: Association for Supervision and Curriculum Development.

Campbell, L. (1988). Holistic, integrative education: Becoming all that we can be. *Holistic Education Review, 1*(2), 4–7.

Carin, A. A. (1993). *Teaching modern science* (6th ed.). Columbus, OH: Merrill.

Chaillé, C., & Britain, L. (1991). *The young child as scientist: A constructivist approach to early childhood science education*. New York: HarperCollins.

Chalmers, A. F. (1999). *What is this thing called science?* (3rd ed.). Indianapolis, IN: Hackett.

Cheek, D. (1992). Introduction. In M. O. Thirunarayanan (Ed.), *Think and act—Make an impact: Handbook of science, technology and society* (Vol. I). Tempe: Arizona State University.

Colburn, A. (2000, September). Constructivism: Science education's "grand unifying theory." *The Clearing House, 74,* 9.

Cole, K. C. (1982, March). Ask a stupid question. . . . *Washington Post Magazine,* p. 18.

De Fina, A. (1992). *Portfolio assessment: Getting started.* New York: Scholastic Professional Publications.

Dickens, S. (2005). How students use empirical evidence to draw conclusions. In H. E. Fischer (Ed.), *Developing standards in research on science education* (pp. 87–92). London: Taylor & Francis.

Doll, R. C. (1996). *Curriculum improvement: Decision-making and process* (9th ed.). Boston: Allyn & Bacon.

Duschl, R. (1989). *Restructuring science education: The importance of theories and their development.* Wolfeboro, NH: Teachers College Press.

Duschl, R., & Hamilton, R. J. (Eds.). (1992). *Philosophy of science, cognitive psychology, and educational theory and practice.* Albany: State University of New York Press.

Eaton, V. (1996). *Differentiated instruction.* Retrieved February 2, 2004, from www .quasar.ualberta.ca/ddc/incl/difinst.htm

Ebert, C., & Ebert, E. (1993). An instructionally oriented model for enabling conceptual development. In J. Novak (Ed.), *Third international seminar on misconceptions and educational strategies in science and mathematics.* Ithaca, NY: Cornell University.

Ebert, C., & Ebert. E. (1998). *The inventive mind in science.* Englewood, CO: Teacher Ideas Press.

Ebert, E. (1994). The cognitive spiral: Creative thinking and cognitive processing. *The Journal of Creative Behavior, 28*(4), 275–290.

Eby, D., & Tatum, R. (1977). *The chemistry of food: A consumer chemistry learning activity package.* Seattle: Unigraph.

Eisenkraft, A. (2003). Expanding the 5-E model. *The Science Teacher, 70*(6), 56–59.

Enger, S. E., & Yager, R. E. (1998). *The Iowa assessment handbook.* Iowa City: University of Iowa Science Education Center.

Enger, S., & Yager, R. (2001). *Attitudes toward science inventory.* Thousand Oaks, CA: Corwin Press.

Enright, J. B. (1993). Asking the right questions. *New Dimensions, 20*(3), 4.

Enyedy, N., Goldberg, J., & Welsh, K. (2006, January). Complex dilemmas of identity and practice. *Science Education, 90*(1), 68–93.

Erikson, E. H. (1950). *Childhood and society.* New York: W. W. Norton.

Fisher, B. (1992, August–September). Starting the year in a first grade classroom. *Teaching K–8,* pp. 57–58.

Flick, L. B., & Lederman, N. G. (Eds.). (2004). *Scientific inquiry and nature of science: Implications for teaching, learning and teacher education.* Dordrecht, the Netherlands: Kluwer.

Gallas, K. (1995). *Talking their way into science: Hearing children's questions and theories, responding with curricula.* New York: Teachers College Press.

Geelan, D., Larochelle, M., & Lemke, J. L. (2002). The laws of science. In J. Wallace & W. Louden (Eds.), *Dilemmas of science teaching: Perspectives on problems of practice* (pp. 22–35). New York: RoutledgeFalmer.

Geography Education Standards Project. (1994). *Geography for life: National geography standards.* Washington, DC: National Geographic Research and Exploration.

Hardin, J. W., & Arena, J. M. (1977). *Human poisoning from native and cultivated plants.* Durham, NC: Duke University Press.

Harmin, M., & Toth, M. (2006). *Inspiring active learning: A complete handbook for today's teachers* (expanded 2nd ed.). Alexandria, VA: Association for Supervision and Curriculum Development.

Harré, R. (1981). *Great scientific experiments: 20 experiments that changed our view of the world.* Oxford: Phaidon.

Hestenes, D. (1992). Modeling games in the Newtonian world. *American Journal of Physics, 60*(8), 732–748.

Hively, W. (1988). How much science does the public understand. *American Scientist, 76*(5), 439–444.

Hope, J. (2005). Student portfolios: Documenting success. *Techniques Making Education and Career Connections, 79*(5), 26–31.

Jensen, M., Moore, R., & Hatch, J. (2002). Cooperative learning—Part 1: Cooperative quizzes. *The American Biology Teacher, 64,* 29–34.

Johnson, D., & Johnson, R. (1987). *Learning together and alone: Cooperation, competition, and individualization* (2nd ed.). Englewood Cliffs, NJ: Prentice Hall.

Keeley, P., Eberle, F., & Farrin, L. (2005). *Uncovering student ideas in science,* Volume 1: *25 assessment probes.* Arlington, VA: NSTA Press.

Kiernan, L. J., & Tomlinson, C. A. (1997). *Why differentiate instruction?* Alexandria, VA: Association for Supervision and Curriculum Development.

Kuehn, C., & McKenzie, D. (1989). Using interviewing as a teacher education technique. *Journal of Science Teacher Education, 1*(2), 27–29.

Kuhn, T. (1962). *The structure of scientific revolutions.* Chicago: University of Chicago Press.

Kuhs, T. M. (1997). *Measure for measure: Using portfolios in K–8 mathematics.* Portsmouth, NH: Heinemann.

Latour, B., & Woolgar, S. (1986). *Laboratory life: The construction of social facts. An ethnographic study of biochemistry at the Salk Institute.* Princeton, NJ: Princeton University Press.

Lederman, N. G. (2002). *Project ICAN.* Paper presented at annual meeting, Association of Educators of Teachers of Science, Charlotte, NC.

Lincoln, Y., & Guba, E. (1985). *Naturalistic inquiry.* Beverly Hills: Sage.

Llewellyn, D. (2002). *Inquire within: Implementing inquiry-based science standards.* Thousand Oaks, CA: Corwin Press.

Louv, R. (2005). *Last child in the woods: Saving our children from nature-deficit disorder.* Chapel Hill, NC: Algonquin Books of Chapel Hill.

Martinez, M. E. (2006). What is metacognition? *Phi Delta Kappan, 87*(9), 696–699.

Mayer, R. (2003). *Learning and instruction.* Princeton, NJ: Pearson Education.

McCloskey, D. N. (1995, February). Once upon a time there was a theory. *Scientific American, 272*(2), 19.

McComas, W. F., Almazroa, H., & Clough, M. P. (1998). The nature of science in science education: An introduction. *Science Education, 7*(6), 511–532.

McGuiness, B., Roth, W.-M., & Gilmer, P. J. (2002). Laboratories. In J. Wallace & W. Louden (Eds.), *Dilemmas of science teaching: Perspectives on problems of practice* (pp. 36–55). New York: RoutledgeFalmer.

Miller, J. D. (2004). Public understanding of, and attitudes toward, scientific research: What we know and what we need to know. *Public Understanding of Science, 13*(3), 273–294.

Miller, R. (2006, March). Cloning. *Science Scope, 29*(6), 70–74.

National Center for Educational Statistics. (2005). *The condition of education 2005.* Washington, DC: Author. Retrieved July 27, 2005, from http://nces.ed.gov/programs/coe/

National Council for the Social Studies. (1994). *Curriculum standards for social studies.* Washington, DC: Author.

National Research Council. (1996). *National science education standards.* Washington, DC: National Academy Press.

National Research Council. (2000). *Inquiry and the national science education standards: A guide for teaching and learning.* Washington, DC: National Academy Press.

National Science Teachers Association. (Prepublication copy, 1977). *Safety in the secondary science classroom,* pp. 4–18.

Newmann, F. M. (1988, January). Can depth replace coverage in the high school curriculum? *Phi Delta Kappan, 69*(5), 345–348.

Nicholson, S. (1972). The theory of loose parts. *BEE,* 1, 3. (Originally published as Theory of loose parts: How not to cheat children. *Landscape Architecture,* October 1971, pp. 30–34)

Nielson, H. (1992). Paper presented at the International Conference on the History and Philosophy of Science in Science Teaching, Queen's University, Kingston, Ontario, Canada.

Novelli, J. (1995, September). Learning centers that work. *Instructor,* pp. 82–85.

Nunley, K. F. (2003). Layered curriculum brings teachers to tiers. *Education Digest, 69*(1), 31–36.

Nunley, K. F. (2004). *Layered Curriculum™: The practical solution for teachers with more than one student in their classroom* (2nd ed.). Amherst, NH: Brains.org.

Oppenheimer, T. (2004). *The flickering mind: Saving education from the false promise of technology.* New York: Random House.

Osborne, R., & Freyberg, P. (1985). *Learning in science.* Portsmouth, NH: Heinemann.

Penick, J. E. (2002). Doing real science while integrating science and technology. *Science Education International, 13*(3), 2–4.

Piaget, J. (1929). *The child's conception of the world.* London: Routledge & Kegan Paul.

Piaget, J. (1977). Problems in equilibration. In M. Appel & L. Goldberg (Eds.), *Topics in cognitive development,* Vol. 1: *Equilibration: Theory, research and application* (pp. 3–13). New York: Plenum.

Posner, G., Strike, K., Hewson, P., & Gertzog, W. (1982). Accommodation of a scientific conception: Toward a theory of conceptual change. *Science Education, 66*(2), 211–227.

Postman, N., & Weingartner, C. (1969). *Teaching as a subversive activity.* New York: Dell.

Powell, D., Needham, R. A., & Bentley, M. L. (1994, April). *Using big books in science and social studies.* Paper presented at Annual Meeting of the International Reading Association. Toronto, Canada.

Price, S., & Hein, G. (1994, October). Scoring active assessments. *Science and Children,* pp. 26–29.

Prigogine, I. (1980). *From being to becoming: Time and complexity in the physical sciences.* San Francisco: W.H. Freeman.

Puls, D., & O'Brien, P. (1994). What's a zoo to do? *Science Scope, 17*(4), 17–20.

Reiss, M. J. (1993). *Science education for a pluralist society.* Philadelphia: Open University Press.

Richards, S. (1987). *Philosophy and sociology of science* (2nd ed.). New York: Basil Blackwell.

Rowlett, R. (2000). *How many? A dictionary of units of measurement.* Retrieved May 2, 2006, from www.unc.edu/~rowlett/units/usmetric.html

Rutherford, F. J., & Ahlgren, A. (1990). *Science for all Americans.* New York: Oxford University Press.

Ryan, A. G., & Aikenhead, G. S. (1992). Students' preconceptions about the epistemology of science. *Science Education, 76*(6), 559–580.

Sanders, M. (1993). Science and technology: A new alliance. *Science Scope, 16*(6), 56–60.

Shulman, L. (2003). Knowledge and teaching: Foundations of the new reform. In A. Ornstein (Ed.), *Contemporary issues in curriculum* (pp. 109–127). Boston: Allyn & Bacon.

Singer, P. (1975). *Animal liberation.* New York: New York Review.

Sizer, T. R. (1984). *Horace's compromise: The dilemma of the American high school.* Boston: Houghton Mifflin.

Smith, E. L. (1991). A conceptual change model. In S. M. Glynn, R. H. Yeany, & B. K. Britton (Eds.), *The psychology of learning* (pp. 43–63). Hillsdale, NJ: Erlbaum.

Smith, L. (1989, July–August). Public understanding of environmental issues. *Environmental Communicator,* p. 9.

Snively, G. (1995). Bridging traditional science and Western science in the multicultural classroom. In G. Snively & A. MacKinnon (Eds.), *Thinking globally about mathematics and science education.* Vancouver: Centre for the Study of Curriculum and Instruction, University of British Columbia.

Stepans, J. (1994). *Targeting students' science misconceptions: Physical science activities using the conceptual change model.* Riverview, FL: Idea Factory.

Sunal, D., & Wright, E. (Eds.). (2006). *The impact of state and national standards on K–12 science teaching.* Greenwich, CT: Information Age Publishing.

Thomas, L. (1978, July 2). Debating the unknowable. An address to the Mount Sinai School of Medicine. *The New York Times,* p. 15.

Tomlinson, C. (1995). *How to differentiate instruction in mixed-ability classrooms.* Alexandria, VA: Association for Supervision and Curriculum Development.

Tomlinson, C. A. (2003). *Fulfilling the promise of the differentiated classroom: Strategies and tools for responsive teaching.* Alexandria, VA: Association for Supervision and Curriculum Development.

United Nations Population Division of the Department of Economic and Social Affairs. (2004). *World population prospects: The 2004 revision population database.* Retrieved May 2, 2006, from http://esa.un.org/unpp/p2k0data.asp

University of Florida. (1996). *Enhanced science helper: K–8* (CD-ROM). Gainesville, FL: Author. Available at learningteam.org.

U.S. Census Bureau. (2005). *School enrollment—Social and economic characteristics of students: October 2003.* Washington, DC: Author. Retrieved August 18, 2005, from www.census.gov/prod/2005pubs/p20–554.pdf

van Horn, R. (2006). Technology: Generation "M" and 3G. *Phi Delta Kappan, 87*(10), 727, 792.

von Glasersfeld, E. (1989). Cognition, construction of knowledge, and teaching. *Synthese, 80,* 121–140.

Vygotsky, L. (1978). *Mind in society: The development of higher psychological processes.* Cambridge, MA: Harvard University Press.

Waks, L. (1995, April). *Citizenship in transition: Globalization, postindustrial technology and education.* Royal Bank Lecture presented at symposium "Life After School: Education, Globalization and the Person," Queen's University, Kingston, Ontario, Canada.

Ward, P. (1994). *The end of evolution: On mass extinctions and the preservation of biodiversity.* New York: Bantam.

Weininger, S. (1990, January 8). Science and "the humanities" are wedded, not divorced. *The Scientist, 4*(1), 15, 17.

Weiss, I. R. (1987). *Report of the 1985–86 national survey of science, mathematics, and social studies education.* Research Triangle Park, NC: Research Triangle Institute.

Wiggington, E. (1972). *The Foxfire book.* New York: Anchor.

Wilson, E. O. (2005). *The future of life.* Environmental Semester Lecture. Knoxville: University of Tennessee.

Wittrock, M. C. (1974). Learning as a generative process. *Educational Psychology, 11,* 87–95.

Yager, S. O., & Yager, R. E. (2006). The advantages of an STS approach over a typical textbook dominated approach to middle school science. *School Science and Mathematics, 106*(5), 248–260.

Zembylas, M. (2005). Three perspectives on linking the cognitive and the emotional in science learning: Conceptual change, socio-constructivism and poststructuralism. *Studies in Science Education, 41,* 91–116.

Index

CORWIN PRESS

The Corwin Press logo—a raven striding across an open book—represents the union of courage and learning. Corwin Press is committed to improving education for all learners by publishing books and other professional development resources for those serving the field of PreK–12 education. By providing practical, hands-on materials, Corwin Press continues to carry out the promise of its motto: **"Helping Educators Do Their Work Better."**